TERROR ON TRIAL

Grounded in court ethnography, this book explores terrorism trials in France. A multidisciplinary research team examines how terrorism logics are reflected, represented, and negotiated within criminal proceedings. Based on hundreds of hearing days – ranging from small terrorism criminal cases to the so-called trials for history, commonly known as the 'Charlie Hebdo' and the 'Bataclan' trials – this study offers a nuanced, bottom-up perspective on the role of courts. Through courtroom immersion, close observation of legal performances, and interviews with judicial actors, it investigates how justice is shaped in practice. Identifying three generations of trials, the book provides original insights into the evolving role of courts in terrorism cases. From an empirical and comparative perspective, it also seeks to make criminal trials of civil law systems more accessible to Anglophone readers, offering a deeper understanding of how terrorism is prosecuted in France, highlighting the role of judges, prosecutors, lawyers, and victims.

SHARON WEILL is Professor of International Law at the American University of Paris and a research associate at La Sorbonne University (PhD, Geneva University). Her research focuses on the relations between armed conflicts, political violence, and the role of courts, using socio-legal approaches including trial ethnography. She is the author of *The Role of National Courts in Applying International Humanitarian Law* (OUP, 2014) and co-editor of the *President on Trial: Prosecuting Hissène Habré* (OUP, 2020). She has been directing several research programmes focusing on the role of national courts as transnational actors.

DENIS SALAS is an author, magistrate and holds a PhD in Public Law and the Sociology of Law (University of Paris I Panthéon-Sorbonne). Since 2016, he has been the Editor-in-Chief of *Les Cahiers de la Justice* (peer-reviewed journal of the *National School for the Judiciary*). He has published more than a hundred articles and over a dozen books.

ANTOINE MÉGIE (PhD, Sciences Po Paris) is an associate professor at the University of Rouen in France, and head of the Political Sciences department. Former Director of the journal *Politique européenne*, he is a member of the editorial board of the journal *Cultures et Conflits*. His research focuses on the role of law in the 'fight against terrorism'. In addition to coordinating several European and transatlantic programmes on the fight against terrorism, from 2017 he has been co-director of several research programmes funded by the Ministry of Justice on terror trials.

CHRISTIANE BESNIER, an anthropologist and research associate at the Center for Cultural Anthropology at the University of Paris Sorbonne, has been working on criminal courts in France and Europe since 2002. She is the author of *La vérité côté cour – Une ethnologue aux assises* (2017).

CAMBRIDGE STUDIES IN LAW AND SOCIETY

Founded in 1997, Cambridge Studies in Law and Society is a hub for leading scholarship in socio-legal studies. Located at the intersection of law, the humanities, and the social sciences, it publishes empirically innovative and theoretically sophisticated work on law's manifestations in everyday life: from discourses to practices, and from institutions to cultures. The series editors have longstanding expertise in the interdisciplinary study of law, and welcome contributions that place legal phenomena in national, comparative, or international perspective. Series authors come from a range of disciplines, including anthropology, history, law, literature, political science, and sociology.

A list of books in the series can be found at the back of this book.

CAMBRIDGE
STUDIES IN
LAW AND SOCIETY

TERROR ON TRIAL

An Ethnography of French Courts

Sharon Weill
The American University of Paris

Denis Salas
French National School for the Judiciary

Antione Mégie
Université de Rouen

Christiane Besnier
Sorbonne University

CAMBRIDGE
UNIVERSITY PRESS

CAMBRIDGE
UNIVERSITY PRESS

Shaftesbury Road, Cambridge CB2 8EA, United Kingdom

One Liberty Plaza, 20th Floor, New York, NY 10006, USA

477 Williamstown Road, Port Melbourne, VIC 3207, Australia

314–321, 3rd Floor, Plot 3, Splendor Forum, Jasola District Centre, New Delhi – 110025, India

Cambridge University Press is part of Cambridge University Press & Assessment, a department of the University of Cambridge.

We share the University's mission to contribute to society through the pursuit of education, learning and research at the highest international levels of excellence.

www.cambridge.org
Information on this title: www.cambridge.org/9781009333221

DOI: 10.1017/9781009333214

When citing this work, please include a reference to the DOI 10.1017/9781009333214

First published 2026

Cover image: © Cour d'appel de Paris (The Paris Court of Appeal)

A catalogue record for this publication is available from the British Library

Library of Congress Cataloging-in-Publication Data
Names: Weill, Sharon author | Salas, Denis author | Mégie, Antoine author | Besnier, Christiane author
Title: Terror on trial : an ethnography of French courts / Sharon Weill, Denis Salas, Antione Mégie, Christiane Besnier.
Description: New York : Cambridge University Press, 2026. | Series: Cambridge studies in law and society | Includes bibliographical references and index.
Identifiers: LCCN 2025054971 (print) | LCCN 2025054972 (ebook) | ISBN 9781009333221 hardback | ISBN 9781009333252 paperback | ISBN 9781009333214 epub
Subjects: LCSH: Trials (Terrorism)–France | Terrorism–Law and legislation–France | Criminal courts–France | Criminal procedure–France | Terrorism–Trials–France | Political crimes and offenses–France
Classification: LCC KJV129.T47 W45 2026 (print) | LCC KJV129.T47 (ebook)
LC record available at https://lccn.loc.gov/2025054971
LC ebook record available at https://lccn.loc.gov/2025054972

ISBN 978-1-009-33322-1 Hardback

Additional resources for this publication at www.cambridge.org/9781009333221

CONTENTS

FIGURES

THE AUTHORS

All of the authors have been involved in a number of research projects funded by the research mission 'Droit et Justice' (National Scientific Research Fund-CNRS/Ministry of Justice), including Jihadist Networks on Trial (2017–2019) and The Trials of the 2015–2016 Terror Attacks in France – Ethnographic, Comparative and Memorial Analysis.

Sharon Weill is Professor of International Law at the American University of Paris and a Research Associate at Sciences Po, Paris. She holds a PhD in international law (Geneva University, 2012). Her research focuses on the relations between law, armed conflict, terrorism, and the role of judges, topics on which she has published numerous articles and book chapters. Her research method combines legal doctrine with socio-political approaches, including trial ethnography. Since 2017, she has been examining the role of French judges as transnational actors in the 'fight against terrorism' as well as the transformation of legal systems in the face of transnational jihadism. Previously, her postdoctoral research, carried out at the Center of Law and Society, University of California, Berkeley, focused on the Guantanamo Bay trials and Israeli military tribunals in the occupied territories. She worked for several years as a research fellow at the Geneva Academy of International Humanitarian and Human Rights at the University of Geneva. She was an expert member of the French National Consultative Commission on Human Rights (CNCDH) and she was nominated by the UN High Commissioner for Refugees to serve as a judge at the French Asylum Court (CNDA). Sharon Weill is the author of the book *The Role of National Courts in Applying International Humanitarian Law* (Oxford University Press, 2014), co-editor of the book *The President on Trial, Prosecuting Hissène Habré* (Oxford University Press, 2020), and the research report (in French) '*Jihadists on Trial: An Ethnographic of French Courts* (2017–2019)'.

Denis Salas is a magistrate and holds a PhD in Public Law and the Sociology of Law, and he is qualified to direct research (HDR, University of Paris I Panthéon-Sorbonne). His doctoral thesis 'Du procès pénal' was published in the prestigious *PUF* (France University Press and re-edited in 2011) and was written under the direction of Professor Mireille Delmas Marty. After having practiced as a juvenile judge and an investigating judge, he was nominated as Deputy Secretary General (1995–1998) at the Institute for Advanced Studies on Justice (IHEJ), where he continued his research into criminal law and the role of justice. A lecturer at the French National School for the Judiciary (1999–2007), he was appointed Vice President of the Tribunal de Grande Instance in 2007. He has since been appointed Scientific Director of Cahiers de la Justice (peer-reviewed journal of the French National School for the Judiciary/edition Dalloz). In addition, he is an international expert on justice issues (for various Superior Councils of the Judiciary, the Council of Europe, the European Union), and a visiting professor at various foreign universities (including Brussels, Tokyo, Ottawa, and Rio de Janeiro). Since 2016, he has been President of the French Association for the History of Justice (AFHJ), an association founded by Robert Badinter. In this context, he directs the collection 'History of Justice' (La Documentation Française) and organises a series of conferences at the Cour de cassation. His work focuses on the following themes: the relationship between justice and politics, the sense of punishment, the history of justice and its representations. He has published more than a hundred articles in various reviews and over a twelve dozen books. In 2020, he edited a special issue on the Charlie Hebdo trial in Cahiers de la Justice. His latest books include (unofficial translation from French): *The 100 Words of Justice* (Presses Universitaires de France, 2018), *The Innocent Crowd* (Desclée de Brouwer, 2018), and *Judging Terror* (1794–1795) (co-editor) (La Documentation Française, 2021).

Antoine Mégie, a political scientist, is an assistant professor at the University of Rouen in France, and an associate researcher at the University of Montreal. A former director of the journal *Politique européenne* (2011–2018), he is a member of the editorial board of the journal *Cultures et Conflits*. His research focuses on the place of law in the 'fight against terrorism'. His thesis at Sciences Po Paris (CERI) under the supervision of Renaud Dehousse and Didier Bigo on the evolution of European criminal cooperation in the fight against terrorism has led to numerous publications in scientific journals. In addition to coordinating several programmes on counterterrorism (Sciences Po Paris, King's College, Toronto University, and Montreal

University), his post-doctorate at the University of Montreal led him to study the transnationalization of counterterrorism norms (Europe and North America). Since 2015, he has been coordinating, with funding from the Ministry of Justice and the Normandy Region, the Jupiter Research Program (Justice à l'épreuve du terrorisme) on terrorism trials in France, and he has published the book '*Chroniques d'un procès du terrorisme: l'affaire Merah*' (La Martinière – Radio France edition, 2019). An expert at the European Parliament, the European Judicial Network and the National School for the Judiciary, he was Scientific Director, from 2015 to 2017, of the European training programme for European magistrates on the theme 'Fight against Terrorism and the Charter of Fundamental Rights of the ECHR'. Currently, he participates in two research programmes funded by the Ministry of Justice on the trials of the November 13 attacks: 'The trials of the terror attacks of 2015–2016 in France. Ethnographic, comparative and memorial analysis' and 'Victims and victims' associations in the trials of the January and November 2015 attacks (2020–2022)'.

Christiane Besnier, an anthropologist and research associate at the Center for Cultural Anthropology (CANTHEL) at the University of Paris Sorbonne, has been working on criminal courts in France and Europe since 2002. Since her PhD thesis was published in 2017, *La vérité côté cour – Une ethnologue aux assises* (La Découverte, Paris, 2017) she has been developing an ethnographic reflection on the oral nature of the actors involved in the trials, and the construction of truth in the courtroom. She has directed several research projects in France, including 'Les filières djihadistes en procès (2017–2019)' (Jihadist Networks on Trial, co-directed with Sharon Weill), funded by the research mission Droit et Justice (Ministry of Justice). In Europe, she has worked on the judicial practices of criminal courts in Belgium and Switzerland ('The construction of the motivation of criminal decisions in court, France, Belgium, and Switzerland', research supported by the Mission de Recherche Droit et Justice, 2014–2016). As part of a H2020 European research project involving fourteen countries on cultural expertise, directed by Livia Holden at the University of Oxford (Centre for Socio-Legal Studies), she was responsible for collecting and modelling the data in France. Currently, she is participating in research on: 'The trials of the 2015–2016 terror attacks in France. Ethnographic, comparative and memorial analysis'. Her analysis focuses on the parallel between the trial relating to the Parisian attacks of

13 November 2015 and the attacks of 22 March 2016 in Belgium. Since January 2008, she has been a member of the editorial committee of the journal Droit et Cultures (a biannual journal published with the support of the CNRS); between 2015 and 2021, she was the Editor-in-Chief of the peer review journal *Droit et Cultures*, University of Nanterre.

ACKNOWLEDGEMENTS

Our group dynamic – horizontal, engaging and collaborative – was possible thanks to the Mission Droit et Justice support and encouragement of multidisciplinary and empirical research on the judiciary. They made it possible for us to meet, to imagine and to collaborate on this long research journey. We would like to thank our academic colleagues (and each other), with whom we continue to collaborate: This book was only possible thanks to that synergy and motivation to work both together and individually, as well as to the encounters with other researchers along the way in court, including those in the PROMOTE group. A special thank you goes to Sandrine Lefranc, with whom we have built not only working partnerships but also a deep friendship that started within the court corridors. Many thanks to Benoît Peyrucq, whose sensitive eye brought the courtroom to life through his sketches. We are thankful to all the professionals we met and interviewed throughout this research. Without their insights and openness to research and intellectual dialogue, none of this would have been possible: Céline Ballerini, Régis de Jorna, David De Pas, Raphaël Kemp, Jean-Louis Periès, Ariel Planeix, Isabelle Prévost-Desprez, Olivia Ronen, Clémence Witt and many others.

A very special thank you to the Cambridge Law and Society series editors, and especially Mark Massoud and Rachel Stern, and to Sharon's Law and Society's family – Sara Dezalay, Jacqueline Hodgson, Malcolm Feeley, Kerstin Carlson, Ron Levy, IN-Court Network and many others – to whom we owe so much for their inspiring critics, intelligence and generosity. Thanks also to Sharon's dearest friend and collaborator, Kim Seelinger (and her beloved family).

Together, we also extend our thanks to the editorial teams at *Culture and Conflict* – especially Didier Bigo – and *Les Cahiers de la Justice*, for providing us with such critical and engaging platforms for French publications.

We are grateful as well to our home institutions.

Sharon Weill wishes to express her thanks to the American University of Paris and her department for their support. Special thanks go to Brian Schiff and Constance Pâris de Bollardière at the Schaeffer Center, whose generous funding enabled her to present early drafts of this work, and to Brenda Torney and the John H. Lewis Jr. Grant, which supported her during her sabbatical to complete the book, and to Susan Perry, who always has new ideas.

Sharon also wishes to thank her students at the AUP Justice Lab and the Sciences Po PSIA Capstone course, who accompanied her to court and became integral to her research. Special thanks are due to Adv. Jeanne Sulzer, with whom Sharon co-created a court-based course at Université Paris 2 Panthéon-Assas. She also extends her gratitude to Professor Olivier de Frouville for his trust and support.

Sharon also wishes to acknowledge the research centres that hosted and supported her during this project: CERI/Sciences Po Paris, with special mention to Nadia Marzouki for always being available to organise talks and seminars, her sharp and insightful analysis, and her smile. Thanks also to the Sorbonne Comparative and International Law Center, and its directors, Isabelle Fouchard and Kathia Martin-Chenut, for being 'undisciplined' researchers – where Sharon could find an intellectual home.

And finally, none of this journey would have been possible without the everyday light and love that Zoe and Maayane, Sharon's daughters and her partner, Bartolo Conti, bring to her life. Like everything else she does, this is for them.

Antoine Mégie wishes to express his thanks to the University of Rouen and his colleagues for their invaluable collaboration over the years, Virginie Sansico as part of the Jupiter programme, Sylvain Antichan, the members of CUREJ, and other colleagues from different Universities: Pauline Jarroux, Hèlène Bellanger, Anne Wyvekens, Aurore Behel, and Sylvie Lindeperg. Thanks to the fellow doctoral students Janna Behel, Mathilde Sergent-Mirebault, and Romane Gorce for including me in their exciting new research and doctoral careers. Thanks to students from the University of Rouen, and more specifically from the Master of Justice and Bachelor of Political Science programmes, our immersion in the world of trials has been recounted and has become the subject of courses and collective reflection.

Finally, I would like to thank those who have become my friends and many more during these years of research: Benoit, Charlotte, Florence, Edith, Céline, Julien, Tymothée, David, Soren, Monia, the team of Paris Victim Support, and special thought to Marie. Last but not least, much gratitude to my family and my two sons, Simon and Camille.

INTRODUCTION

FROM THE LABORATORY OF THE LOWER COURTS TO THE BATACLAN SHOW TRIAL

Three Generations of Terror Trials

In the last decade, the number of youths engaged in transnational jihadism has been increasing, with many of them joining armed forces in the Iraqi–Syrian conflict zone and committing acts of violence in France or abroad. The terrorist attacks on the headquarters of the satirical newspaper Charlie Hebdo and the Bataclan concert hall and surrounding cafés in 2015 can be seen as France's 9/11 and a turning point in its counter-terrorism policy: the war on terror had reached French soil. Against this socio-political setting, French legal institutions have been extensively mobilised. A two-year state of emergency was introduced between 2015 and 2017, gradually becoming part of common criminal law. The number of trials against individuals involved in armed groups on the Iraqi–Syrian front has reached a level unprecedented in the history of French criminal justice: terrorism has become a phenomenon of mass prosecution.

When these cases were only beginning to be prosecuted, in 2016, we proposed to the French 'Mission de Recherche Droit et Justice' – an independent research entity financed by the French National Centre for Scientific Research (CNRS) and the French Ministry of Justice – to study the courts that have the authority to hear these terrorism cases. The method proposed was ethnographic, and the originality of our project lay in its pluri-disciplinary nature. The research team was composed of an anthropologist, a political scientist and sociologist, a jurist (who was formerly a judge), and an international lawyer. They all had previous research experience in studying trials.[1] The project was accepted and funded. The initial research questions, which were to be examined through the lens of our different perspectives and disciplines, were focused on the role of the court and how counter-terrorism law is applied from within the courtrooms. Our methodological starting point was to enter the courtroom and to observe the trials. Together, we attended hundreds of hearings of jihadist terror trials between 2017 and 2022, as outlined in detail in the first chapter.

In line with legal ethnographic research on courts, our aim was to enter the places where the law is performed.[2] Combining anthropological and socio-legal approaches, derived from the European tradition of judicial ethnology begun by Malinowski in 1927[3] and continued in the later works of Norbert Rouland and Jan Broekman,[4] the approach employed for this book is reflected in the physical presence of the researcher in the courtroom for the entire trial period and is extended by theoretical reflection starting from legal norms. 'Participatory observation' as a fundamental qualitative research method allows for understanding cultures, behaviours, and human interactions in various social and political contexts, and in this case, the judiciary.

[1] The international lawyer, Sharon Weill, previously worked on the relationship between conflict, law and the role of judges. She was mainly interested in examining how the global war on terror was managed within local and ordinary judiciaries, and the extent of their dialogue with international law and politics. The political scientist, Antoine Mégie built upon previous work on European judicial cooperation and the transnational dynamics of the war on terrorism between Europe and North America (Canada, United States). The anthropologist, Christiane Besnier has been working ethnographically on criminal hearings in France and Europe since her doctoral studies. Her research focuses on the construction of the truth in the courtroom, and the role of the judges in this context, a notion that she wanted to further explore in terror cases. Denis Salas, judge and professor at the National School for the Judiciary, is also a historian of justice and widely published when it comes to various trials.

[2] Feeley, 1979; Latour, 2002; Weill, 2020; Mégie, 2021; Lefranc, 2021; Gill and Good, 2019; Fassin and Kobelinsky, 2012.

[3] Bronislaw Malinowski is the first ethnologist with an interest in law to conduct extended stays in the field. He bases his reflections not on ethnographic materials collected by other travellers, but on his own fieldwork conducted between 1914 and 1918 on various islands of New Guinea, particularly the Trobriand Archipelago. He documents these experiences in *Les Argonautes du pacifique occidental* in 1922 and *Les Jardins de corail* in 1935. He published two works in 1926 and 1927, *Crime and Custom in Savage Society* and *Sex and Repression in Savage Society*, which are derived from his observations of the inhabitants of the Trobriand Islands.

[4] Rouland, 1988; Broekman, 1993.

Applied to trials and, more broadly, to the justice system, it reveals how the law is practised and experienced, beyond legal texts and formal principles, providing valuable insights into the human and social reality of justice, offering thus nuanced perspectives of the making of the law, *law in action* (as opposed to *law on the books*).[5] The researcher is primarily interested in actual practice: it is the concrete case that serves as a basis for theoretical analysis, as the classical sociology of law leaves us with a 'missing something'.[6] In France, this methodology has been used in the work of Bruno Latour,[7] and it has been more widely developed by the American school of legal realism, ethnomethodology.[8] The aim is to understand the involvement of actors, the 'praxeology of the practice of law': 'This means that it considers absurd the pretention of dealing with the law while ignoring what its practitioners consider essential to their activities, that is, the rules; but it finds it equally indispensable to deal with these rules and the activities that refer to them through their modes of accomplishment.'[9] In this vein, our premise was that the production and evolution of the law do not simply take place through a shift in jurisprudence or legislation, but also through a transformation in the representations and practices of the actors in charge of formulating and applying it.[10]

I.1 WHY DOES ETHNOGRAPHY MATTER? GOING BEYOND DICHOTOMIES

To what extent have liberal democracies been loyal to the rule of law principle? Within law and society studies, it has been well observed that, since the 9/11 terrorist attacks, rule by exception has become a defining feature of liberal democracies.[11] Günter Jakobs' theory of the

[5] Vanhamme and Beyens, 2007; Colemans and Dupret, 2018. [6] Cefaï, 2010.
[7] Latour, 2010. [8] Colemans and Dupret, 2018, p. 18.
[9] Dupret, 2021, pp. 76–77:

> Legal praxeology is the perspective that claims to consider the law through practice ... Particular cases are studied ethnographically in order to elicit the mechanisms that are specific to how they unfold, including what is linked to the law as followed by both its professional and lay practitioners. Legal praxeology's descriptive attention is concerned with the methods proper to the people concerned. One could speak of an interest in "legal ethnomethods".

[10] Dezalay and Garth, 2002. [11] See for example, Abel, 2019.

'criminal law of the enemy' has received renewed attention,[12] identifying criminal law categories created for people who are not 'loyal' to political society, for whom procedural guarantees can be withdrawn if the circumstances require. General discussions on terrorism tend to frame the relationship between the rule of law and the state of exception as a binary opposition[13] that is reproduced in subsequent discussions on security versus rights or militarised security models versus rehabilitative criminal justice. While theories of exception and the permanent suspension of the law have opened avenues for important criticism,[14] this reading remains, however, it is a metatheory that does not allow for an understanding of the political, legal, and social phenomena in all their complexity. Critical scholars such as Bigo and Bonelli have called for the challenging of this doxa of simplified and blinding dichotomy, towards the development of approaches analysing a more complex transformation of practices. Boundaries are dynamic, and by empirically tracing the processes of boundary, a new understanding of the practice of law can emerge.[15]

This book examines how terrorism logics are reflected, represented, and negotiated, from within courtrooms, offering a nuanced approach based on the practice. Our method looks at the role of courts through a bottom-up approach, as performed and shaped within the judicial scene at the local level. It focuses on courtroom scenes to report on the ordinary nature of these legal processes. As opposed to doctrinal legal research on terrorism, which focuses essentially on the study of legislation and precedents of eclectic case studies, we consider the social interaction of the actors and the empirical context of judicial practices.[16] Narratives and interactions often remain outside the text of case law; by contrast, trial observation facilitates a nuanced understanding of how the law is made by the different protagonists, who operate within a specific context.

The French oral procedure has the advantage of offering the public and researchers unique access to the narratives and personal trajectories that led to the accused's involvement in terrorism-related acts, as narrated by the actors themselves. Indeed, one of the few places where the accused's voice is heard publicly is in the courtroom. Criminal trials of terrorism cases constitute privileged moments to

[12] Jakobs, 1985; Linhardt and Moreau de Bellaing, 2017. [13] Agamben, 2003.
[14] Huysmans, 2008. [15] Dezalay, 2020. [16] Cotterrell, 2012.

observe the dynamic management of 'terrorism': how and why indeterminate terms such as 'prevention', 'radicalisation', and 'dangerousness' are understood.

What becomes permissible with these practices, and according to what underlying policy objective? Our study analyses terrorism logics beyond the dichotomies. We examine how they are reflected, represented, and negotiated, from within courtrooms, based on the practice, the routine, and the evolution of the judicial process and the performance of the law, where a variety of actors and policies modulate these concepts through opposition, accommodation, or innovation. Beyond the empirical assessment of such a method, the analysis that emerges goes beyond simplified dichotomies and offers a nuanced, and sometimes contradictory, analysis of the law and practice that derives from empirical findings. As we show, the French judicial scene is constructed as a space for exercising power and, at the same time, seeking 'justice'. It provides spaces for expression and confrontation among the various actors, which can only be observed through ethnography. It is not simply security versus rights, exceptionalism versus the rule of law, repression versus reparation, but a space where conflicting concepts interact in an organic way and modulate justice in the era of jihadism. Beyond dichotomies, 'justice' does not speak in one voice: the application of the law could be at the same time nuanced and mechanical, adjusted and rigid.

I.2 CRAFTING OUR VIEWPOINT: MULTI-LAYERED ANALYTICAL FRAMES

Being researchers from different disciplines, we used complementary methodological approaches, which enriched the analysis of data throughout the entire research process and allowed us to use a multi-level reading grid as each perspective was developed and refined.[17] As the research evolved, it became clear that it was necessary to combine several strands of social science research to deepen our

[17] The strength of interdisciplinary, empirical legal studies when it comes to producing new knowledge and understandings of complex legal environment. Hambly, 2023, p. 20. For a discussion of the theoretical framing see Goffman, 1974; Bögelein et al., 2022.

understanding of the roles played by courts in terrorism cases, both as local and transnational actors, in relation to a wider legal, social, and political landscape. This realisation prompted us to explore a wide array of interdisciplinary approaches, including sociology, political science, law, legal anthropology, and criminology to capture the multifaceted nature of judicial processes in these cases.

Faced with analytical impasses regarding the concept of terrorism itself, an analysis under the lens of bureaucratic logics and the discourse of the actors involved allows us to deconstruct the terrorist 'genre' and its very strong discursive dimension. The analysis of the terrorist scene leads us to re-examine the question of continuity or rupture in the phenomenon since the 11 September 2001 attacks. The value of such an analysis lies primarily in its ability to avoid reducing the terrorist phenomenon to merely those groups that claim violent actions, thereby allowing for a necessary distancing from the term 'terrorism' itself. Indeed, in response to numerous critiques regarding the objective value of the term 'terrorism' for defining groups that use violence as a mode of action,[18] 'terrorism' does not only describe these actors but more broadly a system of power relations between various entities: societies, terrorist groups, political powers, security authorities, and media. The use of the plural to list these entities highlights that we do not consider them as homogeneous groups. The extreme fragmentation of terrorist actors, as exemplified by groups identifying with international jihadism, perfectly illustrates this postulate. This heterogeneity is also evident within security institutions, the media, and societies. Studying these as complex entities constitutes an important research avenue, similar to analysing the interactions that structure these groups of actors among themselves.[19] This perspective particularly helps to understand the dynamic dimension of the terrorist scene around the idea that each group defines and evolves based on the positions of others. Such a relational approach directly aligns with Bourdieu's concept of the social field as a configuration and space of struggles and objective relationships between positions that impose themselves objectively on their occupants, agents, or institutions.[20] The choice of this theoretical orientation is part of a broader approach regarding how security issues should be analysed in their entirety. By focusing on understanding the

[18] Sommier, 2000. [19] Mégie, 2010. [20] Bourdieu, 1987.

processes that shape the security–insecurity relationship within trials, the aim is to undertake a deconstructive task to avoid interpreting security as an objective concept, a natural consequence of the international political environment. From a reflexive perspective, security should be understood partly as a product of discourse.[21]

Convinced of the necessity to examine terror trials through several frames, we constructed a dimensional framework that guided our data collection as well as our analysis. While each of these stands alone as a separate field, together they yield the singular perspective presented in this book, and can serve as a guide for studying courts in other contexts:

(1) The dynamic of the legal doctrines: The inner legal language is an important aspect of analysis, both in terms of tracing the development of the doctrines and their limitations. While acknowledging that any legal doctrine has its underlying socio-political goals, as a doctrine is developed and functions as an independent force, it can eventually achieve other visions through interpretation or fact-finding.[22] Far from being 'neutral', a legal decision is motivated by political choices that shape it. Through an 'internal' critique of the law,[23] we examined how French criminal courts legally constitute the meaning of law and for what underlying purpose, while filling content into vague statutory terminology, such as 'dangerousness', 'radicalisation', and 'terrorism'. We further analyse how judicial actors establish the facts, and to whose vision they correlate (for example, by the use of presumptions or by giving more weight to the narratives of security agents or 'experts').

(2) The role of the human actors: Beyond positivist law, a court decision is a product of the interaction and contribution of many actors, given as a result of a given empirical context of judicial practice. The actors' trajectory, competencies, prior socialisation, and political positioning are key to understanding how court decisions are made. Second, the interactions between these players,

[21] For instance, Ole Waever bases his reasoning on the notion of the 'speech act' (Waever, 1989) drawing on philosophical and linguistic work by authors such as Jacques Derrida and John Austin.
[22] Shapiro, 1986; Kennedy, 1997; Carlson, 2018; Weill, 2014.
[23] The critique of the legal reasoning is done through a politico-legal analysis influenced by Critical Legal Studies (CLS) and Political Jurisprudence.

particularly the extent to which they cooperated, confronted one another, and were impacted by different internal or political struggles or networks, demonstrate how the practices and legal choices of different actors are impacted by power dynamics.[24] Third, the component of 'law in action' – which refers to the court's ritual and the performance of the protagonists: their language, their position, their actions[25] – was at the centre of our attention.

(3) Institutional mass litigation: Hierarchy, routine, and bureaucracy.

The legal work of lower courts is necessarily impacted by the structure of the institution, including by institutional routine, legal bureaucracy, and working conditions.[26] Routines, organised by managers, set the balance between the legal and social dimensions of the act of judging and orient the work of courts towards a bureaucratic goal of efficiency. This is how a trial becomes a work of routine by professionals bounded by institutional bureaucracy, hierarchy, and sometimes personal precarity.

Beyond the confinement of the courtroom, we interrogate wider institutional structures in the courthouse to decipher the extent of their impact on the cases we observed. A judge does not adjudicate a case in isolation from others; rather, judges reproduce their knowledge and perception of the 'truth' from case to case. Each of their individual legal decisions heavily depends on the corpus of their work and previous experiences, which is also attuned to the institutional agenda. They adjudicate cases as part of their routine workload in the context of mass litigation reality, in which the law is applicable as a result of accumulative knowledge, previous experience, and shaped policy. Thus, decisions result from more general dynamics that go beyond just the characteristics of a specific case. It is the omnipresence of several factors such as specialisation, the *massification of case law*, and policy that leads to a certain line of jurisprudence, apparent only while studying the court's practice as developed over their routine work during of long period of time. A case study approach in which an exceptional case, a precedent, is observed, only masks the overwhelming cumulative power of ordinary and banal judgments.[27]

[24] Bourdieu, 1987; Christensen, 2017; Lefranc, 2021. [25] Dupret, 2010.
[26] Latour, 2002; Bigo, 2007; Fassin, 2013. [27] Shamir, 1990.

In relation to broader state hierarchical power, 'terrorist cases' have remained distinct objects of judicial scrutiny due to their contentious nature, often prompting a reconfiguration of state institutions, particularly their penal power. This examination builds on prior literature. For example, in their analysis of situations that examine the state and its bureaucracy through 'tests', Linhardt and Vitale redefine court judgement as a thoeretical and methodological framework that allows for the examination of 'the processes through which the state redefines and reorganises itself in relation to specific contexts and issues'.[28] Likewise, the body of work dedicated to street-level bureaucrats and 'frontline' actors has, from its inception, focused on judges and their role in the implementation of sentences or their alternatives.[29] The recent emphasis on reaffirming the importance of studying judges as key actors in public actions[30] aligns with a broader expansion of ethnographic research within judicial authorities.

(4) Geo/political interdependence and interconnection: Despite judges claiming their underlying capacity to evade political variables, they are not isolated but an integral part of a political process.[31] Starting from this premise, we are first interested in examining the space allocated to politics within the courtroom: how the conflict in Syria is portrayed, and how facts are established against a complex reality that involves a matrix of actors and geopolitical interests. As lower criminal courts render decisions on a case-by-case basis without imposing general policies, their political impact becomes barely visible. It becomes apparent through studying the court's case law over several years. This is not to say that individual judges are not independent, simply that they do engage with politics all the time and have themselves a political role. Drawing on Foucault's reflections, the analysis also looks at the mobility of political powers – between the State, the organs of justice, and individuals – while situating the political role of these courts within the broader context of international political arenas. Michel Foucault, urges us

> not to take power as a phenomenon of domination, massive and homogeneous – domination of one individual over others, of one

[28] Linhardt and Vitale, 1980.
[29] Lipsky, 1980.
[30] Biland and Steinmetz, 2017.
[31] Parsons, 1962; Shapiro and Stone Sweet, 2002.

> group over others... to bear in mind that power, unless considered from very high and very far away, is not something that is shared between those who have it and who hold it exclusively, and then those who don't have it and who undergo it. Power, I believe, must be analyzed as something that circulates, or rather as something that only functions in a chain. It's never localized here or there, it's never in the hands of a few, it's never appropriated as wealth or property. Power works. Power is exercised in a network, and on this network, not only do individuals circulate, but they are always in a position to undergo and also to exercise this power. They are never the inert or consenting target of power; they are always its relays. In other words, power transits through individuals, it does not apply to them.[32]

To conclude, the book brings together these four distinct yet interconnected fields of study – legal doctrines, the role of the human actor, institutional structures, and the political interconnections – to present a comprehensive framework for understanding the judicial scene. By integrating these perspectives, the book demonstrates how each dimension informs and shapes the others, offering a nuanced view of how law is modulated and justice is performed. This approach is novel in its insistence on treating these dimensions not as isolated areas of inquiry but as mutually constitutive forces that together construct the act of judging. The theoretical contribution lies in showing that the judicial process cannot be fully understood without accounting for the interplay of abstract legal principles, human agency, institutional dynamics, and broader political implications. This integrative methodology provides a new lens through which scholars can study judicial systems, emphasising the necessity of a multidisciplinary approach that further research can adopt and expand upon.[33]

[32] Michel Foucault, Il faut défendre la société, cours au collège de France, année 1975–1976, cours du 7 janvier 1976, Paris, Gallimard, 1999, p. 33. Loss translation. See also, Foucault, 1975, p. 55. "'Regimes of Truth', the types of discourse that society accepts as true, the mechanisms that society uses to distinguish true statements from false ones, the techniques and procedures that are valued for obtaining the 'truth.'"

[33] A workshop around these frames was organised by Sharon Weill and Sara Dezalay in the Onati Institute for the Sociology of the Law in 30–31 May 2024. See also Weill et al., 2022.

I.3 THE STRUCTURE OF THE BOOK

After years of collective research, together and separately, numerous conferences and exchanges, reports and follow-up projects, we have endeavoured to write a book together. Alas, many experiences, anecdotes, field notes, data, and analysis must remain beyond its bounds. Bearing in mind that 'writing always means betraying',[34] this book is by no means exhaustive. It is a narrative that we have crafted for this purpose, where we explore the three generations of trials we have identified during the research. While there is a rich store of English-language literature in the area of counter-terrorism, it focuses mainly on common law systems – most notably, the seminal work by Richard Abel on U.S. courts. Too few studies address civil law systems. From an empirical and comparative perspective, a major objective of the book is to contribute to existing Anglophone literature on the civil law judicial system,[35] and to allow English readers access to, and an understanding of, criminal terror trials in France. The first two chapters provide this in detail. The first chapter begins by opening the door to the courtroom, introducing readers to the location, arrangements, and our methods. The second chapter introduces the various counter terrorism judicial actors and the criminal procedure. The chapters that follow on from these (3–5) present our main findings for the three generations of trials, which we have identified. The first generation of jihadist trials took place before the 16th Chamber in the lower criminal courts (Tribunal Correctionnel) in Paris, which centralised all terrorism offences with sentences of up to ten years imprisonment. Between 2014 and 2018, more than 200 individuals faced prosecution, and an additional 1,600 individuals were subject to criminal investigation. These trials are discussed in Chapter 3, entitled *The Lower Courts' Laboratory: Designing the Architecture and Experimenting the Policy*, in which we offer

[34] Fassin, 2013, p. 32, cited in Hambly, 2023.

[35] See the works of Jacqueline Hodgson, published following her ethnographic study of French police stations, prosecutor offices, and the offices of investigative judges and courts (Hodgson, 2005, 2020; Renée Lerner, who wrote a fundamental article on a French criminal trial: Lerner, 2001); Antoine Garapon and Ioannis Papadopoulos, who authored a seminal book comparing the American and French systems: Garapon and Papadopoulos, 2003; and Frank Foley who looked at countering terrorism in Britain and France: Foley, 2013. Recently, the film *Anatomie d'une Chute* (*Anatomy of a Fall*) brought criminal French law to the Oscars in Hollywood and won the award for Best Original Screenplay.

an immersion into the procedure of the 16th Chamber. This includes 'ghost trials'; the recurring practice in this period to put the dead on trial when they did not possess 'official death certificates' from Syria. Our takeaway from these observations is that, with the first generation of jihadist trials, the 16th Chamber operated as the laboratory that designed the judicial response to jihadism. It was forged upon broad pre-emptive approaches and undefined notions of dangerousness and radicalisation, which had been gradually experimented, shaped, and practised. The use of one accusation defined in 1996, the 'association of wrongdoing in relation to a terrorist enterprise' (AMT),[36] allowed the prosecution of vast networks of suspects only very loosely related to one another, and with little evidence, while holding them in prison for up to three years up to the trial. This served as a period for the collection of information. This repressive and preventive approach was put into practice through close collaboration between the investigating judges and the prosecution, alongside the specialisation of the judges. Entrusted with growing authority and resources, these actors have become experts in jihadist networks. We have also seen how the narratives of the accused are co-constructed with the other actors. Yet, despite their specialisation, in the aftermath of the major terrorist attacks carried out in January and November 2015 (including at the Charlie Hebdo headquarters and the Bataclan concert hall), the cases were transferred to the Assize Court, which can impose a punishment of up to life imprisonment, to facilitate a higher punishment. Chapter 4 focuses on these trials, namely the second generation of jihadist trials, in a chapter subtitled *The Slow Justice of the French Assize Court*. Assize Court proceedings are characterised by their oral and protracted nature. The Assize Court hears cases involving the most serious criminal offences and has the authority to apply severe punishments. However, appearing before the Assize Court at that time also meant being heard by non-specialised judges, and for a long period of time in a procedure that has two main features: the oral nature of the proceedings and an investigation into the personalities of the accused. This process allows for the creation of a unique space, in which the accused can (and indeed is expected to) express themselves. During our research, we observed that this process facilitated the emergence of narratives that

[36] In French: *Association de malfaiteurs en relation avec une enterprise terroriste*, hereinafter: AMT Article 421-2-1 of the French Criminal Code. See discussion in Chapter 2.

had an unexpected impact on the final decisions of the judges in terms of punishment. We noticed that the non-specialised judges familiarised themselves with the complex sociological and geopolitical context, which they discovered during the proceedings. The long duration of the Assize Court proceedings offers rare opportunities to hear about the radicalisation process as told by the defendants and their environment. This 'slow justice'[37] procedure had an unexpected, inverse consequence: the judges imposed significantly lower penalties than those requested. The trial judges openly resisted the prosecution policy, which involved a clash of positions within the judicial profession. This struggle around the prosecution policy demonstrates that 'justice' does not speak with one voice; on the contrary, it is made up of different actors with different professional interests and ways of acting.

Our data shows how lower jurisdictions, acting in a transnational context, can offer stronger resistance to state policies compared to the Supreme Courts. This is because of the routine of their work and the banality of their function, and the direct interaction with the accused persons, coupled with the judges' own notions of judicial independence and professional criminal justice ethos. Unlike the Supreme Courts, whose role is more visible and thus under the constant scrutiny of the political branches of the state, lower courts can operate in a more distant, independent space. Supreme Court jurisprudence is doctrinal in nature, often decided without discussing the facts or hearing the sides of the case directly. In a lower court, however, the situation is radically different. Lower judges work on a case-by-case basis, where the accused is present. Through the establishment of the facts, they have room to dissociate themselves from doctrine or jurisprudence; in this space – in an ordinary courtroom, far away from the centre of power and the media – they can resist preventive state policy and promote other values such as stronger criminal rehabilitation approaches. Lower judges may have an important role to play here; under certain

[37] The term 'Slow Justice' (akin to 'Slow Food') was inspired by discussions at a conference organised by Jackie Hodgson, titled 'The McDonaldization of Justice and the Disappearance of Fair Trial?' at the University of Warwick in April 2020. While many legal systems adopt a capitalist and managerial approach of 'efficiency', leading to 'fast' justice, such as the use of plea bargains, terror trials in the Assize Courts present the exact opposite: they are lengthy, with notable space for expressing opinions, and with efficiency seemingly not prioritised: appeals that can be plodged also by the State, are essentially retrials, where everything is re-examined from the beginning.

conditions, it is those judges who can develop an alternative approach to the preventive doctrine.[38]

At the same time, during hearings, judges had to assess the 'potential dangerousness' of the accused and their 'radicalisation' to prevent a future potential act – that is the preventive shift of the Assize Court. The question of 'potential dangerousness' was thus present in all of the trials we followed. On the one hand, there is the objective of prevention, framed by a prevailing climate of suspicion and on the other hand, there is the criminal justice procedure, still committed to the principles of a fair trial and the independence of the judges, both of which are anchored by criminal judges through their professional ethos. During the ethnography, it became apparent how judges position themselves both in relation to their attempts to handle their own personal and societal feelings of suspicion towards those accused of terrorism, and, on the other hand, a professional concern to produce a fair decision. This contradiction leads to mixed feelings: although the process is carried out with attention and openness, offering an important space for expression and nuance, the impossibility of this preventive task renders the process profoundly unjust and arbitrary.

Chapter 5 analyses '*The Trials for History*', the third generation of trials that took place between 2020 and 2022. The Charlie Hebdo and the Bataclan trials involved an exceptional number of diverse actors, including thousands of victims.[39] Characterised by their long duration, extensive media coverage, transnational echoes, and most importantly, the participation of a significant number of victims as civil parties, these trials mark the third generation of jihadist terrorism trials in France. These terrorism trials announced the emergence of 'hybrid justice', with the strong participation of victims integrating explicit restorative goals within the criminal trial, triggering strong emotions within the courtroom, transforming the trials into a platform that reminds us of truth commissions. These trials were performed as big productions, referred to by scholars as 'liberal show trials',[40] namely trials with an explicit societal role. Indeed, these trials were the culmination of the

[38] Weill, 2020.

[39] For a background on the Charlie Hebdo and Bataclan attacks, See box 5.1, pp. 152–154. The 2016 terrorist attack in the city of Nice (and its trial), although mentioned and part of the third generation of trials, is not analysed in this book, as our joint ethnography ended with the Bataclan trial.

[40] Osiel, 2008.

professional expertise accumulated during these years. Interestingly, these trials were not only a peak of repression. They went far beyond merely establishing the criminal responsibility of a few defendants. Modulating criminal procedure 'from within', these trials introduced an important restorative dimension, being significantly open to victims, political actors, social scientists, and the expression of the accused.[41] These trials also posed new questions regarding the link between victims' rights and the right of the defence.

The Bataclan trial included over 2,300 civil parties (victims) and 400 lawyers. In French criminal law procedures, victims have the right to participate in the proceedings as civil parties, and are an integral party to it. The first five weeks were devoted to depositions by the civil parties. If these did not contribute to fact finding, the accumulation of individual stories formed a collective narrative of shared trauma. While it was not obvious the defendants would participate in this justice project, all but two answered the judges' questioning and they had multiple exchanges with the victims that triggered strong emotions. In seeking to understand, civil parties called to the stand *witnesses of context* – including politicians and academics – to shed light on the socio-political context. This undertaking by the French criminal court to fulfil the 'right to truth' once again evokes transitional justice, in the same way that truth commissions can expose the involvement of the state apparatus in repression. Our premise is that these trials may be seen as a new paradigm of *mass crime restorative prosecution*, which could be used to design future ways of carrying out justice.

The final chapter offers a comparative reflection on the trials of the 9/11 attacks in the United States at Guantanamo Bay and the Bataclan attacks in France, highlighting their distinct approaches to handling terrorism through the judiciary. While the 9/11 trial, conducted under the U.S. military commission system, was marked by prolonged proceedings characterised by delays, secrecy, and limited victim participation, the Bataclan trial was conducted within a civilian court system that emphasised transparency, and a strong focus on the voices of both victims and defendants. From these cases, important lessons can be drawn for designing future mechanisms to address trials for mass crimes.

[41] Weill and Lefranc, 2025.

I.4 RELOCATING LOCAL COURT RESEARCH IN A GLOBAL CONTEXT

This research is situated within academic literature on the 'War on Terror' in a democratic context,[42] critical global law and security studies,[43] and courtroom ethnographies.[44] From a global perspective, since '9/11', the United Nations and other international institutions and agencies have developed a global and transnational legal framework to fight terrorism,[45] although the concept of terrorism has never been clearly defined.[46] Scholars have raised deep concerns about the implementation and the uncertain impact of this broad new legislative framework on individual liberty, as it has challenged some of the very foundations of liberal criminal law by introducing the uncertain notion of prevention.[47]

Yet, despite an evolving transnational landscape, in which lower national courts are increasingly asked to perform a transnational role, being directly involved in major geopolitical issues such as the global 'War on Terror', the role of national courts as international players is usually considered only with respect to constitutional/supreme courts.[48] Studies of lower courts, in contrast, are still conducted essentially within a narrow national context, or in a comparative way on a specific issue, and do not usually extend their analysis of international relations. They are carried out either through the lens of criminology, bureaucracy, and process,[49] or through Foucault's 'discipline and punish' theory, addressing the management of dangerous populations and the state's moral control.[50]

Previously approached mainly in a top-down manner, 'Transnational Legal Orders'[51] have provided a larger conceptual framework for

[42] Abel, 2019; Vedaschi and Scheppele, 2021.
[43] Bigo and Bonelli, 2018; Chinkin and Kaldor, 2017.
[44] In the context of terrorism see, for example, Mayur, 2023.
[45] De Londras, 2022.
[46] Cassese, 1989a; Saul, 2020; De Graaf and Schmid, 2016.
[47] Garapon and Rosenfeld, 2016; Scheinin, 2013; Roach, 2015; Krähenmann, 2014; De Guttry et al., 2016; Ní Aoláin, 2018.
[48] Weiler, 1991; Shapiro and Stone Sweet, 2002; Hirschl, 2004; Ginsburg and Moustafa, 2008; Slaughter, 2004; Alter, 2014; Waldron, 2021.
[49] Feeley, 1979; Kohler-Hausmann, 2018.
[50] Foucault, 1975; Feeley and Simon, 1992; Garland, 2001; Fassin, 2017.
[51] Halliday and Shaffer, 2015. This framework of analysis offers an original and flexible lens for understanding legal dynamics. It includes international and national legal processes and assesses the interaction of multiple actors at different levels within

studying the complexity of formation and implementation of transnational norms by international and domestic actors. For example, it identifies the growing influence of domestic legal complexes – composed of different legal actors with varying, and sometimes contradictory, political goals – on international politics.[52] With regard to terrorism studies, it has been applied to addressing different aspects such as United Nations listings and sanctions,[53] the financing of terrorism,[54] and intelligence.[55] Further studies have looked more generally at the matrix of global, transnational, and EU counter-terrorism legislation and actors, while highlighting their challenges to democracy.[56] Yet, transnational legal research tends to produce studies that overlook the routine and local management of justice. It moves too quickly from the local to the trans/global, without taking the necessary resources and time to investigate local practices. Thus, the routine legal practices of national lower courts, which are tasked with transnational issues, with dealing with thousands of people, have remained understudied, and the necessity to conduct further prolonged empirical investigations has been highlighted. In fulfilling this research and methodology gap, we aim to 're-localise' terrorism studies into their geographical space and analyse the trans/national from 'within', through a bottom-up approach based on prolonged localised ethnographies.[57] Reaching all the way down to local practice,[58] our approach echoes the ones used by new legal realism scholars and international sociologists.[59]

organisations, including international bodies, transnational professional networks, and state practices through the inclusion of horizontal and vertical relations, while relying on empirical data instead of pre-made models that transcend the state-centred approach.

[52] See Karpik and Halliday, 2011. [53] Sullivan, 2014, 2020.

[54] De Goede, 2012, 2020. [55] Bigo, 2016.

[56] Murphy, 2015; De Londras, 2019, 2022.

[57] Massoud, 2021; Lefranc, 2021; Baczko, 2021; Mustafina, 2022; Weill, 2020; Braconnier Moreno, 2024.

[58] Shaffer and Ginsburg, 2012; Halliday and Shaffer, 2015.

[59] Merry, 2006; Talesh et al., 2021.

CHAPTER ONE

COURTROOM SCENES AND METHODOLOGY

The rationale of the hearing in the French court is for judicial truth to emerge as the product of a lengthy and collective process. The principle of the *orality of debates*, stemming from the French Revolution, embodies the essence of the French judicial procedure: all facts from the investigation file that are to be considered must be presented orally. The lengthy duration of the hearing aims at allowing for the emergence of an intimate space in which moments of truth could emerge, through the interaction of the different protagonists. The trial represents the public phase of the judicial process, where the hypotheses of the investigating judges are examined collectively and in an adversarial manner, within a defined order.

It is the Paris jurisdiction that centralises all terrorism cases. Depending on their gravity, these cases are tried either by the 16th Chamber of the Paris lower criminal court (Tribunal Correctionnel) or by the Special Bench of the Assize Court, which hears cases carrying sentences of over ten years' imprisonment.

These courtrooms provide a space where each actor has a defined place. Studies have shown that using the courtroom as a theatrical setting, the protagonists engage in a politics of performance[1] which influences the exchanges during trial hearings and may ultimately affect the decisions themselves,[2] or at least create an autonomous social

[1] Arendt, 1963; McEvoy et al., 2022; Allo, 2015; Leebaw, 2011.
[2] Weill et al., 2020; Simonson, 2014.

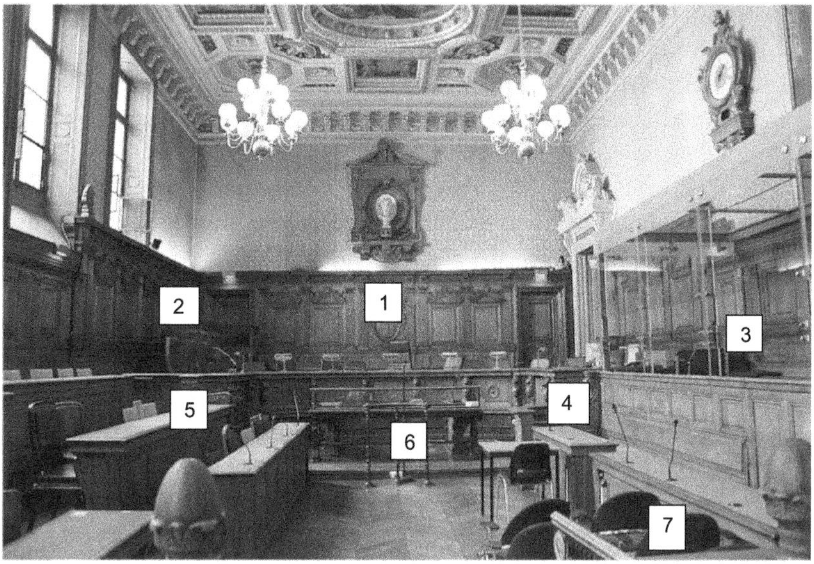

Figure 1.1 The 'Voltaire' courtroom, situated in the historic French 'Palais de Justice'.[3]

space, where political and social dynamics are created.[4] The architecture and the organisation of the space play a major role in shaping these performance dynamics. They contribute to the creation of an atmosphere,[5] which is also influenced by legal rituals, dress, and language,[6] which express and represent the hierarchy and state apparatus.[7] Despite approaches that view this spatial confinement as a distinct unity, the judicial scene – especially in terrorism cases – is in a state of permanent flow with the 'outside', which is omnipresent in the courtroom, and vice versa. Certain fundamental players – such as the investigator and intelligence services – remain unseen, yet play a significant role, being a central element of terrorism trials.[8]

(1) *La Cour* (The Court): The bench is composed of the presiding judge, wearing a red robe, sitting in the centre of a raised platform,

[3] The picture is publicly available at: https://commons.wikimedia.org/wiki/File:Palais_de_justice_de_Paris_-%20_salle_Voltaire_(cour_d%27assises).jpg?uselang=fr

[4] In the Dutch context, see: Immler and Wentholt, 2023; and for the US context: Simonson, 2017.

[5] Garapon, 1997; Bens, 2022.

[6] Besnier, 2007; Bourdieu, 1991.

[7] Bourdieu, 1991.

[8] Bigo et al., 2023; Mégie, 2020; Weill and Robinson, 2020.

surrounded by four assistant judges in black robes, two on each side. The presiding judge is directing the debates and maintains order.

(2) The prosecutor sits on the same level as the judges, in the corner, facing the accused. S/he is questioning the accused after the judges.

(3) The accused, if in custody, sits behind glass, in the so-called box. The 'box' can accommodate up to ten individuals. Each defendant is surrounded by two gendarmes and seated in a way to ensure a clear view for the court. A stand may be placed near the box for an interpreter.

(4) Defence lawyers sit in front of their clients. They can exchange words through a hole in the glass. If the accused is not in detention, they sit next to their lawyer. The lawyers only rarely intervene during the interrogation by the judge or the other actors. They will wait for their turn, and have a final word.

(5) Civil parties (victims) and their lawyers face the accused. Victims have the right to participate in the trial as civil parties, with extensive rights such as the right of access to the investigation file, and the prerogative to call a witness to the stand and to question the accused during the trial. Their civil claim is decided by the same bench immediately after the verdict.

(6) The witness stand: the witness always talks while looking towards the presiding judge.

(7) The public benches (beyond the frame of the picture): The front rows are reserved for experts, families, researchers, and journalists. In certain big trials, large screens bring the proceedings to those beyond the courtroom's walls, sometimes placed in adjacent rooms to accommodate the overflow.

As seen in the figure 1.1 the space where the debate between the parties takes place, led by the presiding judge, is known as 'le prétoire' (1–6). The second area of the courtroom is the audience area where the public sits (7). These two spaces are separated in various ways depending on the courtroom: a door, a barrier, a step, or a rope. *La Cour* (The Court), a solemn assembly is presided by a judge (1), wearing a red robe, seated at the centre of a raised platform. Surrounded by assisting judges in somber black, the scene is one of grave authority.[9] The prosecutor (2), sits at the same level as the trial

[9] See Code of Criminal Procedure, Art. 243: 'The court proper consists of: the presiding judge and the assessors.'

judges, while facing the accused. Elevated on their podium, they cast a gaze downwards upon the accused (3), the defence (4), and witnesses (6), a visual assertion of the state's authority. The defendant, if held in custody, is sitting enclosed in the 'box', behind a glass, next to policemen. Below, the defence lawyers and the defendants (3, 4) face the victims/civil parties and their lawyers (5). This setting presents the victims and the accused in a juxtaposition.

This architectural arrangement contrasts sharply with common law trials, where the prosecutor and the accused are positioned on the same level, symbolising the equality of arms, while the judge stands at an equal distance between the two actors in a triadic structure, with the victims absent. In France, the architecture represents a hierarchical structure, in which the state, through the judicial authorities, looks down on the accused. It seems that all 'arms' are directed towards the accused, in the pursuit of a shared truth to form the basis of a fair judgment that is supposed to be understood and accepted.

The choreography within this space is one of restrained movement. Judges always remain seated; the prosecutor, lawyers and accused rise when they speak but stay rooted in their place. Unlike cinematic portrayals, no one strays from their designated position; only witnesses traverse to the 'prétoire'. Those whose testimonies are very long may be granted the mercy of a seat. Eyes and voices are directed in all times towards the presiding judge. It can be a demanding exercise: lawyers, often positioned behind the witness, lack direct sightlines to the witnesses responding to their questions.

Within this scenography, the accused is at the centre of the interrogation. Starting with the hypotheses set out in the investigation file, constructed by an investigative judge during a long process that preceded the trial, the court, led by the presiding judge, conducts its own independent inquiry and reconstructs the various aspects of the case by directly questioning the accused, as well as other witnesses. While the pre-trial investigation phase is conducted confidentially, the trial hearing represents the public phase of the judicial process, during which all the actors are confronted. The accused has the right to remain silent, but this is quite unusual. Rather, the 'search for the truth' promotes a quite flexible procedure based on narratives and direct exchanges. Unlike common law criminal trials, everything is set to trigger the active participation of the accused, with the procedure much more accommodating, allowing also for spontaneous expression and interventions by the protagonists at different stages of the trial. Thus, it is not uncommon to see, under the strict control of the presiding judge, who remains the master of the courtroom, the accused suddenly interrupting a testimony to engage in a direct and free exchange with the victims or the prosecutor, or to have unexpected events that bring forth new issues. This way of interacting can also lead the prosecutor, by the end of the hearings, to request a requalification of the charges if new understandings emerge.

It is in this setting that our research was conducted. It took place across various sites, following the judicial spaces dedicated to the hearing of terrorism cases, during the years of the 'Global War on Terror', corresponding to the period in which France played an active role on the military front in Syria. Section 1 introduces the courtrooms within the Assize Court and the lower Criminal Court. Section 2 outlines our methodology and our evolving immersion in the court environment and the gradual consolidation of our presence.

1.1 MULTIPLE SITES ETHNOGRAPHY

Our inquiry was conducted through ethnographic research in two main locations in Paris, the 'Palais de Justice', situated in the city centre, and the new, modern courthouse built in the north of Paris – *Les Batignolles* – designed by the renowned architect Renzo Piano.

The collection of first-hand data on hundreds of hearing days, including the major terrorism trials, was made possible by our gradual and intimate immersion in these courthouses, at different sites, both formal and informal. The courtrooms included the assize benches and the 16th chamber of the lower criminal court, both dedicated to terror trials. Within the courtroom, we were able to grasp formal and spontaneous exchanges that would otherwise have gone unheard, most notably the questions of the judges and narratives of the accused, which can only be heard publicly in this setting. It also allowed us to observe professional interactions and organisation in and around the trials. The observations were carried out continuously by the presence of at least one of the members of the team, and often several, who communicated the evolution of the trial to absent members.

Our immersion continued through informal exchanges with lawyers, judges and journalists as well as with the families of the accused.

Beyond the courtrooms, our immersion extended to include other spaces such as the cafeteria, the courtyard, the security lines, and the press rooms. This allowed for the collection of unofficial information, anecdotes, and personal insights, obtained by discussions, daily meetings, and occasional exchanges in the corridors, during the suspension of the sessions, or while waiting for verdicts, sometimes late in the evening. This led to a deeper and more nuanced understanding of how the law can be seen through the lens of routine and the banality of human interaction.[10] During long trials, we could further observe how these sites were transformed into a space with its own social environment, which redefined the roles of those involved.

In addition to prolonged trial observations in these courts, we also attended a few hearings at the French Constitutional Court, where the constitutionality of terrorism legislation was examined, and at the French Conseil d'État, the supreme administrative court, which reviewed state orders during the period of the state of emergency. Further participatory observation was conducted in different professional contexts. Between 2017 and 2019, one of the authors, Sharon Weill, was part of a network created by academics, NGOs, and lawyers, which was coordinated by Open Society and a member of the French National Human Rights Commission (CNCDH). This allowed her to keep up to date with the many legal developments and litigations before the constitutional and administrative courts as well as the European Court of Human Rights, and to interact with judicial actors in different settings.[11] Other members of our group carried out some scientific collaboration with the National School for the Judiciary and organised a series of conferences with the European unit for judicial cooperation in combating terrorism. Our students were also involved in these different networks and joined us in conducting court observations.[12]

[10] Latour, 2002; Dupret et al., 2015; Kohler-Hausmann, 2018.

[11] In addition, Antoine Mégie was the Scientific Director of the European Programme, 'The Fight Against Terrorism in Light of the Charter of Fundamental Rights of the ECHR,' National School for the Judiciary (ENM) – Council of Europe (2016–2018) and of the European Training Programme for judges (ENM France – European Judicial Network): 'The Judicial Treatment of Violent Radicalism in Europe', Paris, November 2015. Denis Salas has organised training sessions on a regular basis at the ENM.

[12] 'Terror in Courts: French counter-terrorism. Administrative and Penal Avenues – Report prepared for the official visit of the UN Special Rapporteur on Counter-

1.1.1 The Assize Court for Terrorism Cases

Our common ethnography commenced in 2017 with the beginning of the first jihadist terrorism cases at the Assize Court. The Paris Assize Court, which has exclusive jurisdiction over cases that are punishable by ten years' imprisonment or more, is situated in the old Palais de Justice in the city centre.[13] During the years of the 'French war on terror', and in response to the growing number of cases linked to acts of terrorism, the number of courtrooms dedicated to criminal cases increased, passing from three in 2017 to four in 2019. Figure 1.1 shows the Voltaire courtroom, the oldest Assize courtroom. We attended several trials in this courtroom, including the Cannes–Torcy case. Additionally, there is the Victor Hugo courtroom, the Georges Vedel Georges courtroom, and finally, the Myriam Ezratty courtroom, which was named after a president of the Paris Court of Appeal.

The bench for the terrorist cases at the Assize Court is composed of a presiding judge alongside four assistant judges ('assesseurs'/assessors), without a jury of ordinary citizens, as is the case with regular Assize trials.[14] This is why it is named the 'Specially Composed Assize Court'. For each trial, a different set of judges sits on the bench. The presiding judge is chosen from the regular pool of Assize judges, while the other four assistant judges can be any judge, regardless of their specialised experience in terrorism. Previously, the court was composed of seven judges, but due to the increasing number of terrorism cases, it was reduced to five members – one president and four assessors – with decisions now being adopted through a regular majority, unlike jury courts. The origin of this special chamber can be traced back to the 1980s, when it initially established jurisdiction solely over crimes related to the military and the safety of the State. By 1986, its

Terrorism and Human Rights' by Sharon Weill and her students of The Capstone Course, PSIA, Sciences-Po, Paris (May 2018); 'Terrorisme et état d'urgence – Jurisprudence des hautes juridictions françaises', Capstone Course on International Crimes and Counter-terrorism, under the supervision of Sharon Weill, Sciences Po Paris (April 2017); Promete, 2021.

13 For a historical description of this courthouse, see Jackson, 2023.

14 Article 706-25 of the Code of Criminal Procedure (Title 15: On the prosecution, investigation, and trial of acts of terrorism): This article refers to, regarding the composition and functioning of the court, Article 698-6 of the Code of Criminal Procedure.

jurisdiction had expanded to include terrorism and, later on, organised crime. On 3 December 1986, during the trial of a member of the anarchist terror group 'Action Direct', the jurors and a few journalists were threatened. The following day, a majority of the jurors submitted medical certificates to officially justify their decision to no longer serve. This courtroom event is unanimously cited as the moment that officially shifted the previously postponed decision in favour of specialised judicial authorities in matters of terrorism cases. While opponents objected to its exceptional nature of being specialised, the Constituional Court has declared it to be in accordance with the Constitution and the principle of equality.[15]

For the first two years, from 2017 to 2019, we observed all terrorism Assize trials, including their appeals, namely thirteen trials over 138 days of hearings.[16] Some of these trials extended over two months, while others were shorter, lasting a week. A significant portion of the cases focused on individuals who had returned from the Syrian front, and the charges primarily related to joining an armed terrorist group. Notably, these cases did not involve victims, nor any terrorist acts committed within France. Only two trials dealt with terrorist acts that were actually carried out – the Merah and Cannes-Torcy trials – and they included victim participation and important media coverage. Later on, from 2020 to 2022, we attended the so-called trial for history, commonly known as the 'Charlie Hebdo' and the 'Bataclan' trials. These trials prosecuted individuals who were accused of being involved in the major terror attacks that took place in France in 2015 and 2016.[17]

1.1.1.1 The Charlie Hebdo Trial Courtroom in the New Courthouse

The 'Charlie Hebdo Trial' refers to several attacks, which took place in Paris on the 7th and 9th January 2015. It first targeted the offices of the French satirical newspaper known for its controversial cartoons, resulting in the killing of twelve people, including cartoonists, journalists, and police officers. It was followed by a second coordinated attack on a Kosher supermarket, resulting in the deaths of four people and leaving others injured. The trial was held five years after the events, from September to December 2020, in a courtroom in the new modern Palais de Justice de Batignolles. It was decided to hold the trial there

[15] Decision dated 3 September 1986 (No. 86-213 DC).

[16] See Table 6A.1 in the Annex 6A.

[17] For more details on these cases, see Annex 6A.

because it was easier to secure, being in a remote place in the north of the city. Having the tribunal located on the periphery of the city, near major highway exits and some distance from major commercial activity, makes the Batignolles location a suitable place to hold such a security-sensitive trial. Built by the renowned architect Renzo Piano, the new judicial court building defines a new scenography of justice with the prevailing values such as transparency rather than the visible symbols of the hierarchy of the judiciary and the State.

This trial was deeply influenced by external events, with a constant stream of outside events affecting its proceedings. Firstly, several acts of violence occurred in parallel to the trial, including the murder of school-teacher Samuel Paty for teaching about the Mohammed cartoons' controversy. In this tense context, some of the civil parties were assigned security guards, which influenced the atmosphere inside the courtroom. Secondly, the trial took place during the initial period of the COVID-19 pandemic, and the courthouse was relatively empty. Despite movement restrictions due to the pandemic, we were able to observe the hearings. The COVID-19 context also impacted the trial's schedule, as hearings were frequently interrupted when defendants tested positive, with the added surrealism of attending hearings while wearing masks and maintaining physical distance from one another.

Figure 1.2 The Charlie Hebdo Trial courtroom, New Paris Tribunal.

1.1.1.2 The Specially-Built Courtroom for the Bataclan Trial in the 'Palais de Justice'

The attack on the Bataclan Theatre on 13 November 2015 during a concert, as well as the shootings in nearby cafés, resulted in the loss of 130 lives with hundreds more injured. Six years later, the Bataclan trial lasted for an extensive period of ten months and was a focal point of public attention. It was the most important trial in terms of its political role, victim participation, the level of responsibility attributed to the accused, national and international media coverage, as well as its considerable cost and duration. 2,300 victims were recognised as civil parties, and 400 of them gave a deposition in court. The significance of the trial was further underscored by the construction of a temporary courtroom within the historic Palais de Justice. This dedicated courtroom was specifically designed to accommodate the large number of victims and their lawyers, allowing their participation and representation throughout the proceedings. It was named the 'grand trial' courtroom. The location and the architecture had to respond to the 'victims' demand, who expressed their desire to see the trial unfold in a place of justice rather than in a conference room, gymnasium, or auditorium, as had been contemplated. Their lawyers also supported this preference. Furthermore, the victims expressed a wish to be in the same courtroom as the accused.

The institutions faced enormous challenges, both in addressing the victims' requests and in making the trial a moment that was collectively and symbolically shared by French society. Several options for the location of the courtroom were considered. Ultimately, it was decided, for reasons of solemnity and security, to construct a custom-made courtroom within the Paris courthouse (Palais de Justice) itself, located in the city centre. The construction lasted over a year and was completed at the end of spring 2021. The cost of building the courtroom amounted to almost eight million euros. With a capacity of 550 people, the 750 square metre courtroom, which is fifty metres long and fifteen metres wide, is equipped with a secure dock that can accommodate the defendants and their escorts as well as ten cameras to facilitate the recording of the 'historic' trials. According to one of the architects, as there was no underground passage connected to a transit room where the defendants arrived from prison, they 'had to imagine having the defendants arrive from above. A walkway, located

Figure 1.3 The Bataclan trial courtroom, specially built at the Palais de Justice, (Photo by Romane Gorce 13 June 2021). For an explanation of the various positions, see above.

above the *Salle des Pas Perdus*, covered with a mirror coating, provided a secure route for them, totally invisible to the public'.[18] Unable to gather all the civil parties in a single room, ten direct broadcast rooms were made available to victims, in addition to the main courtroom. The Paris courthouse could thus accommodate over 2,000 people simultaneously when all of these rooms were in use. An eleventh room was open to the public.

- One main courtroom with a capacity of 550 people.
- One transmission room for journalists with 130 seats.
- Ten additional transmission rooms for civil parties with 150 seats.
- One room for the public.

We attended this trial for ten months from September 2021 to June 2022. After the end of this trial, the room continued to hold other terror trials, including the City of Nice trial and much smaller trials. It was dismantled in March 2025.

[18] Beatrice Mouton, one of the architects involved in the design of the courtroom, cited in Hayaert, 2023. In this article many interesting aspects regarding the two courthouse's architecture are highlighted.

Figure 1.4 Back door entrance to the Palais de Justice.

1.1.2 The 16th Chamber of the *Tribunal Correctionnel*

In parallel, we irregularly attended hearings at the lower criminal court, known as the Tribunal Correctionnel, which handles all terrorism-related offences punishable by up to ten years imprisonment. One of the authors, Antoine Mégie, had been closely following these trials from 2015 onwards. With a bench comprising three trial judges, this court has accumulated substantial expertise in handling numerous cases against foreign fighters and returnees from the Iraqi–Syrian front. This Chamber was situated in the same courthouse, on the ground floor, identifiable by the large mosaic in front of the grand staircase.

In this part of the courthouse, there are a number of trial chambers spread over two floors. Among these chambers, with relatively identical architectural styles but very different sizes, is the correctional chamber where terrorist cases are tried: the 'sixteenth' chamber. Just before, the gendarmes set up a detector to search bags. In front is the judges' office. There are very few benches for the public in these old courtrooms. This courtroom has become increasingly crowded, particularly in cases with

Figure 1.5 The 16th Chamber in the new courthouse.

numerous detainees and extensive media coverage. It is in this courtroom that, from 2015 to 2018, all the trials of jihadist networks will be held in France.

In June 2018, the move of the 16th Chamber to the new Paris Tribunal marked the end of an era.

Throughout our observation period, we witnessed the construction of this new facility, and the relocation of the counter-terrorism investigative unit and the lower criminal court. This move was accompanied with the transformation of the old 'Palais de Justice' into a place that was much less busy than before. A larger courtroom and more modern technical facilities are changing the atmosphere of the trials and the conditions for observation. For researchers, this change of scenery will also have a major impact on access to the actors. Whereas in the old courthouse, access to the players in the trial was possible all around, including the judges' offices, in the new court, access requires badges, which are different for magistrates and lawyers. Each actor therefore has to follow an even stricter path and placement, severely limiting the possibilities for interaction and for participant observation. It is in this courthouse, and more specifically in the new sixteenth courtroom, that the trial of the Charlie Hebdo attacks took place in 2021.

During our observations, we all had a field diary for containing verbatim reports, informal exchanges, drawings, and observations from the hearings. They are an important source of our study, capturing details such as 'the president wants the defendant to say something' or 'the defendant is adopting a posture of repentance'. Accompanying the participant observation, the field diaries played an essential role in uncovering judicial practices. It contributed to the gradual construction of the narrative of each trial and, more broadly, our analysis of the evolution of justice in the time of the war on terror.

Extract from Antoine's research diary, written in the 16th Chamber (2017):

> After passing through the security archway and undergoing a thorough bag search, two large, padded brown leather doors come into view. We step into a wooden vestibule, softly illuminated by glass portholes that offer a glimpse of the courtroom beyond. Entering the vast room, characterised by old wallpaper and high wooden panelling. To the right are long, narrow wooden windows, while on the left, a blank wall is adorned with a single, imposing wooden clock. The clock, which draws considerable attention during prolonged proceedings, symbolises the judicial time that, due to the overburdened schedule of the 16th Correctional Chamber, results in lengthy and late hearings. Terrorism trials have become a routine exception for this court.
>
> The courtroom is divided by two facing docks, separating the public from the judicial space where debates unfold. These docks are where the 'returnees' from Syria, seized by the justice system stand and sit. Located two metres from the front rows, typically occupied by journalists, these wooden docks, topped with narrow glass, have evolved into 'glass cages' since 2018 in the new Paris courthouse. Over time, a strange intimacy has developed between observers and the defendants within these confines. The docks, which can hold five or six individuals along with their gendarme escorts, such as those for the Forsane Alizza group in 2015, the Strasbourg network in 2016, or Orléans in 2017, where a dozen or more defendants might appear. In such cases, the density and potential tension in the room are palpable, as the docks often seem too small to contain the defendants and their escorts, many of whom have a muscular physique or commanding posture. This arrangement lends a unique atmosphere to

the proceedings from the moment one enters the room. Fully occupied docks inevitably suggest a 'significant' case. While this impression can be misleading, a more accurate assumption is often confirmed: 'this trial will last several days due to the number of defendants'. On other days, when only a single person is being tried, the docks remain empty, creating a very different visual impression. The courtroom's scenography becomes more oppressive, with defendants appearing lost on the vacant benches. At the request of the officers, one must quickly take a seat on the public benches. The third-row seat on the right, next to the central aisle, offers distinct advantages: it ensures good audibility while providing a comprehensive view of the various actors and their interactions. In this courtroom, the public benches are either accompanied by desks or arranged closely together. Spectators generally crowd the benches, while students and journalists use the desks, giving the impression of being 'regulars' of the justice system. These benches, covered in worn green vinyl and notably uncomfortable, like most courtroom benches, may also be supplemented with folding chairs during high-profile trials.

Figure 1.6 An investigating judge compared moving from the historic Palais de Justice to the new courthouse to working in a Zara store.

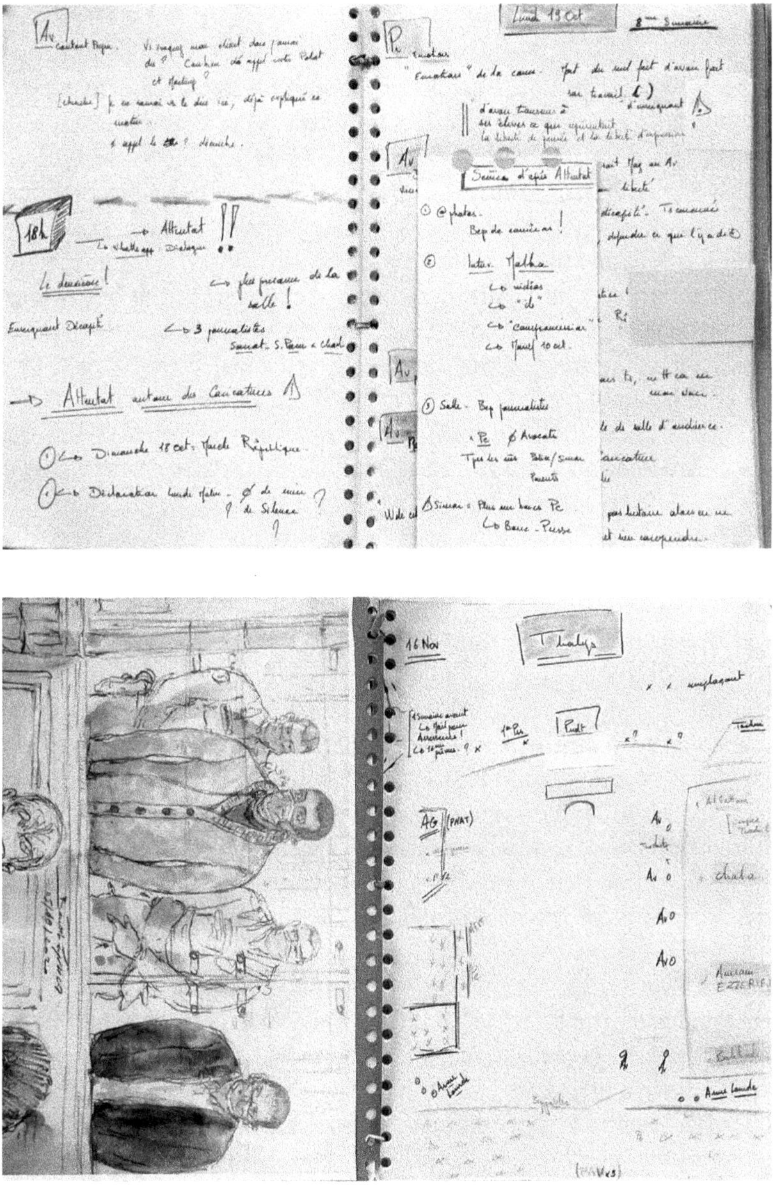

Figure 1.7 The note book of Antoine.

1.2 A RESEARCHER IN THE COURTROOM?

Being immersed in courtrooms transforms the researcher into part of the judicial scene.[19] However, reaching this point requires establishing a sense of legitimacy to gain acceptance from key actors. Initially, we had to gradually secure access to the courtroom and define the boundaries of our presence within this space. At first, even obtaining the hearing calendar was a significant accomplishment, the result of extensive negotiation. Our position evolved over time. At the beginning of our research, we could enter the courtroom incognito with our notebooks, being a part of a small audience who had little interest in us. We could simply merge into the room without being singled out. For instance, in one trial, we regularly sat next to the father of the main person accused: his son noticed us and asked his father who we were.

With time, however, the way we, as researchers, were perceived by the actors evolved during the long research period. As we became more and more visible, our status gradually changed: we were allowed to bring our laptops and even use phones in the courtroom. Access to legal documents was, at times, easier and we became more and more familiar with the people who worked there who provided us with inside information and documents from and off the record. This process reached its peak at the start of the Charlie Hebdo and Bataclan trials. There was now an official list of accreditations to access the courtroom, restricted to only the civil parties, lawyers, security personnel and a limited number of journalists and researchers.[20]

The first time that researchers were given accreditation to enter the courtroom was for the trial of Charlie Hebdo, which was the first trial with restricted access, for security reasons, COVID-19 and numerous victims. Our accreditation was as 'journalists' because there was no other category such as 'researcher'. We were generally required to explain and re-explain, with each change of the gendarmerie team, why we have a press badge but not the accompanying professional card, and what our profession entails. We became used to negotiating for access and to humorous remarks: 'What are you searching for? Gold?' (Police Officer, October 2020), or 'Research? Is that the name of your

[19] Cefaï, 2010, p. 637.

[20] The researchers of whom there were now dozens, were working on various projects, under the umbrella of a new collective called Promete (2021).

newspaper?' (Police Officer, October 2021).[21] Eventually, at the Bataclan trial, for the first time, 'researcher' accreditation was separate from press accreditation. The possibility of being specifically accredited as 'researchers' subsequently facilitated the work of the authorities and, by extension, the research group. It has now become institutionalised, as the term 'researcher' has become official for accreditations to trials at the Paris courts. Researchers had orange badges, lawyers black, victims red, and those affiliated with the court blue:

> The badge, beyond granting access to the scene of the trial, situates the body of the person wearing it within a constellation of hierarchised actors and within the bounds of their relationship to others. In other words, wearing the badge, much like a lawyer dresses in a robe or the judge wears a robe trimmed with ermine, is a display of the distinction between those who belong to, or are close to, the legal field and those who are distant from it. It is a claim to a status within the micro society sheltered by the court; it also means navigating with less effort between the thus separated universes.[22]

At the Bataclan trial, each of these groups was assigned a particular space to sit. As journalists and researchers were attributed the same space, we could mix together: we exchanged information, clarified a misunderstood word, and sometimes shared documents. This socialising and the personal relations established during the long hearing days resulted in the researchers often being approached by the media: we were all invited to be interviewed by all of the major TV, radio, and newspaper outlets, both local and international, including *Le Monde*, *the Financial Times*, *the Washington Post*, *the New York Times*, and *France 24*.[23] We have been developing together the narratives about the trials. Indeed, during the 'historic trials', our position was visible, recognised and identifiable by the judicial authorities and actors, as well as the general public.

1.2.1 Open Access or 'Favours' for Insiders?

While French terror trials are public and reflect the notion of 'open justice',10 they should be put in context. Firstly, there are no hearing transcriptions available. The oral nature of the trials leaves no trace;

[21] For a collective analysis of this experience regarding the place of researchers at terrorism trials, see Politika (2022).

[22] Politika (2022).

[23] See for example: Nossiter, 2018; Abboud, 2021; Bienvault, 2020; Jacquin, 2020; Noack, 2021.

the richness of the interactions at the hearing is often lost. As this is the only place where the voice of the accused can be heard, important stories disappear once the trial is over. In fact, their existence depends on the more or less haphazard attention given to the trial by the media. One must be present in the courtroom throughout the entire trial to have a record of what is being said. Judgments and the motivations behind sentencing, although public documents, are very difficult to access, usually very short, and they do not reflect, or reflect very little, the verbal exchanges. Lastly, public seating is relatively limited in small courtrooms. Many times, we could not access the hearing, simply because of a lack of space. In the historic trials, access was only allowed to an accredited, pre-selected audience, and that did not include the general public. Very few seats were available in the transmission rooms, leaving the public to rely on media narration. The filming of the Charlie Hebdo, Bataclan, and Nice trials, was a notable exception to the absence of a court record. However, despite being filmed, the footage was not broadcast live, and it remains stored in an archive, inaccessible to the general public for fifty years.[24]

Researchers faced major difficulties in accessing written sources. Even though the judgments are public documents, they are not easily accessible, as they are not published electronically. Regarding the indictment, even if the legal framework seems to allow free access to these documents once the public reading in court has begun,[25] during

[24] The Badinter Act of 1985 made the filming possible. This law was adopted on the eve of the prosecution of Nazi collaborator Klaus Barbie, who was found guilty of seventeen crimes against humanity and sentenced to life imprisonment for deporting hundreds of Jews from France. It marked a turning point in the history of French justice, as it opened up, for the first time, the possibility of recording trials to create audio-visual archives, essentially filming 'trials for history'. Since then, only a few trials have been filmed and archived in the National Archives, including trials related to the genocide of the Tutsis in Rwanda, Nazi collaborators in France, and most recently, terrorism trials such as the Charlie Hebdo, Bataclan and Nice trials. More recently a new law 'Confidence in the Judiciary' entered into force (Law no. 2021-1729 of 22 December 2021), which added that 'The sound or audiovisual recording of a hearing may be authorised, for a reason of public interest of an educational, informative, cultural or scientific nature, with a view to its dissemination.' Today only researchers can have access to these achieved films. For more details see Bellanger et al., 2023.

[25] Article 38 of the Law of 29 July 1881 on the freedom of the press prohibits the publication of criminal or correctional procedure documents before they are read at a public hearing.

the years of our research, access to indictments remained extremely opaque, even though many journalists possessed them even before the opening of the trials! It came as a great surprise for us to discover several minutes before the trial began that the journalists in the front row had already prepared their articles using the official documents, including the indictments. We were even more surprised when, according to the rules of criminal procedure, the two assistant judges of the lower court, the Tribunal Correctionnel, did not have access to this document. While the investigation files are secret and kept secret from the public – we encounter a few 'exceptions'. For example, on the eve of the Bataclan trial, in August 2021, a comic book was published, revealing the facts as established in the investigation file.[26] It was written by a *Le Monde* journalist and a researcher from the think tank CAT, with information based on the investigation file:

> We used several investigation files, the main one being that of 13 November, which runs to a million pages, divided into fifty-two volumes. It is one of the biggest files in the French justice system. Fortunately, I kept reading it as the investigation progressed. I had a clear picture of how the events unfolded and what triggered the investigation. The main part of the job was to select the material from these thousands of pages.[27]

To obtain access to these 'confidential' documents, we developed a network of personal ties with journalists or lawyers, and sometimes even the judges. It very quickly became apparent that obtaining the indictments was done as a favour – part of a ritual for those recognised as being 'part of the scene'. This ritual of providing documents to journalists and other players takes place informally, marking a boundary between the 'insiders of the terror hearings' and others. Getting access to these documents, including the decision itself, gradually improved, as did our position as 'insiders'. These 'deals' create bonds of obligation and collusion: 'If you have this week's order, I'm interested!' – a system well known to everyone. Discretion is required.

These exchanges of documents and information, including those that are reserved or secret, reveal the importance of developing links, a network, with players who can also benefit from disseminating them.

[26] Seelow et al., 2021. [27] Soren Seelow, reproduced in Tardy-Joubert, 2022.

1.2.2 The Alternative Sites: The Coffee Machine, the Queue, the Bistrot

Once inside court, we developed our own positioning and mode of observation, which requires a certain level of modesty, curiosity, and sensitivity. The researcher does not need to know in advance what they are looking for: in a flexible and open manner, they have to connect with the space and explore situations. Emotion, our emotions, also played a significant role. We encountered the same people daily, developing close relationships with some of them, sharing lunch and late evenings. Naturally, it was not all fascinating; we also endured lengthy, boring moments, such as during the technical testimonies, when police officers appeared on video under encrypted identities, or when PowerPoint presentations were delivered in a monotone voice. We also shared moments of sadness with the victims, and situational anger with the defence lawyers.

Our position was consolidated as a result of our unstinting presence behind the scenes of the courtroom hearing, within the courthouse. It was by assiduously frequenting these backstage areas that we were able to meet a large number of players in the terrorist judicial scene. This was an essential part of our understanding of the multiple realities of terrorism trials. Different kinds of interaction can be transformative outside the courtroom. A place for socialising par excellence, several places in particular proved invaluable: the security queue, the coffee machine, and the outside courtyard, inhabited by smokers. The security queue is the first place the observer comes across when trying to access the courtrooms. This immediately reveals a hierarchy between the people wishing to enter the courtroom, such as lawyers, defendants, and certain journalists, who are given priority. Sometimes, being in the queue just behind a defendant (who had not been detained prior to the proceedings) allowed us to identify their family member, who accompanied them and whom we could find ourselves sitting next to, or to identify security services officers, who were following the trial from the public benches.

An area which proved particularly important for our research was the coffee machine. This machine was in the covered courtyard just a few metres from the entrance to the chapel. A daily meeting point in the historic courthouse, it is a place where all of the people who work, visit, or are summoned by the courts pass through. During breaks in the hearings, this special place was the scene of many interactions between those involved, including lawyers, journalists, researchers, police officers, and sometimes the families or even some of the defendants appearing freely.

On the night of the verdict of the Bataclan trial, after ten months sharing this collective experience, the trial was over, and we took part in an unforgettable scene: prosecutors, defence lawyers, assistant judges, victims, defendants, journalists, and researchers all spontaneously gathered at the bistrot, Les Deux Palais. This bistrot, just across the road, used by everyone daily, had a surrealist allure: within a mingling crowd, where everybody was drinking and talking to each other without robes, defendants, who were now free as their punishment amounted to their pre-trial detention period, asked for forgiveness from the victims and shook hands. It was a very powerful gathering for the victims and for us all, which shows the importance of these informal moments and spaces, which ultimately contribute to 'doing justice'.

1.2.3 Formal Exchanges

These observations and interactions were complemented by dozens of semi-structured interviews carried out by the members of our group with various judicial actors. From the start, we had relatively privileged access to the judges to carry out interviews, for three main reasons. Firstly, the research was financed by the Ministry of Justice, and they facilitated access by providing an official letter. Secondly, one of the authors, Dénis Salas, was a judge earlier in his career and has become an author of high esteem, which has facilitated access to various players in the justice system. Lastly, many of the judges were personally interested in academic research in general and more specifically in terrorism and their own work. We exchanged further communication with those involved while we presented and tested our hypotheses, in the context of training sessions at the National School for the Judiciary, at lectures and conferences we organised at our universities, at which they participated.[28] These

[28] We organised two major conferences at Sciences Po Paris. The first was the launch of our first report, 'Jihadists on Trial: An Ethnographic Study at the French Assize Court (2017–2019)' (CERI 2020), in an interdisciplinary colloquium with the participation of judicial actors including the French Counter-Terrorism Prosecutor, the President of the Assize Criminal Court, a counter-terrorism investigative judge and a defence lawyer. The program is available at www.sciencespo.fr/agenda/ceri/fr?event=1953. The second conference was held in November 2022 following the Bataclan trial: 'The Bataclan trial seen by the social sciences: an ethnographic and multidisciplinary approach' (CERI, 2022). The programme is available at www.sciencespo.fr/centre-etudes-europeennes/fr/evenements/journee-detude-le-proces-des-attentats-terroristes-du-13-novembre-2015-vu-par-les-sciences-sociales-que-dit-le-proces-v13-de-la-societe-francaise/. See also Weill, 2022. www.sciencespo.fr/centre-etudes-europeennes/fr/actualites/la-societe-face-au-terrorisme-

exchanges strengthened our immersion and our ability to understand the way in which these judicial actors create, think, and represent their professional practices. Repeated interviews with the same person not only helped to build a relationship of trust but also prompted the interviewees to further contemplate their own actions and experiences reflexively. Becoming 'insiders' of the scene allowed us to develop an additional methodological tool. From the end of 2017 onwards, during a trial and at the end of the day's proceedings, several 'on the spot' interviews were conducted with the presiding judges and the lawyers, to reinforce our observations on the practices, representations, and even emotions of the actors we had been observing. By observing the person '*in situ*' and conducting an interview on that specific situation, we gained a deeper contextualisation, allowing the interviewee to comment on specific issues raised during the hearing, making the discussion more concrete and revealing personal insights.[29]

1.2.4 Cross Analysis with the Multidisciplinary Research Team

Our multidisciplinary research group operated both collaboratively and independently. Our individual approaches only reinforced our collective and horizontal relations within the group: we could achieve more together than each of us could have done separately. Additionally, the special political moment and active public debate added another dimension to the significance of this research. Our meaningful engagement, collaboration, and political timing created such a synergy that resulted in a lasting experience, strongly shaping our approach to future court research.

During the entire research period, we had regular discussions within our research group, through periodic meetings in the office and routine

quel-role-pour-les-proces/. Other conferences have been organised by members of our teams at the universities of Rouen (October 2019) and Limoges (January 2023). At the French National School for the Judiciary, where one of our team members teaches, we have, since 2018, organised and participated in a dozen panels with the participation of various people from the legal profession.

[29] As Julie Colemans noted:

> interviews make explicit what is implicit by highlighting incorporated professional knowledge, ordinary interpretation procedures and common-sense knowledge. The interviews make it possible to shed light on areas that were obscure during the observations due to the researcher's lack of practical skills. Having taken part in the same hearing, the researcher and the legal professional can compare their perceptions and interpretations of the key moments, bodily cues and emotions expressed (Colemans, 2015).

exchanges in the courtroom. Being researchers from different disciplines, we used complementary methodological approaches, which enriched the exchange and analysis of data throughout the entire research process. We then collectively produced a report, as well as joint publications. Working as a multidisciplinary research group is not a new practice in many fields, and the virtues of this approach are well established. However, it is rarer for such groups to work together on the same subject, at the same time and space, and to produce a collective piece of writing. From a methodological point of view, this was an innovative experience that allowed us to have a multi-level reading grid as each perspective was developed and refined through joint discussions. Writing together allowed these different perspectives and analyses to become a common reflection. Our first report was submitted in December 2019.[30] The report was circulated widely within professional legal circles and became a tool for exchanges. Our network with prosecutors, judges, and lawyers played a crucial role in disseminating the report. Additionally, our funder played an important part, as one of its aims is to support research into dialogue with legal professionals for institutional improvement. Follow-up research projects were then funded, now focusing on the 'historic trials'.

1.2.5 The Challenges: Observer or Player? On the Distance and Positioning of the Researchers

As the research evolved, it allowed us to 'take an active role in the institutions and phenomena we studied'.[31] Nevertheless, this position raises important epistemological and ethical questions, particularly concerning the role of the researchers and their research. The researcher has to be conscious of their own impact. The longer the immersion is, the more the dividing line fades between the actors and the observers, and the relations between them evolve. Stéphane Beaud noted that the place of researchers in his ethnographic approach should not 'have the intention of diverting the action from its ordinary course, nor of involving the participants in acts different from their own perspective. [. . .] The observer must be reserved, must not overdo things, and must understand what he can do'.[32] Was this the case? At certain moments, we clearly became a player in the process, such as when one of the defence lawyers cited a report written by one of the

[30] Besnier et al., 2019. [31] Starr and Goodale, 2002, p. 7. [32] Beaud, 1996.

legal researchers on the Merah appeal. When we became very close to certain civil parties and supported them in their path. When we spoke with the judges at public conferences. When journalists interviewed us. When those involved read our publications.

Being in the courtroom, we could grasp certain aspects of the legal process: ones that are open to the public. Focusing on the trial scene, some fundamental players, such as the security services and court clerks, and important moments, such as investigations and deliberations, were not only absent but also hidden from the public. Therefore, while observing hearings, it is necessary to consider not only what is visible but also what is invisible, especially in terrorism trials where secrecy – and the imaginative thinking that goes with it – has a growing presence. The trials establish a legal truth: they highlight certain aspects while obscuring others. Depending on the political and legal system in which they occur, access to terrorism trials and related information is often limited, both for the accused and the public. Indeed, while the trial is supposed to be transparent and accessible, it largely relies on secret information provided by security agencies. This contradiction, namely the public-secret dichotomy, is at the heart of terrorism trials, which are supposed to be both a public forum for revealing information transparently and accessibly, while simultaneously preserving secrets. How is confidentiality managed? What can we know and not know? What is eventually known? Is the trial revealing the truth or obscuring realities?

While observing a trial presents a unique approach to understanding the nuances of legal practice and the human experiences within the justice system, research in such a context requires particular attention to ethical issues, especially when it comes to confidentiality, the informed consent of the participants, and the treatment of personal and emotional data.[33] This is a significant challenge, particularly in a research context marked by a seal of secrecy, such as the fight against terrorism.[34] More generally, the challenges in this study echo the usual problems of ethnographic research. Spending so much time in close proximity to the actors involved raises the question: how do we say what we cannot say?

There was something addictive in observing justice, being in the courtroom every day, hearing fascinating human stories, and being part of a collective. And yet, the researcher has to know how to remove themselves from their immersed experience and be able to translate the

[33] Beaud, 1996, p. 235. [34] Daho et al., 2020.

endless anecdotes and experiences into a theoretical framing, while being detached from the individuals who accompanied this long journey, and the accompanying strong emotions.

Being able to leave the courtroom was a major challenge. The distance between the field research, the object, and the researcher is a crucial aspect to consider. Ethnography is an immersive method, embedded in the environment it studies, with the researcher in close contact with the object they are studying and with which they interact to conduct their research. In our case, we were dealing with a field of research with major political and social importance, locally and internationally, an object that we were observing but also one in which we were involved in constructing. This distance from our object became challenging, as it involved a daily commitment and very close proximity to the players in the field, including the family of the accused, victims, and the judicial actors. Sociologist Loïc Wacquant has stressed the importance of this proximity and deep immersion in the field of study, but at the same time, the danger of being too immersed and not being able to have the required distance to pursue the analysis and to relocate the object into a larger historical and political context.[35] Striking a balance between immersion and distance is a constant consideration in ethnographic research. It is essential to be mindful of these dynamics and continually reflect on their potential impact on the research process and outcomes. Writing, in itself, is a crucial part of the process. Before entering that phase, we took the necessary time to disconnect from the field research. However, the findings can only reflect our own stance and distance from the object of study.

[35] "Crossing a boundary (. . .) consists of "going native", as the Americans say, in other words . . . embracing "the point of view of the native". . . to immerse yourself in it . . . you also have to give yourself the means to come back from it, to make the return journey, to gain some distance thanks to theoretical tools" (Wacquant, 2023).

CHAPTER TWO

THE TRIAL ACTORS

'In the Name of the French People'

A legal decision is the result of many contributors working in concert, both in and beyond the courtroom, all central to this collective production.[1] Within a 'structured structure' that is the judicial scene, to borrow Bourdieu's word,[2] each of the players has a defined role. We can distinguish the 'repeat players',[3] who are the professional protagonists, from the 'one-shot' players, who are the ordinary individuals involved in a trial – the accused or the witnesses. Naturally, the trial scene, its special arrangement, management, and the roles attributed, reflect the hierarchy and power relations outside this space that predefine the borderline[4] between the actors, designed to create the authority of 'producing the truth'.[5] Yet, unlike a theatre play, the trial scenario is not repeated and not entirely known in advance. It is, to a large extent, also an organic and constitutive process. Thus, while the 'repeat players' interpret their roles as part of longer-term professional experiences and routines, modulated by their accumulated expertise and knowledge that has been constructed over time, and are more familiar with the language and hierarchical relations among actors, it is the

[1] Weill et al., 2020. [2] Bourdieu, 1987. [3] Galanter, 1974.
[4] Bourdieu, 1987.
[5] For Foucault, the law maintains a prominent role in the exercise of power, providing for it the discourse of legitimacy. As he had highlighted: 'On one side, the legal rules formally delimit power, and on the other side, the effects of truth that this power produces, that this power leads to, in turn, reinforce this power. That is a triangle: power, law, truth.' Cours du 14 janvier 1976, Foucault, 1994.

freshness of the 'one-shot' players that can set a different tone due to the relatively relaxed procedural constraints on expression in France. Bearing in mind the underlining power relations as a starting point for any analysis, while in court, we observed that this space also creates its own social space, which is unpredictable and develops as the trial progresses. This evolution depends on the actors themselves, leading to a redefinition of the relations and expressions that can emerge – at least for the duration of the trial. While legislation, prosecution policy, and jurisprudence grids are produced according to policies, there is, in between, this space where the law is performed. This performance follows rules and rituals but also allows for spontaneous oral expression and the interactions of the actors, who collectively form a constitutive process. External factors, including social and political debates, also contribute to make each trial unique.

The actors' engagements, their perception of professionalism and the strong personalities of some of them create nuanced situations where, within this court setting, new practices have emerged, even if they sometimes remain in the margins. The relatively brief decisions of the court, often written in prefabricated languages, rarely reflect these exchanges. The following section looks more closely at the practices of each actor engaged in the 'collective search for the truth', to examine in a concrete way who has the authority to determine it, and how it is done in practice.

2.1 THE TRIAL JUDGES AND THE TRUTH

> *'When the judge asks the accused to acknowledge the facts . . . he is asking the accused to do him a wonderful service, he is asking the accused to say: yes, your honour, I'm claiming the punishment, I am punishing myself, it is not you, I am exonerating you judge . . . in fact, it is the judge's innocence that is at the heart of the trial. It is not really a question of the innocence of the accused, everyone knows his culpability . . . but the innocence of the judge, that is what the judge wants to obtain with the judicial ritual' (Michel Foucault).*[6]

The Assises court, which is competent to hear cases carrying sentences of over ten years imprisonment, is composed of a presiding judge and

[6] Foucault, 1977.

four assisting judges.[7] The President is the central figure of the bench, mastering time and space. In charge of organising the court schedule, facilitating interactions between those involved, and maintaining order, s/he directs the 'debates' and allocates speaking time to the various parties. As noted by Lerner, "The inquiry . . . has the effect of allowing witnesses – including the defendant – to speak freely, in their natural voices. The French word for trial session – *les débats* – suggests this free speech; it means, among other things, debate or discussion. And indeed trials in the Cour d'assises resemble an ongoing discussion, directed by the president."[8]

The French criminal procedure is composed of two stages: the investigation of the personality and the establishment of the facts. The investigation into the accused's personality is an important phase, which usually takes place at the beginning of the trial, just after a brief summary of the charges. It allows for an understanding of their life trajectory within their family and social environment, and considerable time is devoted to it. The desire to understand the facts through the lens of the accused's personality is the main characteristic of an assize trial. As said by a judge, 'the act and the person are not separable'.[9] In the trials observed it took on average, a day, depending on the severity of the case. The presiding judge addresses the accused's childhood and schooling, as well as their professional and personal experience through different professional reports corroborated by testimonies from family members and others connected to their environment. The second part of the procedure establishes the facts. The trial judges conduct their own inquiry based on the investigation file, in an adversarial manner, allowing the parties to question in turn. The file contains all the necessary elements for the indictment and the accusation; however, the bench is not bound by the conclusions of the investigating judge. Assisting judges often play a more passive role during hearings; however, during the deliberation process, which takes place at

[7] This part focuses mainly on the Assise court. In the lower court discussed in Chapter 3, the proceedings are quicker, and the bench is composed of only three judges.

[8] Lerner, 2001, p. 9. When Prof Malcolm Feeley went with author Sharon Weill to watch a trial in 2021, he told her that French trials look like a symposium to him.

[9] Jean-Marie Fayol-Noireterre, Magistrate, President of the Chamber at the Court of Appeal of Grenoble, President of the Assize Courts of Grenoble and Valence. See also Besnier, 2017, p. 125.

the end of the trials, decisions regarding culpability and punishment are made by majority vote, with all judges holding equal voting power.

2.1.1 The Presiding Judge: Crafting the Atmosphere

After reading of the indictment and the list of witnesses, the presiding judge starts the interrogations, first of the accused and then of all other witnesses. Particular moments may reveal instances of emotion and authenticity. For this to happen, beyond merely directing the debate, the presiding judge tries to establish a connection with each person being questioned, and the fluidity of the exchanges depends on the atmosphere created. The personality of the presiding judge is of paramount importance. For example, a president may display a rather paternalistic demeanour, often addressing the accused with arrogant remarks like 'I asked you to concentrate' and 'think before you reply'.[10] This intimidating tone aims to remind and produce a hierarchical relationship, and as we could see in our ethnography, it does not necessarily lead to the revealing of a new truth or the triggering of sincerity, quite the opposite. However, in other trials, the judge created an empathetic environment, even for the accused. This was the case, for example, in the Cannes–Torcy network case, where the nineteen defendants were all from very different backgrounds and social environments. After fifty-five days of trial, the final words of one of the defendants were: 'I thank the judges for listening to my story. For the first time, someone has taken the time to listen to me'.[11] In the Bataclan trial, when the main person accused appeared in court, Salah Abdeslam, who had participated in the deadly attack and had not spoken during five years of pre-trial investigation, said, 'Mr. President, I do not know if I will answer your questions.' He then spoke for three hours.[12] A different attitude on the part of the president can lead to a different result, affecting how the debates are managed, how the actors – starting with the defendants – engage themselves, and assume responsibility for the acts committed. Ultimately, even the verdict itself can be impacted.

In principle, the trial must allow sufficient time for all parties to express themselves and react to the arguments of the opposing side,

[10] Audience statement, defendant, Paris Assize Court, April 2024.
[11] Audience statement, defendant, Paris Assize Court, 22 June 2017.
[12] Audience statement, defendant, Paris Assize Court, 9 February 2022.

while ensuring that neither the accused nor the victims are unheard, or feel that they cannot express themselves. Since a testimony can last anywhere from five minutes to several hours, the schedule must allow for a degree of flexibility. The presiding judge must also avoid anything that unnecessarily prolongs the debate. Balancing these opposing interests and managing time is, in a sense, alchemy.

The president's role as the master of time and space, and its impact on the trial's atmosphere was particularly evident in the major terrorism trials such as the Charlie Hebdo and Bataclan trials. The decision to allow the testimonies of hundreds of victims at the start of the trial (and not, for example, after the fact-finding phase) set the tone of the trial and prioritised their depositions. This choice order was not neutral. Judge Régis de Jorna, presiding judge in the Charlie Hebdo trial, explained his approach to this point:

> The schedule is the backbone of a trial. Everything revolves around it, and it's up to the presiding judge to establish it. Before the trial begins, the judge must determine the order of the investigators, witnesses, and experts, schedule the hearings for the civil parties, the questioning of the accused, consider the time needed for requisitions and pleadings, and factor in time for deliberation ... For the Charlie Hebdo trial, it was necessary to schedule the testimonies of the 144 witnesses and 14 cited experts, to allow the 287 constituted civil parties (e.g. victims) and their 71 lawyers to express themselves, without omitting that, first and foremost, the trial remains that of the accused, those who are accused of the facts, who must explain themselves, and who face heavy penalties if found guilty ... The entire challenge – gamble, even – was to ensure that each victim could speak and be heard, that each accused could assert their defence arguments, that the consecutive contradictory debate following each testimony or interrogation could take place without time being considered limited, all while respecting a daily schedule and reasonable end-of-session hours.[13]

2.1.1.1 *Trials Under Pressure*

One of the roles of the presiding judge is to police the audience. Managing a criminal hearing is also about calming tensions, managing disturbances, and maintaining calm so that speaking and listening prevail. When the presiding judge is compelled to demand silence from a restless room, their authority should be respected. The suspension of

[13] Interview carried out by our team, published in Jarroux et al., 2021.

the hearing is used when debates veer off verbally or physically, when tensions run too high, or when insults or threats are made against the opposing party. When there is a divergence of opinion between the presiding judge and the lawyers on the conduct of the proceedings, a report of an 'incident of the audience' can be filed.

> I do not want to be too strict, but sometimes it is necessary to demonstrate authority to ensure the proper conduct of the proceedings. … However, sometimes a bit of relaxation helps the proceedings to run smoothly and without tension. It should be noted that during the trial, almost all of the accused observed Ramadan, which led me to slightly shorten the session times to avoid discomfort or remarks from the defence attorneys.[14]

During our ethnography, we observed numerous incidents triggered by external events that infiltrated the courtroom. Terror trials, in particular, have a unique dimension. They do not merely represent a microcosm; these trials often deal simultaneously with ongoing violence, sometimes directly connected to the proceedings. Widely scrutinised by the media, the courtroom proceedings are not conducted in isolation from their environment. Studies on political reactions to the 2015 attacks in France reveal a broad spectrum of mobilisations and political demonstrations with various emotional and memorial dimensions.[15] Terrorism trials, too, are spaces through which we can examine the effects of the attacks as a test of justice and its procedures, when faced with terrorist violence. Since 2017, several violent attacks have taken place during trials, and it has been up to the president to manage them. Each president has managed it differently.

The Charlie Hebdo trial probably stands out most for the series of three attacks that disrupted the proceedings, and which had a direct link to the trial.[16] A first suspension was implemented by the president of the court when the entire audience in the courtroom learned via text message of the attack on the former Charlie Hebdo offices on 29 September 2020. Only a couple of weeks later, the courtroom audience was informed of the murder of teacher Samuel Paty. The proceedings were again disrupted when a solemn statement was made

14 Interview with the President of the specially constituted Assize Court, Cannes-Torcy trial, reproduced in Besnier et al., 2019, p. 177.

15 Boussaguet and Faucher, 2018; Gensburger and Truc, 2020.

16 For facts, see box 5.1, pp. 152–154.

by the presiding judge informing the courtroom of the killing of a teacher 'for having taught his students what represented freedom of thought and expression'.[17] The heightened security in the courthouse and the provision of security guards for the civil parties also confirmed this context. For the defence, these attacks and their representation in the media, along with the ensuing public emotion, inexorably put pressure on their position and that of the accused. They requested in their plea that the court 'apply the law . . . We do not ask you to judge history but men'.[18] This was to emphasise the responsibility of the professional judges overseeing this special assize court to set aside public opinion and its emotions.

Presiding judges also faced incidents internal to the hearings. A notable incident to illustrate this point occurred during the Bataclan trial, when the audience in the courtroom, primarily consisting of civil parties, applauded when the main accused spoke – an act done to silence him. On that day, the defence lawyers left the hearing in a coordinated protest against the presiding judge's handling of the order. This decision followed the Presiding judge's failure to address the clapping and a subsequent escalation involving one of the defence lawyers. This event was reported in detail by the daily newspaper, *Le Monde*,[19] ending by being the journalists who police the judge.

As matter of routine, judges need to manage dozens of issues regularly. One exceptional event happened during the reading of the verdict in the Bataclan case. The courtroom was packed, with hundreds of people inside the room as well as in the transmission rooms. In the courtroom, there was silence. The judge solemnly read out the verdict. Suddenly, the video was cut, and further transmissions were not possible, either to the dozens of international and national journalists in the parallel rooms or to the general public. We learned later that the Wi-Fi had failed. The presiding judge decided to proceed with reading the verdict for the defendants present in the courtroom, and a select group of journalists. The following day, the judge had to return to court to read the verdict again. This time, without the defendants and without the public – it was recorded and filmed for 'history'.

These examples show how courtroom proceedings are caught in a wider socio-political environment and are not heard or adjudicated in a

17 Audience statement, President, Paris Assize Court, 19 October 2020

18 Audience statement, defence lawyer, Paris Assize Court, 19 October 2020.

19 Seelow, 2022.

sterile and detached space, impacting the position of the judges, who are under constant external and internal pressure through which they have to navigate while rendering justice. It also highlighted the importance of the personality, experience, and attitude of the central figure in the room, the president.

2.1.2 The Assisting Judges

Once the presiding judge has completed their questioning, it is the turn of the assisting judges to ask further questions. The assisting judges, who have taken the place of the jury since 1986, are not necessarily specialised in criminal law nor terrorism. They are appointed to the bench on a volunteering basis, and for the duration of the trial. Unlike the presiding judge, the assisting judges at first did not have access to the file. They discovered the facts orally during the hearings. This led to a feeling of exclusion among certain of them, as mentioned to us in 2017 in an interview with an assisting judge who sat in the first jihadist assize trial, the Cannes–Torcy trial. At that time, he was an investigative judge at the specialised unit for crimes against humanity and war crimes:

> Assisting judges are treated like jurors, with no access to the case file, which is regrettable ... it would be preferable to involve the assisting judges in a form of collegiality: sharing topics to be addressed, questions to be asked... The role of 'assessor judge' should be valued in the career path of a judge in order to inspire vocations. This Assize Court must maintain its nature, that is, judges who are not specialised.[20]

This lack of access to the file contrasts with the access of other parties, including journalists, established a dissymmetry among the actors, that was modified in 2019, when the assisting judges were given access to the file, probably also due to the complexity of the cases. This was the first step in the specialisation of the bench. Further specialisation occurred with the creation of a designated list of judges, including a significant number of judges, who were previously in the 16th Chamber of the lower courts. This new configuration led to a specialised mode of function within the Assize Courts. This is part of a broader specialisation process that began in 1986 with the abolition of the jury. At that time, the official position for doing so was based on security

[20] Interview with an assisting judge (12 July 2017), reproduced in Besnier et al., 2019, pp. 180–181.

concerns for the jury members. However, opponents of this reform saw this special designation as a 'court of exception', intended to ensure higher sentences.[21] This specialisation process, through the pre-selection of assisting judges and granting them access to the file, has continued to evolve towards this goal of harshening the punishment, as discussed in detail in Chapter 4.

2.1.3 Decision Making: Intimate Conviction and the Freedom to Assess Evidence

Article 427 of the Code of Criminal Procedure states that 'offences may be established by any means of proof, and the judge decides based on their intimate conviction'.[22] Intimate conviction is a method of judgment that considers all means of proof: verbal, scientific, and psychological, and also the overall understanding of the judge. While the system of legal evidence from the Middle Ages relied on professional justice – the judge was required to justify their decision in writing – the French Revolution acted as a rupture and introduced a system of intimate conviction based on the assessment of jury citizens who deliver a verdict based on the arguments debated adversarially before them. Their sole guide is their conscience and reason. Since then, in the French legal system, every piece of evidence is subject to 'intimate conviction'. There is no rule where evidence is hierarchised. Even confession is not the ultimate evidence as the trial continues. Any evidence, whether scientific or subjective, is admitted and subjected to contradictory debate, including counter-expertise, or testimonies. It is the judge's role to assess the evidence that prevails through successive layers of factors considered first plausible, then probable, and finally certain, forming tiers on a scale of graded judicial truth.

Deliberations take place at the end of the proceedings. Decisions on guilt and sentencing in terrorism cases are made by a simple majority, unlike in jury cases.[23] The fact that a simple majority suffices in terrorism cases reflects 'a desire to facilitate conviction, and thus to

[21] Kampf, 2024; Mégie and Sansico, 2021; Pereira Rui, 2017.

[22] 'Hors les cas où la loi en dispose autrement, les infractions peuvent être établies par tout mode de preuve et le juge décide d'après son intime conviction.' (Loose translation.)

[23] In ordinary assize trials with a jury, decisions that do not favour the accused must be made by a qualified majority when it comes to guilt (at least 6 out of 9 votes in the first instance and 8 out of 12 on appeal), and by an absolute majority of voters when

intensify the repression that guides the modification of the majority rules applicable to the assize court'.[24] By its very nature inaccessible, the deliberation room is the subject of numerous representations. Featured in testimonial books, documentary films, and cinematic works, this secret space appears as a symbol of justice with democratic appearances, as in Sidney Lumet's film *12 Angry Men*. A group of defence lawyers acting for those accused of the attacks of 13 November 2015, wondered how it was possible to resume a trial after ten months and, within forty-eight hours, to issue a decision of 146 pages.[25] It was not uncommon during our years of observation to hear that certain decisions were the result of a vote that was not unanimous among the judges and that the president was in the minority: 'It is that, when issuing judgments with only professional judges, the role of the president may be less important than when dealing with a lay jury in which he occupies a fundamental place'.[26] We can see how the role of assisting judges is evolving. Initially, in 1986, designated as unspecialised judges functioning like a jury, they are transitioning into becoming more specialised and experienced judges. This shift involves a reconfiguration of the distribution of powers within the bench.

Our ethnographic experience confirms the necessity of going beyond an exclusively judge-centred perspective and analysing the broader context of judgments – be it social, legal, or political. The near-daily mass hearings, initially before the 16th Chamber and subsequently before specially composed assize courts, have led to the development of a jurisprudence that significantly influences the sentencing process: 'We have progressively refined our way of judging and sentencing. If we sentence a network to seven years for organising trips to Syria, the subsequent network that has fought in Syria will have to be judged through the prism of this decision.' Beyond ruling in line with established jurisprudence, mass litigation implies that judges do not adjudicate cases in isolation from others, as the public might imagine. Instead, judges reproduce their knowledge and perception of the 'truth' from case to case. Furthermore, penal policy represents another important

it comes to sentencing. The maximum sentence of imprisonment can only be imposed by a majority of at least 6 votes in the first instance and at least 8 on appeal.

24 Alix, 2010. 25 Collective of defence lawyers, 2022.

26 Interview with a judge at the Paris Court of Appeal in 2018, reported in Mégie, 2020.

contextual factor. Since 2016, the public prosecutor's office has consistently appealed judgments that deviate from their original requisitions. Thus, the convictions handed down in terrorism trials result from broader dynamics that extend beyond the specific characteristics of the case and the judges responsible for ruling. The omnipresence of several factors, such as specialisation, the massification of case law, and prosecution policy, challenges the principle of individualisation of sentences. Instead, an encompassing action aimed at punishing those labelled as the terrorist enemies of France has been put in place.

2.2 THE INVESTIGATING JUDGE AND THE FILE

The trial's foundation lies in the file compiled by the investigating judges. It serves as its cornerstone, playing a decisive, though not final, role in the process. According to the rule procedure, 'The investigating judge, in accordance with the law, carries out all necessary investigative actions deemed useful to uncovering the truth.'[27] In France, unlike common law systems, it is a judge who independently carries out the investigation, collecting incriminating and exonerating evidence for the 'manifestation of the truth'. During this phase, the investigating judge constructs the investigation file, which contains all the material relating to the enquiries, with the statements and evidence gathered during the investigation. At the end of the investigation, if there is enough incriminating evidence, the indictment will be issued. Interestingly, the investigation phase is called a *judiciary information* (and not investigation) as 'investigating judges are here to inform an eventual court'.[28]

While the trial judges are not bound by the findings of the investigating judge and the hearing may reveal other narratives and facts, the file is the hypothesis on which the trial's debates are based. Thus, the 'collective search for the truth' is not the prerogative of a single judge: it starts with the investigating judge. In a way, based on the findings of the investigating judge, the accused is, more than innocent, presumed guilty. As noted by Antoine Garapon and Ioannis Papadopoulos:

[27] Code of Criminal Procedure, Art. 81. [28] Trévidic, 2024.

> The inquisitorial procedure operates through a series of successive assumptions about guilt, as evidenced by the ability to detain a suspect before trial ... In France, the outcome of assize trials often leaves little doubt, as indicated by the very low number of acquittals ... Acquitting at a trial in France amounts to invalidating the work of the judges who, though they deny it, have already taken a stance on the substance.[29]

In terms of counter-terrorism investigations, the investigative judges are centralised in the jurisdiction of Paris within a specialised unit created in the 1990s. The increase in the amount of resources spent over the years is evident: in 2000 there were only four judges, and in 2018, the unit comprised thirteen investigative judges: 'Today, each investigating judge in the anti-terrorism unit is handling between thirty and thirty-five cases as the lead judge, in addition to cases in which they are co-lead, which can represent a very significant workload.'[30]

Investigating judges have wide-ranging authority that includes the ability to seek arrest until the end of the proceedings, directing the police, and allowing special investigation methods, as well as summoning witnesses. The investigating judges are also the competent body to recognise victims as civil parties at any time during the investigation phase. While this phase is not public, the different parties – the defence, the victims, and the prosecution – have access to the file and can suggest avenues for investigation, propose summoning a witness, and can appeal the judge's decision to the investigation chamber.

In terrorism cases, the practice has been the systematic use of joint investigation, which collectively constructs the investigation strategy.[31] The joint appointments are tailored to the complexity of the case: two or three judges are designated for network cases (i.e. without victims), three judges for terrorist plots in France and for attacks abroad; three to six judges for the most complex attacks, such as the Paris attacks of 2015. Joint appointments with other specialised units (financial and crimes against humanity units) are possible when certain aspects of a case require the sharing of expertise with one of these units. Investigating judges affirm that the diverse backgrounds of the judges ensure a rich expertise in joint appointments: 'We are making every effort to ensure that the anti-terrorism unit is a place of collective work, even if – obviously – our personalities and professional backgrounds are

[29] Garapon and Papadopoulos, 2003, p. 98.
[30] Les Cahiers de la Justice, 2017.
[31] Code of Criminal Procedure, Art. 83-2.

different.'[32] 'To ensure the effectiveness of our work, it seems essential to us to avoid any form of personalisation.'[33] And yet, despite their hidden and confidential work, there are strong personalities among the investigating judges who have become public figures, as was the case with Marc Trévidic, a famous investigating judge with important experience in the counter-terrorism unit, who wrote books on the subject and enjoyed extensive media coverage.[34] However, due to an important turnover in the French justice system, which limits the term for a judge in office to ten years, a number of investigating judges, even in complex cases, had no prior experience in counter-terrorism, while experienced judges had to change positions.

Investigations are primarily based on interrogations. Investigating judges spend long hours with the individuals under investigation for terrorism: 'Their profiles are very diverse; we need to understand their background, motivation, ideological conditioning, and demonstrate (or not) the reality of the charges against them.'[35] The methods of investigation often depend on the distinction between 'network cases', which aim to prevent, and cases where terror acts have been committed: 'In attempting to achieve this goal, we rely on procedural frameworks and investigative techniques established for combating organised crime, such as surveillance, infiltration, investigations under pseudonyms, audio surveillance, etc.'[36] During the investigation, investigating judges collaborate closely with counter-terrorism police services and get support from cyber specialists and geopolitical analysts. These are generally very complex cases, with ramifications in numerous countries, in which international cooperation is often needed. Investigative judges have affirmed that they also closely collaborate with other judicial actors. They interact with victims' lawyers and with the prosecution, 'always respecting the role and prerogatives of each'. Additionally, they organise various exchanges, including with the presidents of the criminal courts or meetings with experts in the field. They further participated

[32] Les Cahiers de la Justice, 2017. [33] Robinson, 2021.

[34] Marc Trévidic was an investigating judge at the Paris anti-terrorism unit for ten years, a position that came to an end on the eve of the November 2015 attacks. Judge Trévidic will not be part of this important investigation; interestingly he was invited by the civil parties as a witness to the Bataclan trial. In his testimony in court, he spoke about a 'deadly failure' (Trial hearing, 16 March 2024). He is the author of a number of books including: Trévidic, 2011, 2013, 2014, 2020.

[35] Trévidic, 2024. [36] See Les Cahiers de la Justice, 2017.

in training sessions at the National School for the Judiciary,[37] which 'constitute valuable moments of exchange and reflection that enrich our practices'.

Indeed, the close relations between all of the different actors involved have consistently been reinforced. And what about the defence? According to the investigating judges, the defence lawyer has a major role in this phase: 'They are tenacious, and our exchanges are characterised by loyalty.'[38] Defence lawyers have quite a different view. Interviews with defence lawyers regarding the investigation phase echo the famous phrase coined by Malcolm Feely, 'the process is the punishment'. It appears that this is the case and not only for the defendants but also for their lawyers. Already in 1999, an NGO reported that 'it is clear that the central figures in the investigation of alleged terrorist offences, the investigating judges, tend from the outset to assume the worst when it comes to those who are under investigation'.[39] More than two decades later, a defence lawyer on the Charlie Hebdo trial reaffirmed this statement, when she told us about the defence of her client, who was not radicalised but was likely to provoke fantasies among the investigating judges:

> There is something that always strikes me as very surprising, and that is the difference between how charges and personalities are perceived during the investigation and at the trial ... there is such a difference compared to how my client was treated during the investigation ... it was incredibly violent ... During the investigation, the presence of fantasy and the terrorist nature of the procedure were too dangerous for my client.[40]

This highlights how investigations during times of social anxiety tend to adopt a suspicious attitude, creating a structural asymmetry between the accused and their defence.

2.2.1 Pre-Trial Detention and Isolation

Those accused of terrorism, with only minor exceptions, are systematically held in pre-trial detention and often in isolation. The legislative amendments of 2016 brought procedural changes, including the

[37] See Les Cahiers de la Justice, 2017, p. 273.
[38] See Les Cahiers de la Justice, 2017, p. 273.
[39] Citation from an FIDH human rights report written in 1999 which, according to the lawyer, is still valid today. See McColgan and Attanasio, 1999.
[40] Levy et al., 2021.

lengthening of pre-trial detention exclusively for those who could be tried for 'association of wrongdoing in relation to a terrorist enterprise' (AMT). Codified in Article 421-2-1 of the French Criminal Code, AMT is the main charge used, as it is a 'preventive' crime that requires relatively little evidence. Thus, those suspected of AMT can be held for up to three years prior to trial in cases of offence and four years in cases of felony, compared to only two years for those suspected of any other terrorism-related offence. The term can be lengthened twice for an additional period of four months each time.[41] This underscores the fact that the notion of AMT serves the purpose not only of securing convictions but also of justifying and lengthening pre-trial detention.[42] The investigation phase lasts between two and four years, although, for complex terror trials, pre-trial detention might span more than five years.

In practice, the decision on pre-trial detention is taken by the liberty and detention judge, in the nearby office of the investigative judge, behind closed doors, in the presence of defence lawyers.[43] Public access to these procedures or to the decisions is not available. It is very rare for the detention and liberty judge not to follow the request of the investigative judge.[44] While in 2023, the share of prisoners awaiting trial stood at around 27%,[45] French returnees from Syria, who are suspected of having joined a jihadist group there, are systematically detained until the end of the trial proceedings. Once the investigation is complete,

[41] See French Code of Criminal Procedure, Art. 706-24-3, modified by Law No. 2016-731 of 3 June 2016, Art. 7.

[42] Alix, 2014.

[43] According to Art. 144 of the French code of criminal procedure, the liberty and detention judge may order a provisional detention in the following circumstance: for the preservation of evidence, the prevention of pressure against witnesses or victims, the prevention of fraudulent consultation with co-perpetrators or accomplices, the protection of the person under investigation or the prevention of the renewal of the offence, or to end an exceptional and persistent disturbance to public order. It should be noted that the use of alternatives to detention – such as restriction of movement and house arrest – depends also on the political environment. For example, electronic bracelets have been practically abandoned in favour of pre-trial detention since the attack at Saint-Étienne-du-Rouvray, which was committed by an individual placed under such a judicial control measure (interview with a defence lawyer specialising in terrorist cases, 24 April 2018, on file with author).

[44] Interview with a counter-terrorism investigating judge, March 2018, Paris. On file with author.

[45] Mestren, 2023.

the accused may await their trial for another year; this period can be prolonged twice for an additional six months.[46] The investigative judge or the liberty and detention judge can order solitary confinement for detainees in pre-trial detention.[47] A detainee in pre-trial detention (or a convict in prison) can be subject to solitary confinement also as a result of a decision taken by the penitentiary administration, where it could be justified on the basis of the threat posed by the individual as well as the risk of proselytism and influence over other detainees.[48] There are no available data on how many people have been placed in solitary confinement, but it was a practice largely used during last decade.[49]

As a result, persons who are presumed innocent can be held in detention for an extremely long time. For example, in the Merah case that was ruled in the first instance in 2017, the Assize Court adjudicated facts from 2012, and the accused was in pre-trial detention – and isolation – during this entire period. As of the beginning of 2019, the 16th Criminal Chamber of the Court of First Instance has been hearing cases dating from 2015 to 2016.

Furthermore, regarding the inequality of the arms of the parties, the defence lawyers have to go to the prison to meet their client, where they are subjected to harsh security controls. Further, the lawyers, who are usually very young, tend to be overwhelmed by the size of the files and the quantity of investigative materials, which include a lot of digital data, such as phone transcriptions, etc. Naturally, relatively

46 French code of criminal procedure, Art. 181. Thus, a suspect in pre-trial detention, once indicted, can wait for his trial in detention for two more years. However, according to the Court of Cassation, an extension of the time period cannot be granted because of institutional material problems such as lack of judges. See Mercier, 2016.

47 French Code of Criminal Procedure, Art. 145-4-1.

48 This is for up to one year, with a periodic review every three months. Beyond one year, the Ministry of Justice can extend the confinement measure, in the absence of any maximum duration provided by the French code of criminal procedure. See French code of criminal procedure, Arts 726-1, R57–7-64 to R57–7-68. The Supreme Administrative Court ruled in 2008 that solitary confinement could only be used in circumstances of strict necessity and that detainees had the right to appeal against a decision of solitary confinement. See Conseil d'État, Litigation Section, 31 October 2008, Decision No. 293785.

49 At the end of 2016, 15% of detainees convicted for terrorism-related offences were in isolation. Interview with the French Section of the International Observatory of Prisons, 28 March 2018. On file with author.

young defence lawyers who are appointed by legal aid do not possess such resources. Many told us how they had 'devoted their life' and had to reduce the number of other clients they had, endangering their firm.

The very long time in custody, sometimes a few years before the trial, is used for surveillance. The information gathered about inmate behaviour in prison is yet another tool to understand the actions of suspects under investigation. This long detention period allows the investigative judges to gather information, subjecting suspects to various medical and psychological examinations and including them in different prison programmes. Indeed, confronted with jihadism within their walls, prisons have become a privileged space for intelligence services in their fight against terrorism, maintaining ties linked with the judiciary.[50]

After years of inquiry, the materials in the investigation file comprise several volumes. In the Bataclan trial, it was composed of a million pages. The investigation process reaches its full conclusion when drafting the closing orders and identifying the infractions for the indictment: it can be either dismissal, referral to the lower criminal court (for a sentence up to ten years), or indictment before the assize court. The file then returns to the magistrates of the public prosecutor's office, who act on behalf of the State, and submit a request to the investigative chamber for a decision on the indictment, known as an OMA (Ordre de Mise en Accusation). This indictment is a comprehensive document based on the facts contained in the file. In complex cases, they may span hundreds of pages. The investigation file and the OMA are meant to be kept confidential and unpublished until the conclusion of the proceedings and the archiving of the file. However, it has been a practice to circulate the OMA 'unofficially' among journalists or researchers who had personal connections to judges or lawyers. When the trial starts, the file is physically brought to the courtroom, left in dozens of boxes behind the judges; it is also available electronically for the trial judges. Its physical visibility in the courtroom serves as a reminder to all parties of its foundational role. During the hearings, it is rare but not impossible for an investigating judge to be summoned by the defence or the civil parties.

[50] For example, Camille Hennetier, who was the deputy public prosecutor for several years and prosecutor in the Bataclan trial, was appointed Head of the National Prison Intelligence Service.

2.3 COUNTER-TERRORISM PROSECUTORS AND THE PROSECUTION POLICY

The 'Attorney General' (or 'ministère public', 'parquet') is the generic term used to refer to the judges who occupy the position of the public prosecutor. Prosecutors in France are magistrates by profession. They have the same training as the trial judges. After completing law school (undergraduate studies), they undergo five years of study at the French National School for the Judiciary (ENM), forming a distinct professional corps.[51] Throughout their career trajectory, they will occupy various interchangeable positions, including serving as prosecutors ('parquet'), investigating judges, or trial judges. They often share similar backgrounds and training, and typically belong to the same professional milieu. In the context of terrorism – they all work at the same location, within the Paris Tribunal, and eat at the same tribunal's canteen. Despite the judges of the parquet being under the hierarchy of the Ministry of Justice, there is a culture of proximity that leads to a certain cohesion among the judges. All those who trained at the ENM have strong professional and personal ties that link them. Lawyers (defence or victims' lawyers) belong to a separate professional grouping and are organised under the bar association.[52]

Charged with representing society's interests, when the trial judges conclude their questioning, it is the turn of the prosecutor to present enquiries. The public prosecutor must demonstrate, in the closing arguments, proof of the guilt of the defendants and request the level of corresponding punishment. It is not uncommon for unexpected events to influence the course of the hearing, bringing forth new issues. At the end of the trial, the prosecutor's requisitions resume their role at this phase, and they may ask to requalify the charges if new understandings emerge. In their requisition, with the frequent request for long-term imprisonment, the only conceivable purpose of punishment is the one Durkheim assigns: to restore 'the moral unity of society' by removing from action those who sought to disrupt it.[53] At the very least, this is the message sent to the court and, more broadly, to society.

Up until 2019, all terrorism cases were handled by the Paris Prosecutor's Office (C1 section). It was then reformed into the National Anti-Terrorism Prosecutor's Office (PNAT), which consists

[51] On the work of prosecutor in general see: Hodgson and Soubise, 2016.
[52] See Lerner, 2001, p. 26. [53] Durkheim, 1893.

of three units: the anti-terrorism division, the division for the execution of sentences, and a division for crimes against humanity.[54] Their role begins at the very early stages of the judicial process, with the arrest of the suspect in police custody (*garde à vue*), when the alleged crime is classified as terrorism.[55] Regarding persons who were engaged in Syria, upon arrival in France the individual is arrested.[56] Then, until the case is transferred to the investigative judge (within a period of a maximum of ninety-six hours),[57] it is the prosecutor's office that leads the interrogations with the police. In the 1990s, the public prosecutor's office played a more restrained role in the immediate management, as the investigating judge was involved earlier.[58] Once the investigative judge issues the indictment, the case returns to the magistrates at the public prosecutor's office, who then represent the State during the trial. Thus, the prosecution office is the only entity that follows each defendant from the arrest phase, through the indictment, and up to the trial hearings and prison sentencing. This uninterrupted monitoring of cases, characterised by overall continuity and by magistrates often transitioning between services, results in a particular expertise, bolstered by specialised police and intelligence teams: 'We have the opportunity to follow cases from their inception, with privileged contacts with intelligence services. It is worth noting the smooth exchanges with them, which reflect the trust that exists. Furthermore, this monitoring continues until the judgment is handed on, without omitting our essential role in the execution of sentences and the monitoring of convicts.'[59]

[54] Despite its misleading title, this office groups under the same umbrella as the war crimes and crimes against humanity units. It is the second autonomous national prosecutor's office after the creation of the national financial prosecutor's office in 2013. In 2018, for example, it was composed of thirteen magistrates at the special National Antiterrorism Prosecution Service, and thirteen investigative judges.

[55] See Criminal Code, Art. 113-13, amendment introduced in 2012.

[56] According to an agreement, initiated in September 2014 by the former French minister of the interior, Bernard Cazeneuve, Turkey is supposed to inform France in case a French (presumed) member of an armed group is expelled from Turkish territory. Following this notification, French police officers are sent to Ankara and accompany the individual until their boarding on a flight to France. According to Sofia Koller, as of July 2018, 193 individuals had returned to France through the procedure outlined in this agreement. Koller, 2023, p. 6.

[57] Code of Criminal Procedure, Art. 706-88-1.

[58] National Anti-Terrorism Prosecutor, Jean-François Ricard, 2021.

[59] Deputy Prosecutor, Jean-Michel Bourles, 2021.

Less visibly, the prosecution continues to monitor and control the punishment long beyond the point of requisition in court. It is responsible for determining the course of action regarding individuals released from prison and establishing follow-up procedures.[60] Thus, the punishment extends beyond the prison sentence imposed by the trial judges. Concerns about recidivism, more than rehabilitation, terrorism convicts are registered in various databases, allowing for broad interference in their privacy and limiting their professional and social activities after their release from prison. These practices resulted in a blurring of boundaries between judicial and administrative authorities.[61] Between 2018 and 2023, around 350 administrative measures have been carried out regarding convicted terrorists leaving prison.[62]

Apart from the continuous management of the case, the prosecutor's office was also heavily involved in the organisation of major trials including security control, badges for accredited journalists, and the integration of the victim: 'We had a detailed reflection on the circuits, controls, assistance; everything must be planned: if someone, especially a victim, feels unwell, we need to be able to anticipate their evacuation.'[63] Defence lawyers in the Charlie Hebdo trial complained that similar attention was not given to the accused:

> I filed several incident reports for degrading and disproportionate searches in the detention centre ... it hindered the work of the defence ... My client was very tense because of this. They underwent

[60] 'Judicial measure for the prevention of terrorist recidivism and reintegration', created by the Law of 30 July 2021 The Intelligence Act of 24 July 2015 has been revised to take account of changes in the technologies and modes of communication providing intelligence services new means of control, through algorithmic surveillance, in particular the through intercepting satellite communications.

[61] Guittet et al., 2021.

[62] 'Every time a prisoner convicted of terrorism leaves prison, he or she is closely monitored ... Each of them is assessed on a chart, with a level ranging from 1 (very dangerous) to 3 (not very dangerous). According to this classification, a specific intelligence service is assigned to them. For the most dangerous, the Direction générale de la sécurité intérieure (DGSI) is responsible for monitoring them ... In addition, numerous administrative control and surveillance measures (MICAS) are taken when prisoners convicted of terrorism leave prison. 80% of these MICAS are taken when the person leaves detention, and almost 95% of those leaving are targeted by administrative measures'. . 'France: 84 détenus condamnés pour terrorisme sont sortis de prison depuis le début de l'année, selon le ministère de l'Intérieur', in: *France Info*, 4 December 2023.

[63] Deputy Prosecutor, Jean-Michel Bourles, 2021, p. 212.

searches, including thorough body pat-downs, every time they entered and exited the box. Whenever they went to the bathroom, they had to leave the door open with a police officer watching.[64]

2.3.1 Monopolising the Public Sphere?

The role of these magistrates has seen a growing pivotal role in the interplay between politics, law, and security, where they assume a central and varying position. Being under the authority of the Minister of Justice, the prosecution office is tasked with implementing ministerial directives, thus making judicial action a fully-fledged public policy. Most notably, along with its responsibility for representing the State in trials, managing convictions, and overseeing sentences, it has developed recognised expertise and engagement in media dissemination and operational oversight of post-attack investigations. Since the first proclaimed jihadist attacks on French soil by Mohamed Merah in the city of Toulouse in 2012, and amid a proliferation of terrorist incidents, the counter-terrorism prosecutor's office has assumed increasing responsibility for generating and disseminating official communications. Over time, and especially since the 2015 attacks, it has come to effectively monopolise this communication space, led by its highest authority, the Paris counter-terrorism prosecutor, François Molins. Through regularly delivering official statements at press conferences, Molins has become, for both the media and the public, the quintessential 'face of counter-terrorism'. Operating within a continuous flow of information, his interventions frequently take place amidst crisis conditions, exerting a tangible impact on the content and form of judicial discourse: 'We understand that these interventions have become important in times of crisis, to inform our citizens of the event, the progress of the investigation, but also to provide a framework for the media. In situations like terrorist attacks, there is an extremely strong need, a legitimate expectation from citizens who want to know.'[65]

This growing recognition of their expertise is shown in their frequent participation in investigative committees, specialised training programmes (such as those at the National School for the Judiciary), and media production. It has developed the ability to navigate across various realms of public

[64] Interview done by our research team with a defence lawyer reproduced in Les Cahiers de la Justice, 2021, pp. 241–242.

[65] François Molins, Paris Public Prosecutor (2012–2019), lecture, 16 June 2017.

spaces owing to its recognised expertise on jihadist terrorism, participating in a range of activities, from providing testimonies before committees of the National Assembly and the Senate, organising and drafting legal documents, to holding press conferences in the aftermath of terrorist incidents. Additionally, they are present at police and security meetings, addressing radicalisation, and notably, they represent the State in court hearings and in monitoring the punishments of convicts. This role they assume within different areas of criminal policy allows them to directly shape the boundaries of what has been defined as a legitimate public action.[66] This institution has become the 'owner' in defining these politically charged issues.

2.4 CIVIL PARTIES/VICTIMS AND THEIR LAWYERS

At trial, following the prosecutor's questioning, the lawyers for the civil parties, representing the victims, take their turn.[67] Victims do not merely attend the trial; they can actively participate in the criminal trial. They are a party, just like the accused and the prosecution: 'The raison d'être of the trial is not only punishing the criminals but also for the victims in their "search for the truth".'[68] The jurisprudence dating back to the early twentieth century gives victims a central role in the French judicial system, distinguishing it from common law models. This is known as the status of 'civil party', which serves three main purposes: it grants victims the right to initiate a prosecution just like the prosecutor; it allows them to participate in the judicial process with access to the case file; and it enables them to seek compensation. These three objectives – prosecution, participation in the trial, and compensation – are the basis of the French model. In contrast, in common law countries, the victim remains outside the criminal trial: they are merely a witness and only intervene in civil courts. This is a specific right of citizens in France, rooted in a distrust of the omnipotence of the public prosecutor and seen as a right to resist oppression. In this context, it represents a genuine exercise of public freedom rather than merely a civil action.

To be legally recognised as a civil party, within the meaning of Article 2 of the Code of Criminal Procedure,[69] victims need to prove

[66] Edelman, 1971. [67] See Code of Criminal Procedure, Art. 2, 3, and 375.

[68] Lienhard and Szwarc, 2021.

[69] Code of Criminal Procedure, Art. 2: 'The civil action for compensation for damage caused by a crime, an offence, or a misdemeanour belongs to all those who have

a *direct* link between the crime and the prejudice; it is mainly a geographical criterion of being directly exposed to the crime. They can be attributed the status of a civil party at any time from the opening of the investigation, and even during the trial, up to the requisitions of the attorney general. It is the investigating judge or the trial judge who has jurisdiction to decide on the matter. Once their status is recognised, they are an integrated party of the procedure; they are granted access to the investigation file, can summon witnesses, and during the trial, they can question the defendants and all other witnesses.

Since the terrorist attacks of the 1980s and 1990s, victims in France have gradually obtained specific rights through the jurisprudence. The attacks of 2015 were unprecedented in scale: during the trial for the Charlie Hebdo attack in January 2015, there were 292 civil party applications and 2,322 during the Bataclan trial, with victims able to constitute themselves as civil parties until the prosecutor's requisitions. In the Nice trial, the Court of Cassation recognised the expansion of the status of civil party to persons who tried to intervene or who fled after realising that an attack was taking place. The harm suffered, which must be 'direct and personal', has been expanded by jurisprudence to include 'harm from imminent death anxiety' and 'harm from concern' for relatives.[70] Several weeks were dedicated to hearing civil parties by the court. The unprecedented participation of victims in these terrorism trials has led to the emergence of new practices and an evolving role for the victims, introducing what we named a 'hybrid justice', discussed in Chapters 5 and 6.

2.4.1.1 *Compensation*

Generally, the participation of victims as civil parties in a trial holds significance for the issue of reparations: in French legal procedure, the civil claim is an integral part of the criminal process. In an ordinary criminal trial, following the determination of culpability, the criminal bench also adjudicates on the civil claims put forth by the civil parties. However, in terrorism cases, the scenario differs and has also been

personally suffered from the damage directly caused by the criminal act. Waiver of the civil action cannot stop or suspend the exercise of public action…'

70 Court of Cassation, Criminal Chamber, 15 February 2022, Appeal No. 21-80.264. Further, in 2022 civil parties who are not direct victims but relatives, friends, or partners of those murdered, seeking recognition – reluctantly – for the harm caused by 'imminent death anxiety', became an autonomous harm.

notably strengthened: in addition to the possibility of applying to join as a civil party, a victim of a terrorist act can request a guarantee fund to assess the amount of their compensation after an expert evaluation. This fund, The Victims of Terrorism and Other Offences Guarantee Fund (FGTI), is financed by a €6.50 tax that is mandatory on every household insurance, in other words, through national solidarity. The decision of this fund can also be appealed before the Judge for the Compensation of Victims of Terrorist Acts (JIVAT). The objective of this jurisdiction, established in 2019, is to consolidate all litigation related to victim compensation under one judge, independent of the criminal process, which often proves to be lengthy. Consequently, while the criminal bench is responsible for determining the admissibility of civil party status in the criminal trial, the civil claim itself will be transferred to the specialised jurisdiction JIVAT, which exclusively adjudicates civil interests.

2.4.1.2 Representation

These rights would not have developed as they have without the efforts of lawyers and associations. Civil party lawyers are usually insurance lawyers, but they can also be criminal lawyers. For the major terrorism trials, all of the civil party lawyers intervened under legal aid (AJ). In the Bataclan trial, legal aid was estimated at €50 million and was fully funded by the State.[71] While defence lawyers caution that 'we cannot have 300 prosecutors',[72] some civil party lawyers see their involvement as complementary to that of the public prosecutor. They not only voice their clients' concerns but also contribute to the investigation: having access to the case file, they request investigatory actions, interrogate defendants, challenge investigatory hypotheses, and present their own interpretations during hearings. Meanwhile, associations provide support to victims who can quickly fall into forgetfulness and solitude. Organisations like 'Life for Paris' and '13/11/15' have offered crucial support to this circumstantial community of victims before and

[71] Legal aid was granted for the representation of each civil party at a rate of €1,000 per day. Several lawyers represented large groups of clients, numbering in the dozens, leading to criticism of the imbalance in the payment of legal aid to defence lawyers. A system of digression was installed in the amounts received by civil parties: for the first party, 100% of legal aid, for the 2nd, 80%, then 60%, and finally 40% for all others.

[72] Creux-Thomas, 2022.

during the Bataclan trial, fostering a sense of solidarity that became a collective strategy fully expressed during the trials.

Despite the very large number of civil parties, and in contrast to international criminal trials held before *ad hoc*/hybrid tribunals originating in civil systems, in French terror trials, victims were not compelled to be represented by one of these victims' associations. From a comparative perspective, in the majority of international trials for war crimes, crimes against humanity, and genocide, victims only participate as witnesses, reflecting the legal system of common law. This was the case with the military tribunals of Nuremberg and Tokyo, the two *ad hoc* criminal tribunals for the former Yugoslavia and Rwanda, as well as the Special Court for Sierra Leone. When invited to participate, it is often following an authorisation procedure, as seen in the International Criminal Court, where they are referred to as 'participants'. Even when they are granted the status of civil parties in mechanisms originating in civil law legal systems, as in the case of the Extraordinary Chambers in the Courts of Cambodia (ECCC) or the Extraordinary African Chambers in Senegal (CAE), their position remains fragile. They are obliged to regroup and be represented,[73] forced to form a bloc despite their differences, perceived as forming a single voice. However, as the French major terror trials demonstrated, civil parties do not constitute a single entity but rather the aggregation of multiple sensitivities and experiences.[74] Allowing them to keep their individual representation had been proven possible.

The transformation of the role of lawyers representing victims in the major terrorism trials has been remarkable when compared to ordinary trials: it has impacted the course of the hearing, the strategy of the actors, and the shift towards restorative justice[75] with the inviting of major political figures and experts to give testimonies. Such summonses as 'context witnesses' included the President of the Republic and the Prime Minister at the time, as well as heads of intelligence services who had to answer for their participation in the international coalition when France waged war against the Islamic State.

[73] Marchand and Werner, 2020; Trujillo, 2022; Sperfeldt, 2022; Weill and Sulzer, 2021.

[74] Antichan et al., 2023.

[75] See the book written by the father of a Bataclan victim and the father of one of the terrorists as they engage in dialogue: Amimour and Salines, 2022.

As we will explore in detail in Chapter 5, the simultaneous presence of victims and perpetrators – and their encounter – can be understood within the framework of restorative justice, as highlighted by a civil party lawyer:

> The civil party is fundamental because they share a history with the perpetrator, and their presence is equally important for the perpetrator. The legal narrative that unfolds with the civil party accompanies the victim in their process of reconstruction and the perpetrator in accepting their sentence. We saw moments of restorative justice during the trial thanks to the timing of the discussions, which allows for communication and exchange.[76]

2.5 THE DEFENCE LAWYERS AND THEIR CLIENTS

The trial's sequential order ensures that the defence ultimately has the final word.[77] All along the interrogations by the diverse actors, the debates are adversarial, allowing for the refinement of charges as investigations progress, with defence lawyers playing a vital role. The vast majority of lawyers involved in jihadist network cases have been appointed by legal aid. The defendants' limited financial resources have led them to 'choose' these defence counsels.

Legal aid lawyers are, in many cases, members of the prestigious 'Conférence du stage', selected each year after eloquence competitions of the Paris bar association, open for lawyers aged below thirty-five years. During a year, the twelve selected members of the Conférence are in charge of the Paris legal aid with jurisdiction over terrorist matters. The importance of these lawyers has continued to grow since 2015, with successive promotions and the hyper-specialisation of some of them. Safya Akorri was defending one of the accused in the Charlie Hebdo case:

> For the past three years, I have dedicated myself to terrorism cases. Sometimes, I am chosen because the detainees know me, my name circulates in detention, but most often, I am appointed by legal aid because I belong to the Bar Conference of Paris. I was elected secretary

[76] Salas and Besnier, 2023. p. 117.

[77] Code of Criminal Procedure, Art. 460: 'The accused or their lawyer shall always have the last word'. See also European Convention on Human Rights, Art. 6.

of the Conference in 2018. I am one of the few lawyers authorised to be appointed by legal aid for terrorism-related cases.[78]

The few lawyers who do not come from the Conference regularly point out this monopoly. The result is a high degree of specialisation among a handful of lawyers. As an indication of this phenomenon, some of them come to listen to their colleagues on the public benches to 'grasp what's going on in this special chamber'.[79] Some lawyers play up this specialisation in their line of defence, while others, less experienced, emphasise their lack of specialisation and their distanced viewpoint. Some of the strategies of these outsiders may seem surprising to the more experienced lawyers: 'This lawyer is crazy. He gets to the 16th Chamber, and he wants to plead acquittal. You can't plead acquittal in this chamber. He's heading for the wall and risks dragging us into it!'[80]

Social science research generally depicts the courtroom scene of terrorist trials as a forum used by the accused and the judiciary to publicly discuss the legitimacy of their commitments.[81] In the mid-1980s, members of the radical left group Action Direct continued to fight in the courtroom, whether through their statements or actions such as a hunger strike. In response, the justice system used the trial as an opportunity to assert its position of strength, legitimising its 'democratic values' and condemning the defendants' violence as 'illegitimate'. The defence strategies gradually developed in post-2015 terrorist trials do not follow this trend. Lawyers and defendants define defence strategies that fade the political dimensions of these trials. Oscillating between repentance, claimed innocence, and even speeches inclined to suggest the existence of psychopathological disorders, the statements of these defendants often seem far removed from the propaganda claiming 'armed jihad'. This evolution differs from previous defence strategies in other terrorism-related cases involving Corsican, Basque, or extreme left-wing groups, which often featured the rhetoric of political 'breaking up'/rupture. In the trials we observed, there was almost no use of such a strategy.[82] Defendants respond into microphones, sometimes whispering to each other, questioning their lawyers.

[78] Besnier, 2023. [79] Interview with defence lawyer in October 2017.
[80] Interview with defence lawyer in October 2018.
[81] See for example, McEvoy et al., 2022; Allo, 2015.
[82] The attitude of not answering the court's questions in order to assert one's opposition has only been seen in very few cases. In one case, this opposition was related to the defendant's protest against the conditions of his detention, and his transfer to a

While the ineffectiveness of this type of strategy is at times mentioned to justify the end of the rupture defence, it is the improbability of these defence lawyers to support their clients' ideology that leads to the rejection of this strategy. 'Lawyers for the cause' do not exist in the current litigation, unlike other movements claiming to be part of the armed struggle. The mere mention of this hypothesis is always rejected: it would be neither possible nor even conceivable in the current context.[83]

Defence lawyers also face the challenge of assuming their role as 'defenders of terrorists' in the national public debate. Press articles appear on those who, sometimes barely older than their clients, and in the context of the 2015 attacks, agree to defend those whom many describe as 'indefensible'. Understanding the role of lawyers in terrorist cases raises broader questions about the social and political place of defence in societies struck by such violence: 'But how can you defend terrorists? That's what people say to me every time I talk about one of my terrorist clients. It's not always easy to make people understand, but that's often the problem with being a criminal lawyer!'[84] These lawyers then publicly dissociate themselves: 'We don't share their ideology. We are their lawyers, with the aim of upholding the rights of the defence, and justice.' Lawyers from the Conférence du stage have confirmed that they have only taken on these cases because of their membership of this bar association. Moreover, as a general rule, only a few of them want to specialise in this minority type of litigation. As a result, they seem far less politicised than lawyers working on so-called political cases, particularly in relation to the increasing criminalisation of so-called ultra-left movements. The testimony of lawyer Henri Leclerc, who, since the 1950s, has represented many defendants in terrorist trials, remains most enlightening on this subject:

special unit at a high-security prison. In another hearing, a defendant declared that only God's justice could be recognised, and that he would therefore not respond to the president of the court. Such cases do exist, but they were very much in the minority considering all of the trials we observed.

83 Israël and Malatesta, 2012: 'The tension inherent in the lawyer's profession consists of making it an honour to uphold the right of everyone to be defended, while at the same time creating, with varying degrees of difficulty, the concrete defence of certain defendants.'

84 Interview with defence lawyer in October 2018.

> Today, we are dealing with terrorism that is carried out in the name of an ideology that is difficult to understand. When we defended people during the Algerian war, we could defend them in the name of an ideal that they themselves were pursuing, by finding links between this ideal and the foundations that are also the foundations of the Republic. We could do what Vergès did. [. . .] Today, we find it impossible to use this type of defence![85]

While the political justification is not pursued as an explicit strategy, jihadist trials have nevertheless led to a redefinition of political discourse. Defending the rights of the accused has become the new focus of lawyers currently representing jihadist defendants. These lawyers actively defend their rights and the principle of a fair trial, constantly reminding the court of the context of derogatory anti-terrorism laws. Some rely on the European Convention on Human Rights and the jurisprudence of the European Court of Human Rights to ensure that defendants receive a fair trial. They therefore oppose expedited trials and collective convictions based on the vast definition of AMT, emphasising the need to protect civil rights, including those of alleged terrorists, within a rule of law framework and not to conduct 'impressionist justice'. Consequently, a plurality of political arguments is co-produced, although the religious interpretation of engagement remains predominantly favoured by judicial authorities. Political considerations, such as the war in Syria, coalition bombings, or the issue of discrimination against 'Muslims' in Europe, do not disappear but are reformulated through a new co-production between the accused and judicial actors. Terrorism trial hearings become spaces where these various political issues are continually discussed and confronted.

Equality of arms?

An element that is particularly striking in terrorism cases is the vast amount of investigative material resulting from the prolonged pre-trial detention period and the reinforcement of the units in terms of resources. As discussed above, while the investigating judge works in collaboration with many actors, and with an important number of resources allocated, the defence – almost entirely based on legal aid – is much less supported, and lawyers have expressed how they devoted 'their lives' to working on

[85] Henri Leclerc, lawyer, at La Maison des Avocats during la Conférence du Barreau de Paris, reported in Parmentier, 2018.

some of the cases while sacrificing their firm. They found themselves overloaded by the quantity of documents, playing the role of private investigators. According to a defence lawyer, in the Bataclan trial, he needed to read hundreds of pages of investigation, including lists of hundreds of telephone exchanges, to try to compile a defence. Similarly, a defence lawyer from the Charlie Hebdo trial told us:

'I was assigned by legal aid to ensure his defence just a few days after the January 2015 attacks … I found myself facing a twenty-four-year-old young man who did not seem radicalised and had not fully grasped the extent of the matter … I fought for his release from pre-trial detention, which I obtained after thirty-nine months, and for the requalification of the charges against him, which occurred at the conclusion of the investigation, after four years. It is the most worked-on investigative case of my life, visiting my client more than twenty-five times in prison and making numerous requests for actions and medical expertise.[86]

A more difficult situation is when the lawyer is nominated at the end of the investigation:

> When I arrived to defend the accused [the main person accused in the Cannes-Torcy case], the investigation was completely finished. The case consisted of four or five CDs that I collected from the registry. This represented 90 volumes of procedures, which is colossal. The investigation had been lengthy, and in less than six months – I had to meticulously go through these 90 volumes of procedures. Not all of it concerns him, but that's precisely what I needed to verify … I was defending someone who had spent four years in extremely difficult detention conditions, as he was in solitary confinement. He hadn't had any human interaction for at least the last two years.[87]

The relationship with their client is also impacted by the security constraints that apply to defence lawyers. Attorney Kempf describes how he went to visit his client daily in the highly secure prison at *Fresnes*, where the defendant in the Bataclan trial was detained in isolation until the end of the proceedings. They both had to undergo intense search methods and isolation; before and after each meeting, his client was strip-searched, suggesting that even the lawyer was suspected.[88]

[86] Les Cahiers de la Justice, 2021, pp. 238–239 and 241.

[87] Interview with a defence lawyer, Cannes–Torcy trial, reproduced in Besnier et al., 2019, p. 200.

[88] Kampf, 2024.

Finally, this imbalance is reflected in the hearing itself, and more specifically in the order of speaking, as we have witnessed in the prolonged hearings of the major terror trials. The large number of civil parties created disadvantages for the defence, which was the last to intervene. Defence lawyers contended that with dozens of victims' lawyers conducting questioning, defendants are often left exhausted, and with a dominant narrative already shaped, when the turn of the defence finally arrives. While it is evident that the flow of proceedings is no longer the same because there are hundreds of additional interlocutors, the creation of such an order was not a procedural obligation, but a choice of the presiding judge. Further, the presence of so many civil parties also completely changes the logistics of the hearing, and considerable financial and human resources were deployed to accommodate and support them, while similar attention was not given to the accused. The focus of the trial was shifted: it was no longer the trial of the accused but that of the victims.

According to a defence lawyer, 'Civil parties certainly need a space to express themselves: they could do so before the JIVAT. One could imagine that, once the criminal judgment is rendered, victims could come to express the harm they have suffered, the severity of their trauma before this judge.'[89] And yet, in the Charlie Hebdo trial, one defence lawyer, who was highly critical of the way the investigation was conducted, recognised that:

> this trial was very special for my client, as if it was the first time that the public authorities had given him so much importance. From an educational, geopolitical, cultural, and historical point of view, he learned things. It will remain, even though it's tragic to think that this boy – who comes from the most disadvantaged areas of the Paris region – had to be involved in a criminal procedure to interest someone and see so many people say interesting things on such varied subjects.[90]

2.6 THE ACCUSED AND THEIR NARRATIVE

Behind the lawyers stand the defendants. Held in custody, they are brought from prison every day and placed in the 'box'.[91] The accused

[89] Besnier, 2023, p. 106; See also Weill and Sulzer, 2021.

[90] Le Cahier de la Justice, 2021, p. 251.

[91] The use of glass or plexiglass enclosures is officially mandated for keeping the defendants secure from the public. These measures have been criticised by the

speaks into a microphone, with a lack of formality, in a very direct and spontaneous way, wearing civilian clothing, usually casual attire such as jogging pants or trousers, and a shirt. In some cases, their clothes, as with their hairstyle, express a particular model of self-presentation corresponding to a particular affiliation, expressed especially by young people who joined Daesh. Defendants appearing freely, accused of minor charges, enter the courtroom alongside the public.

At the start of the hearing, the presiding judge informs the accused of their right to intervene during the proceedings: 'Do not hesitate to intervene', the judge says to the defendants. 'Feel free to ask for the floor. You may speak whenever witnesses contradict your version of events.' In the French system, in principle, forming a conviction relies heavily on the accused's own narration of events. The court seeks to hear their account of the actions, motivations, mental state at the time, and perspective on the future. The *cour d'assises* requires the accused to reveal who they are, to provide a nuanced understanding of the facts. In these cases, the accused is an active participant in his or her trial, not merely a passive figure. This approach contrasts sharply with common law proceedings, which focus on external testimony and largely disregard the accused's version of events or their personal background.[92] This attitude is indicative of the philosophy of this judicial system, which is to understand the trajectory of the accused and the context in which the crime was committed, including the socio-political reasons surrounding the crime.

During the debates, the accused is repeatedly asked to react and to talk. Whenever a new witness is heard or a new element is introduced, the judge seeks the accused's version of events, bringing him or her back to the discussion. At any point, they may share their observations, respond to a testimony, or introduce new elements to the discussion. In contrast to the common law system, where the accused is largely passive, the *cour d'assises* places the accused at the centre of the proceedings, actively encouraging their participation as it is,

French Lawyers' Union, who condemned the 'glass cage'. They argued that this setup hinders the proper conduct of proceedings by reducing the visibility of certain defendants and complicating communication with clients. Some enclosures have since been modified to address lawyers' concerns. Interestingly, the term 'box' is usually used to describe a compartment in a horse stable, designed to isolate them while giving them space to move.

92 See for example, how the work of Mayur on terror trials in India reveals the importance of 'legal technicalities' (Mayur, 2023).

fundamentally, 'their' trial. The accused is expected to contribute to uncovering the truth. Although the order of addressing the court is regulated, their interventions are always allowed, even if is the turn of a witness or another actors to speak. At any point, they may share their observations, respond to a testimony, or introduce new elements to the discussion.

However, while every effort is made to hear the voice of the accused, their speaking turns and their voice are highly regulated by the various phases of the proceedings, and subject to the primary need to establish his or her possible responsibility. The accused is the main player, but their participation (and voice) is strictly normed. Indeed, they are required to play within a space, a milieu with specific codes – such as given rhetoric, posture, language, and norms – which are often alien to them and which they hardly understand. Moreover, various phases contribute to framing the trial and formatting their voice. The 'investigation of personality' phase provides a large amount of information, including antecedents, childhood, family relationships, and actions carried out. This framing starts earlier, with the investigative judges, from the moment of their arrest until the end of the proceedings, and can last several years. For the vast majority of defendants, there is the detention phase, during which the accused is the subject of observation, producing information that will have a major impact during the trial. In this period, the accused are 'screened' to assess their dangerousness and their degree of radicalisation, and also to obtain information that will be used to discipline them during the trial phase. The information obtained during detention, collected by a wide range of actors, will influence the debate, the defendants' statements and, ultimately, the judgement.

To understand the importance of the incarceration phase in counterterrorism trials, it is worth briefly reviewing recent developments in the French prison system, in particular following the recent terrorist attacks on French soil and the departures (and then returns) to the Iraqi–Syrian front of thousands of young French citizens. In fact, the successive reforms have created a system centred on detection and evaluation, in which the prison's 'Radicalisation Assessment Units' (in French: Quartiers d'évaluation de la radicalisation, 'QER'), the flagship of the policy to prevent and combat radicalisation, play a major role and characterise the French approach to prevent and fight radicalisation.

Initially, five dedicated units were set up in the aftermath of the 2015 attacks to avoid radical Islamist proselytism in prisons and to provide effective care to so-called radicalised individuals imprisoned for terrorist acts.[93] However, as observed by Bartolomeo Conti, a sociologist who has conducted prison ethnography for several years, the notion of care very soon became secondary, and these 'dedicated units' were transformed into the QER.[94] The role of the QER is essentially evaluation and securitisation: detainees are evaluated by a multidisciplinary team over the course of seventeen weeks during successive sessions involving a variety of prison staff.[95] The primary function of this evaluation period is to identify their level of radicalisation, and the objective is to assign the detainee to an appropriate prison. Daily interviews with psychologists, educators, and specialised prison staff are conducted to evaluate the individuals' degree of radicalisation. This work is carried out by specialised and trained personnel, such as religious mediators and experts in Islam and religious texts who possess geopolitical understanding, enabling them to assess the ideological immersion of those they evaluate. Following the assessments, the majority of prisoners are transferred to ordinary detention, whereas others, those considered to pose a risk to fellow prisoners, are transferred to prisons designed specifically for violent or dangerous detainees, and they are sent to specialised units for managing radicalisation. Some are incarcerated in isolation because of the level of danger.

The periods of detention, and in particular the QERs, have another important function, as they are also a pivotal source of information during trials, particularly through the reports produced by the various detention services. In all of the trials we have observed, the question of the 'potential dangerousness' of the accused persons was extensively debated in particular the sentences. One of the ways to assess the 'potential dangerousness' of the accused was through the prisons' QER reports, which were frequently read during the proceedings. Consequently, the presence and influence of prison has become omnipresent within the courtroom: it is not solely a means for potential

93 Conti, 2020.

94 According to official data, as of 5 December 2023, there were seven radicalisation prevention quarters (QPR), with a total capacity of 189 places, including one for women – a second is due to open soon. DNA, 2023.

95 On this subject, see in particular the study carried out for the DAP by Chantraine, Scheer and Depuiset in 2018, *Enquête sociologique sur les « quartiers d'évaluation de la radicalisation » dans les prisons françaises*, Rapport DAP, as well as the reports by the Contrôleur général des lieux de privation de liberté, 2015.

punishment. It has become a quasi-evidentiary resource that can offer insights into the person. We have also to consider that, before arriving in the courtroom, the accused – whether associated with jihadist ideology or not – has spent a significant amount of time in the prison environment, which contributes to shaping, among other things, their interpretation of the acts committed, the explanation they give for their trajectory, the interpretation of his or her choices and the possibilities around thinking about reintegration.[96] It must also be borne in mind that the accused has not only lived in prison since his or her arrest, but will in all likelihood spend many years there after the trial, which can affect their attitude during the trial, from two opposing points of view: to collaborate and recognise a certain responsibility, with the risk of appearing to be a traitor in the prison environment, or to keep a fixed ideological position and defend their status among incarcerated jihadists?

2.6.1 A Sociography of Jihadist Commitment

Since the attacks of 2015, France has invested significant effort in attempting to understand an unprecedented phenomenon, that of a significant number of young people – born and raised in France – who travel to the Middle East to join jihadist groups or 'just' to perform *the Hijra*, that is, to emigrate to a society considered 'authentically Islamic'.[97] Social research has had to, first and foremost, confront a lack of empirical work on the subject, a problem that was by no means limited to France, and which affected our understanding of the causes and the modalities, the 'why' and the 'how' of radicalisation and extremism.[98] As Amélie Blom rightly points out in her work on jihadist martyrs in Pakistan, 'the motivations attributed . . . are induced by the sources selected'.[99] In France, as in other countries, the lack of empirical studies has been a major methodological factor that has directly affected the response to the question of motivation, though this gap has been filled over the past decade.

[96] In this regard, see in particular the empirical study conducted by Conti, 2023, p. 217.

[97] According to the data that we have available (Pawella, 2019), around 1,700 French citizens have joined the Iraq–Syria front since 2014. To this number, one must add those who would have wanted to leave, but who were apprehended before their departure or were simply prevented from going (Thomson, 2014, 2016).

[98] Schmid, 2013, Beck, 2015. [99] Blom, 2011, p. 891.

As described in the report presented at the National Assembly on 29 May 2019, in France, 21,039 individuals are registered in the File for the Processing of Reports for the Prevention of Radicalisation of a Terrorist Nature (FSPRT), of which 12,809 cases are considered 'active', meaning subject to official monitoring (these data includes all kinds of radicalisation and terrorism, not only jihadism).[100] The report emphasises primarily that there is no 'typical profile' of people who are radicalised, nor a typical process of radicalisation. It concludes that there exists not one, but several types of radicalism. Nonetheless, certain characteristics of this phenomenon have been identified, drawing from the main studies on French jihadists conducted during the last decade, mainly by sociologists and political scientists, who made use of primary data, such as interviews conducted in prison or working groups specifically created or of secondary data, such as prisoner files or data produced by security services.[101] Despite some disagreement, we can retain the following main characteristics of people accused or condemned for jihadi terrorism.

The first characteristic concerns age, as jihadism is a phenomenon that mainly involves young people. According to data provided by the parliamentary report, less than 5% of registered individuals are over 50, and only 3% are minors.[102] According to data provided by Crettiez and Seze, the average age at the time of incarceration is 28 (and 24 for women).[103]

A second characteristic concerns gender. Jihadism is, in fact, a predominantly masculine phenomenon since men represent 78% of registered individuals. However, the growing number of radicalised women – and the role they play in the construction of the Caliphate – is a new and notable phenomenon compared to previous

100 According to data from the French Prison Service, by the end of 2024, there will be 373 people incarcerated in French prisons for terrorism (TIS) and 511 persons convicted of ordinary crimes but accused, monitored or suspected of radicalisation (RAD). In addition, there are 225 TIS and 300 RAD monitored for radicalisation outside of prison.

101 Khosrokhavar, 2017; Sèze and Clément, 2021; Bonelli and Carrié, 2018; Hecker, 2018; Crettiez and Seze, 2022; Ferret and Khosrokhavar, 2021; Settoul, 2022; Conti, 2024.

102 Bonelli and Carrié, 2018. Yet, as minors are subject to particular procedures and treatments it is not possible to have a precise perception of the phenomenon in quantitative terms.

103 Crettiez and Seze, 2022, p. 38. They worked on a panel of 350 prisoners based on secondary sources.

radical or terrorist movements. As of December 2024, of an estimated 400 French women who went to Syria, 50 women and 100 children remain in camps in Northern Syria, controlled by Kurdish armed groups, while the others have fled or been repatriated.[104]

Initially, almost invisible or perceived solely as victims, over time, women jihadists have emerged as pivotal figures in the courtroom. Despite their significant number, the rate of prosecutions and indictments for women has been much lower than for men. Up to 2016, the judicial treatment of women reflected their marginalisation and lack of visibility in both politics and armed conflict. Consequently, the concept of the female terrorist has been largely overlooked.[105] Only in the spring of 2016 did the anti-terrorist prosecutor's office decide that, from then on, female returnees would also be subject to the same judicial procedures as male returnees. The case of the 'gas canisters at Notre Dame de Paris' in September 2016, in which a group of women attempted to carry out an attack in the centre of Paris, constitutes a founding event in the official narrative for this change of policy, used to 'show the importance of women in the phenomenon of jihadist network'. 'We were already well aware of the place and role of women in the Syrian networks … but it's true that the Notre Dame episode clearly showed us how dangerous women are and how they can act after their departure for Syria'.[106] From 2019, the issue of French women and children imprisoned in Syrian and Kurdish camps as a result of the destruction of cities held by the Islamic State and the military defeat of the terrorist organisation became an issue of major attention. Yet the decision to repatriate was not fully on the agenda until the summer of 2022, after France was found by the UN Committee on the Rights of the Child and the European Court of Human Rights to have violated its legal obligations.[107] This ruling largely contributed to the acceleration of the transfer of some of the children from these camps; yet women are largely prevented from returning.[108] Upon their return, these women are systematically

104 Wilhelm-Olympiou and Köse, 2023. 105 Freedman, 2012.

106 Interview, Procecutor, PNAT, October 2018.

107 United Nations Committee on the Rights of the Child, 2022; European Court of Human Rights, 2022.

108 See for example at: www.diplomatie.gouv.fr/fr/dossiers-pays/syrie/evenements/actualites-2022/article/rapatriements-du-nord-est-syrien-20-10-22. Until 2022 women could they return on their own via Turkey, when all French women were still able to return voluntarily.

arrested at the airport, placed in police custody, and then placed under investigation and pre-trial detention. Their children are placed with family members, host families or institutions, with siblings typically kept together. Today, with the use of AMT, the focus is on activities such as cooking for the fighters, raising their children, and providing emotional and material support to their husbands. In effect, the domestic sphere has been criminalised, leading to extremely severe punishments (between six and seventeen years of imprisonment), harsher than in any other European country. As observed by Constance Wilhelm-Olympiou, over the past few years, the policy shift has been quite radical: from a patronising attitude (treating these women as mere victims) to a what the PNAT has termed a 'feminist' approach, in which they criminalise even domestic activities as being part of the fight.[109]

Another important characteristic to note is the social status of these individuals. The majority of them come from poor social backgrounds or have very limited resources, which is also a notable difference from previous experiences with terrorist political violence. In particular, this contrasts with other armed struggle movements such as the Red Brigades, Action Directe, the Red Army Faction, and separatist groups. This disparity can be attributed to the allure of the caliphate project, which creates a fantasy of a life of wealth and abundance. Similarly, individuals from precarious backgrounds tend to lack significant professional stability.

Regarding the geographical specifics of terrorists or radical people, they originate from across the entire country. However, the majority come from urban environments, with rural areas being notably underrepresented. As Crettiez and Seze show, the main areas from which French jihadists originate are large population centres with working-class neighbourhoods with a high migration density, the French suburbs (banlieue). In this regard, it's important to note a very uneven distribution across areas, with central and eastern France providing a large number of jihadists, while the western part of the country provides relatively fewer. Their research also notes that a significant number (45%) of female members of Daesh are converts from Christianity, as opposed to a minority of males (25%).

[109] Wilhelm-Olympiou, 2024.

Most of the accused are French nationals, with foreign nationals constituting only a small fraction. These figures challenge the perception that terrorism is predominantly driven by migration flows from Iraq or Syria. The jihadist phenomenon is therefore not an imported product, resulting from the opening of the European Union's borders to migrants driven to Europe by poverty and war, but concerns young people who have grown up and lived in France, even if some of them may have foreign origins. All of the studies underline the crucial role played by social networks, in particular in the dynamics of socialisation and involvement in violent radicalisation of those young people suffering isolation, anomic conditions, and exclusion.

The family dimension also appears to be central, as we have also observed at the court hearings. In this regard, the studies are often controversial. According to various empirical research studies, a lot of radicalised people come from dysfunctional families,[110] while other studies disqualify the image of dysfunctional families. Another criteria to be considered concerns the presence of male siblings, which is very significant. This could be interpreted as a strong element, revealing that engagement in a struggle that involves violence and death requires reliance on trusted support networks. Children are an important feature in the jihadist dynamic, as the aim of Daesh was to create a new ideal society, based on an ideal traditional Islamic family. In most armed struggle movements, fighters with children typically leave the struggle. However, this is not always the case among jihadists. On the contrary, radicalised individuals view the caliphate mission as a societal project, leading them to involve their families in their departure.

When it comes to the relationships of individuals convicted of terrorism with criminality, research shows that 57% of the sample examined do not have a criminal path, while the remaining 43% had problems with the law during their life.

Finally, psychological disorders are not a major explanatory factor for joining the jihadist movement or committing terrorist acts. If people with a psychological disorder are present among those convicted of terrorism-related offences, this should not be pathologised, as the proportion of individuals with such disorders is not significantly higher than in the general French population. However, recent studies underline how those most recently incarcerated tend to suffer more from

[110] Ferret and Khosrokhavar, 2021.

psychiatric disorders or weaknesses. The collapse of the Islamic State has prevented them from structuring their struggle, leading them to act in its name, and the Islamic State subsequently opportunistically claimed responsibility for the attacks. The lack of future prospects, in which society plays a key role, contributes to pushing some of these individuals into a state of poor mental health and isolation.

A final characteristic that deserves mention concerns addictions. A high rate of addiction to alcohol or drugs is notable among jihadists, with radicalisation often serving as a means of escaping addiction. This data can be analysed alongside the weak religious background of many people convicted of terrorism-related offences, who usually did not practise Islam before their radicalisation process.

***

This chapter has shown how the trial's actors, from diverse backgrounds and trajectories, tied by social and institutional affiliations that shape their choices, and influenced by varying interests and power dynamics, interact and engage in a public performance for the duration of the hearing. Strictly governed by the framework of legal grammar and procedure, they co-construct not only a case but also, more broadly, a judicial policy. The next four chapters examine this evolution, beginning with the first cases in the lower criminal courts.

CHAPTER THREE

THE LABORATORY OF THE 16TH CHAMBER

Designing the Architecture and Experimenting the Policy

The 'first generation' of jihadist trials took place before the 16th Chamber in the Lower Criminal Court (Tribunal Correctionnel) in Paris, which centralised all terrorism offences with sentences of up to ten years imprisonment. Between 2014 and 2018, more than 200 individuals faced prosecution, and an additional 1,600 were subject to criminal investigation. The counter-terrorism judicial experience of the 16th Chamber during those years played a crucial role in the unprecedented rise in jihadist network trials and the enhanced specialisation of the courtroom actors. This Chamber operated as a judicial laboratory, modulating the judicial response to jihadism, while experimenting the application of vague notions such as 'dangerousness' and 'radicalisation'. The use of these broad pre-emptive approaches was developed and implemented during the official 'State of Emergency', in close collaboration between investigating judges and the prosecution, who were given increased authority and resources, alongside the specialisation of the judges and the other actors of the courtroom. Dealing with numerous cases, the Chamber developed significant expertise in handling such cases and established a repeated ritual, designing the boundaries of the law and the narratives, setting the level of punishment. Various actors contributed to the co-construction of the first generation of jihadist trials, including the defendants and their lawyers. This chapter examines these structures and practices from the inner perspective of the courtroom, highlighting the central role of this first generation of trials in shaping the contours of the judicial response to the war on terror in France.

3.1 FROM 'EXCEPTION' TO 'EVERYDAY' JUSTICE: FRENCH COUNTER-TERRORISM JUSTICE IN PURSUIT OF SPECIALISATION

From the beginning of our observations in June 2015, we noted that the terrorist trials in the 16th Chamber of the Paris Criminal Court followed a ritual similar to other criminal cases.[1] These criminal trials often exhibited a form of 'normalcy' far removed from the dominant public perceptions of terrorism cases. It included the easy public access, the close proximity between the public benches and the defendants' dock, and the direct contact observers could establish with lawyers, defendants (when they are not in pre-trial detention), and their families. This ritual of everyday justice was also characterised by the proximity of the diverse courtroom actors to one another, as reflected in the judges' perspective: 'We are used to encountering defendants and especially their families or friends in the courthouse corridors or at the exit... but this is different, right?'[2] These terrorist trials, from the start, were characterised by elements of a routine where the 'exception' became ordinary, even banal. This initial sense of routine evolved over time, leading to the specialisation of all actors involved. It was within this context that the 16th Chamber shaped what came to be known as 'counter-terrorism justice'.

3.1.1 Specialisation of the Actors

Most of the cases tried between 2015 and 2019 related to acts committed between 2014 and 2017, as the legislation was modified to allow pre-trial detention of up to three years.[3] In November 2014, the first defendant tried for participating in a network travelling to Syria was sentenced to seven years in prison. At that time, judges, like other actors, were relatively new to this exercise. They began to 'learn' how to conduct these trials, which were becoming increasingly numerous. During a period when intelligence from Syria was still scarce, these criminal investigations marked the beginning of an intelligence-gathering process that would only grow stronger in the months to come. From these early months of the ethnography, we discovered a judicial scene where the same faces reappeared behind the judges' bench and

[1] Mégie and Pawella, 2017; Weill, 2018.

[2] Interview, presiding judge, 16th Chamber of the Paris Criminal Court, May 2017.

[3] See previous chapter for more discussion.

public prosecutor's tables, as well as among the lawyers and journalists. The courtroom actors meet almost daily and develop courtroom dynamics through shared experiences across trials. This growing specialisation was well described by a lawyer during an interview in January 2018: '*They all know each other and are specialists in these cases, it's a special chamber... very special!*'[4]

The specialisation of the actors in this court has thus become the primary characteristic of the 16th Chamber, whether among judges, prosecutors, lawyers, or defendants. As for the bench, which is composed of a presiding judge and two assisting judges, following several replacements in the chamber, ten presiding judges, accompanied by approximately ten assistant judges, were present in the sixty trials observed. The specialisation of the actors in terrorism matters has developed over the course of the cases, and their personal investment varied according to their personalities, experiences, and career stages. This specialisation is reflected in a uniform courtroom structure that combines a chronological approach to the facts, questions on the degree of radicalisation, and consideration of the future convicts' 'dangerousness'. Further, the judges of the 16th Chamber have gradually become experts on jihadist networks. Some of the presiding judges have invested heavily in studying the cases to acquire 'knowledge of the networks, codes, and how it all came together. We had to seek information on the subject, maps, academic studies, and others on these movements, on the Syrian conflict'.[5] While penal policy has been set and applied uniformly by the prosecutors, the presiding judges have more detached and personal approaches: 'It is currently impossible to fully grasp the impact of our decisions. But perhaps what is more problematic is that we often struggle to understand the consistency of the sentences we pronounce', a presiding judge remarked in December 2017. In the context of the increasing number of trials, judges naturally tend to construct a judgment scale based on the evidence, the defendants' responses during the trial, and their own degree of specialisation: 'If we cannot clearly understand the defendants' statements during the trial, the judgment will be harsher... and certainly more so in terrorism cases,'[6] declared a presiding judge in an interview in November 2018.

4 Interview, defence lawyer, May 2018.

5 Interview, presiding judge, 16th Chamber of the Paris Criminal Court, February 2016.

6 Interview, Presiding, 16th Chamber of the Paris Criminal Court, November 2018.

She added, 'they can no longer tell us just anything; we have seen so many cases over the years.' Indeed, as seen in other specialised jurisdictions, the routine makes the judges harsher in their judgments.[7]

3.1.2 Trial Based Exclusively on 'AMT'

From a legal perspective, although the French Criminal Code has continuously evolved to include more and more criminal offences specifically adapted to the changing modes of international terrorism, such as new offences concerning apology for terrorism, financial support for terrorism, and recruitment, almost all cases of prosecuting terrorism, involve the long-standing offence of 'association of wrongdoing in relation to a terrorist enterprise' (AMT). Codified in Article 421-2-1 of the French Criminal Code in 1996, AMT is defined as participation in a group constituted for the preparation of a terrorist act. There is no requirement that the individual contributes materially to the committing of the terrorist act itself, nor that the terrorist plan is executed; merely participating in a group that has a plan to commit a terrorist act, with the knowledge that that group has such a plan, is enough to satisfy the elements of the crime. AMT is sometimes translated in English as a conspiracy offence. At the same time, it resembles in many aspects the criminalisation of membership of an illegal organisation, because mere participation in a group that has a plan to commit a terrorist act is enough to qualify as a terrorism-related crime. AMT, punishable today by a sentence of up to thirty years (and life imprisonment for AMT leaders), allows the judicial authority to intervene long before the act is committed, as a preventive norm.

AMT is a very broad offence and allows for even remote acts to be qualified under its scope, with its range constantly increasing.[8] Significant for the prosecution of 'returnees' was the amendment of 2012 that provided for the extraterritorial jurisdiction of AMT and thus enabled the prosecution of French citizens or residents for participation in AMT abroad based on the principle of 'active personality'.[9] According to the French Ministry of Justice, it is 'the keystone of the fight against terrorism',[10] allowing the suppressing of terror plans at the preparatory stage. The preventive role of this infraction is clearly

[7] Ní Aoláin and Gross, 2013; Ramati, 2020. [8] Cahn, 2016.
[9] French Criminal Code, Art. 113-13 (amendment introduced in 2012).
[10] French Ministry of Justice, 2016.

articulated by Camille Hennetier, the French vice counter-terrorism prosecutor:

> The evolution of the threat in France, the attacks, the increase in activities by individuals on the national territory, leads to the desire to bring them to court as early as possible, to neutralise individuals deemed potentially dangerous, to achieve zero risk. In practical terms, with regard to the Iraqi–Syrian zone, this allows people to be brought to court in the early stages – people who only wish to go there in the context of a radicalisation process, even though integration into a terrorist group in the area is not yet effective... this allows the arrest of suspects at the intention stage, materialised by more or less operational exchanges, sometimes at the commencement of the preparatory act.[11]

Defence lawyers have highlighted in numerous interviews that this offence, AMT, has allowed the prosecution of vast networks of suspects only very loosely related to one another, with little evidence.

3.1.3 Departures, Stays, and Returns from Syria: A Repeated Courtroom Ritual

A central issue faced by the 16th Chamber was related to departures, stays, and returns from Syria. This was a significant phenomenon for French society, involving more than 1,600 people (both men and women, and in some cases, children). Thousands of other young French citizens also attempted to leave and join this zone, but without success. During our ethnography, we observed numerous trials addressing these attempts and departures, and we noted how each actor developed a narrative to explain this phenomenon through a co-construction, in which oppositions played a major role.

In the trials of defendants who unsuccessfully attempted to reach Syria and 'returnees' from the Iraqi–Syrian war zone, a recurring sequential triptych emerges in the organisation of the debates, imposed by the presiding judges. Following a chronological approach to the cases, the debate developed according the three phases: organising the departure ('having joined a network'), the stay in Syria ('having received military training, particularly in handling weapons and participating in terrorist group activities'), and the conditions of return to France ('potential preparation for violent acts'). These categories – preparation, action, and return – regularly frame the presentation of

[11] Camille Hennetier, cited in Mégie, 2017.

facts, their legal qualification, and the evidence. The judges' objective is to confirm or refute these elements through adversarial debate.

Regarding the departure phase, the discussed facts relate to both the motivations for leaving and the concrete preparations for it. In this phase, the central task is to establish whether the individual left with the intention of engaging in 'armed jihad'. To this end, when the purchase of equipment (such as a tactical vest, scope, gloves, survival blanket, weapons, etc.) is documented in the file, it strongly supports this accusation and frames the interpretation of the motivations for leaving. AMT is demonstrated through meetings between network members (at bars, homes, mosques), as well as evidence of contacts with a recruiter or smuggler at the Turkish–Syrian border. These socialisation or organisational elements that frame the departure weigh heavily when it comes to the judges' opinion, especially when surrounded by precautions that aim to keep the action secret (meetings without mobile phones, lying to relatives). Finally, the sending of finance to the combat zone may also be discussed to show its link to the endeavour when facilitated or orchestrated by a 'recruiter'.[12] These elements, present in the preliminary investigation by the prosecution and the investigative phase, are thus presented to the court. The defendants are asked to explain, a difficult exercise for many of them, not used to rhetoric exercise. As a judge explain: 'We ask them to explain themselves. We need to understand how their involvement unfolded and thus define their responsibility. But it is also very important to hear how they are prepared to explain their actions'.[13]

The judges' decision may also cite participation in sports training in France, violent written or oral statements under surveillance by the General Directorate for Internal Security (DGSI), and the consultation of Islamic State propaganda as incriminating elements. The search for, and sometimes compulsive consultation of, images of atrocities or propaganda via social media is usually accompanied by socialising that

[12] The use of consumer credit or social security benefits is also regularly at the heart of debates to demonstrate the reality of the business. Scams involving cheques and telephones are also present in some cases. For example, a defendant embezzled money from a priest's bank account (without knowing the identity of the victim of the fraud) to finance his departure for Syria. Women are often involved in logistics to provide financial support. See Bouvier and Martelet, 2018.

[13] Interview, Presiding, 16th Chamber of the Paris Criminal Court, September 2019.

supports this virtual activity. In court, these videos are cited as having encouraged their commitment and desire to go to Syria.

The second phase of the debate focuses on the defendants' stay, most often in Syria. The first step is to identify the organisation opposed to Bashar al-Assad that the defendant joined: the Islamic State of Iraq and the Levant (ISIL), Jabhat al-Nusra or the Free Syrian Army, followed by the geopolitical context of the organisation at the time of the stay. In this regard, defence lawyers sometimes remind the court of France's political position in 2013, which strongly condemned Bashar al-Assad's actions against his people. This geopolitical framing of the Syrian conflict often appears disconnected from the personal trajectories of the defendants. Judges and prosecutors present a range of jihadist organisations as options available to recruits, whereas the defendants' accounts often suggest their departure was shaped by an organisational choice imposed by recruiters or social media contacts. The complexity of the geopolitical context and the confusion surrounding recruitment dynamics often surface during court debates, until the prosecution's closing arguments and the judges' decisions. Instead, they adopt a more rational and ideological interpretation of these choices.

The analysis of the stay also focuses on the defendants' actions, even if affiliation with a specific group on the ground is not clearly established. This was particularly valuable for the trials between 2015 and 2017. The returnees must explain their possible participation in training, handling weapons, surveillance, or potential combat and atrocities, as well as any allegiance to ISIL or other groups. Was the defendant assigned to villa guards, checkpoint control, combat, or participation in atrocities, or did they only perform kitchen or cleaning tasks? When found on their computers and phones or their public Facebook profiles, photographs, and videos of the defendants armed in the combat zone are presented as incriminating evidence. In these images, the poses, attitudes, and smiles, often accompanied by an ISIL flag and/or a raised finger, are noted to indicate their level of adherence to jihadist ideology and the absence of coercion in this adherence. Defendants and their defence usually oppose these accusations based on images, by justifying them as a desire to reassure family members in France or 'show off' being armed to friends or potential romantic interests. They also pragmatically recall the principle of taking and posting images on social media, which is to present oneself in a favourable light. They highlight the fact that they are part of a generation that makes extensive use of social networks and images, which do not always reflect the reality of the situation.

Judges and lawyers regularly describe the trial as the moment for defendants to explain themselves and provide their version. However, most defendants are not very cooperative in identifying these activities during the investigation and at trial, often giving multiple versions. These changes in statements between the investigation and trial can have an impact on the sentence, as they raise the criterion of the defendant's credibility and his 'dangerousness'. Defence lawyers emphasise the impossibility of these young men or women refusing to pledge allegiance to ISIL, declining military training, or showing any form of dissent. The confiscation of identity documents and phones upon arrival in Syrian territory is sometimes cited in support of this hypothesis. Actions in Syria are difficult to verify, and the judges' own specialisation and knowledge of the different networks become crucial: 'Yes, we are aware of this information… it is well known in this chamber'.[14]

Finally, the third phase, the return to France, is regularly dissected from the perspective of intention. The aim is to determine whether the return to France was a result of defection, a renouncement of the jihad, or simply relocating the armed jihad to French soil. The disenchantment felt in the combat zone – usually fitting the initial humanitarian journey narrative – was widely used by defendants in the early trials. In fact, a distinction emerged between those who left for Syria and returned during a phase when they were not sufficiently aware of the actions carried out by ISIL, and those who were fully aware of the actions of this organisation. Its credibility, however, was often ridiculed in court regarding later returnees from Syria (between 2018 and 2019), as they stayed longer in the area: 'You tell us it was difficult and dangerous, yet you stayed there … with women and children. It didn't seem to bother you?'[15] Further, judges regularly emphasise that they could not have been unaware of the associated crimes or ISIL's violent nature, due to media coverage. 'But how could you not understand the violence of these groups and attacks in 2016?' the presiding judge asked. The defendant's response was: 'Actually…

14 Audience statement, Presiding, 16th Chamber of the Paris Criminal Court, September 2019.

15 Audience statement, Presiding, 16th Chamber of the Paris Criminal Court, October 2018.

I was in my bubble. That's all I saw. It seemed normal to me. I know it's shocking; I don't know how to explain it.'[16] What emerges here is the difficulty some of these young people face in explaining actions that the rationality of the debate renders simply unjustifiable and absurd, in contrast to the stories shared on the internet or in conflict zones.

While the motivations for leaving Syria are difficult to determine, similar challenges arise in assessing the conditions of return. The difficulty of leaving Syria is often interpreted as evidence of a genuine ideological and militant defection from the terrorist organisation. For instance, a defendant describing being forced to crawl across the border hidden in a flock of sheep is perceived as more credible by judges and prosecutors than one who was handed their passport and assisted by a quasi-official smuggler to cross from Syria to Turkey. Subsequently, phone surveillance, including in prison, can further cast doubt on the authenticity of their motivations for returning. Some express clear defiance or even hatred towards French institutions, while others speak of their desire to return to Syria. Some returns to France are indeed considered temporary, motivated by health reasons (the need for treatment after a gunshot wound, childbirth, etc.) or emotional reasons (a family visit). The defiance towards French institutions expressed in recorded conversations with relatives is rarely articulated in the same terms and publicly during the trials.

3.1.4 In Search of 'Dangerousness' and 'Radicalisation'

> *The problem is that everyone says 'radicalised', but I don't see how my practice of Islam is radical!*[17]

The issue of the convicts' future is crucial, posing the problem of recidivism and hence dangerousness, which takes on a unique social and political dimension in terrorism cases. A judge reminded us during an interview of the absence of a margin for error in such cases. For example, in a case involving the habitual consultation of propaganda and dissemination websites, the judge explained: 'The two-year prison sentence could theoretically be adjusted, but on the one hand, the court does not have convincing elements regarding his integration, and

[16] Audience statement, Presiding, 16th Chamber of the Paris Criminal Court, September 2019.

[17] Audience statement, defendant, 16th Chamber of the Paris Criminal Court, October 2018.

on the other hand, it is essential to avoid any form of recurrence.'[18] Two highly politically charged concepts are influencing the trials in the 16th Chamber, especially after the 2015 Bataclan terror attacks in Paris, which also involved people returning from Syria: dangerousness and radicalisation.

In forming their judgment, a question quickly arises during the trials: that of 'radicalisation', which has now become a crucial issue in the adversarial debate in the vast majority of cases. Often embedded in the defendant's trajectory, 'radicalisation' as a judgment criterion has also been defined as evidence of 'dangerousness.' This increasingly strong assertion of the 'dangerousness' criterion has been empirically observed through trial observations, thus linking it with existing doctrinal reflections.[19]

This evaluation of dangerousness is closely linked to the controversial question of disengagement indicators.[20] The uniqueness of terrorism litigation lies in the centrality of elements such as recidivism and the intentionality or religious motivations for engagement, which are at the heart of adversarial debates yet rarely addressed directly. The term *radicalisation*, a key concept in public discourse since 2015, is systematically but cautiously employed by judges. Their struggle to frame questions about religious practices and their potential connection to violence highlights the difficulty of addressing this aspect of *armed jihad*, which remains distant from the professional and personal experiences of judicial actors.

Caught between hesitation and the desire to demonstrate their understanding of jihadist ideology while carefully avoiding putting *Islam as a religion* on trial, judges have to navigate in a politically sensitive realm. They develop their own formulations during the proceedings, which remains largely affected by a polarised debate within French society. These formulations are systematically repeated, as a translation of their specialisations: 'I note that you perform your five prayers, but what is the degree of your religious commitment?'[21] 'You come from a Muslim family, but that is not in question here. How do

[18] Audience statement, Presiding, 16th Chamber of the Paris Criminal Court, October 2016.
[19] Henrion-Stoffel and Lazerges, 2016; Linhardt and Moreau de Bellaing, 2017.
[20] Conti, 2019.
[21] Audience statement, presiding judge, 16th Chamber of the Paris Criminal Court, November 2016.

you practise Islam?'[22] 'What branch of Islam do you follow? Would you say you are Salafist? … What do you think about Sunni-Shia relations?'[23] Some may also choose a provocative tone: 'The question is not just about the length of your beard!'[24] 'Does your ideology allow you to steal from the French state? Fraudulent benefits align with your beliefs? I don't think so!'[25]

Most often, these debates about religion integrate more general elements about democracy and the defendants' ability to define themselves as members of the nation: 'The Quran is more important than the laws of the Republic?'[26] 'Do you believe you can live your religion here in France? Or do you think you need to leave?'[27] 'How do you react to the November 13 and Nice attacks? By posting messages for IS and wanting to return to Syria? What did you think about these attacks at the time? […] And now?'[28] The risk of shifting from the political to the religious or social domain is very high. The boundary is subtle and tense.

Faced with these questions, the defendants' responses alternate between an inability to explain, repentance, and only rarely, political and religious claims. The defendants are required to construct an explanatory narrative, in a particularly hostile context, which portrays them as the public enemy. Expected responses must demonstrate a disengagement from violence and ideological influence, both of which are intertwined during the debates. Defendants often struggle to find the right words and to distance themselves from their previous engagement. Dispersed or fluctuating statements are considered incriminating in the prosecution's closing arguments or the judgment's motivations. Defence lawyers emphasise the difficulty of demonstrating these

[22] Audience statement, presiding judge, 16th Chamber of the Paris Criminal Court, May 2017.
[23] Audience statement, presiding judge, 16th Chamber of the Paris Criminal Court, June 2017.
[24] Audience statement, presiding judge, 16th Chamber of the Paris Criminal Court, October 2016.
[25] Audience statement, presiding judge, 16th Chamber of the Paris Criminal Court, March 2017.
[26] Audience statement, presiding judge, 16th Chamber of the Paris Criminal Court, September 2017.
[27] Audience statement, presiding judge, 16th Chamber of the Paris Criminal Court, October 2016.
[28] Audience statement, presiding judge, 16th Chamber of the Paris Criminal Court, September 2017.

changes and the defendants' feeling of being trapped: 'They know they will be found guilty and given heavy sentences no matter what they say,' stated a lawyer during an exchange in February 2018.[29]

3.1.5 Co-Construction of the Narratives: 'I Went to Do Humanitarian Work in Syria!'

'The defendants' statements do not correspond at all to the classic model of terrorist trials we knew before,' declared the presiding judge of the 16th Criminal Chamber in 2016.[30] In reality, rather than disappearing, political considerations are reformulated through a new co-production between defendants. Oscillating between repentance, claimed innocence, and even statements suggesting psychopathological issues, these defendants' declarations often seem far removed from propaganda advocating 'armed jihad'. They appear as expressions of explanatory models developed to counter the accusations, created and disseminated primarily on social networks or within the prisons where these individuals are incarcerated. However, rather than the political dimension disappearing, since 2015, we have been witnessing a redefinition and formulation of the political discourses and settings revealed during trials. The significance of the 16th Chamber lies in this opportunity to observe the formation of these argumentative frameworks from the outset, before each participant became entrenched in routine, specialisation, and explanations that dominate the courtroom debate. It is at this point that we can trace the emergence of arguments, interpretations, and even interactions that shape the dynamics of actors in French terrorism trials. The co-production of judicial debates by courtroom actors emerges from the specialisation of judges, lawyers, and defendants alike. This co-construction evolves along increasingly defined lines, such as the geopolitical context, group ideology, personal trajectories, religious connections, and assessments of dangerousness. While the repetition of adversarial debates may sometimes seem tedious to the observer, it is crucial for understanding how these recurring themes are helping to shape new political dimensions specific to these trials.

Religion occupies a central place in courtroom debates. Presiding judges approach it differently, either very directly or through life stories

[29] Interview, defence lawyer, February 2018.

[30] Interview with the presiding judge of the 16th Criminal Chamber in 2016, in Besnier et al., 2019, p. 137.

aimed at identifying the presumed moment of 'radicalisation'. While judges' interrogations may lead to unclear and repentance-tinged responses, a significant number of defendants respond in an engaged manner, with the political element far from absent. Between outbursts and long declarations, many adopt a defiant posture, generally against their lawyers' wishes, claiming that their commitment is above all political:

> 'I know my statements, my videos are radical, and so am I. And I know you don't like it! You don't like my questions about Syria! 'Radical' is like a disease for you. In detention, it's ridiculous. Their goal is to make us change our minds about something they don't know. Evaluation, de-radicalisation, it's useless. It's over!' declared a defendant in 2017.[31]

At the stand, 'travel plans' to Syria are often presented by defendants as quests for meaning accompanied by religious and geopolitical considerations. A rhetorical reasoning allows some defendants to bridge the viewing of violent images and the argument of seeking individual and communal meaning. This quest is embodied in the desire to help the 'widow and orphan' in Syria or to fight Bashar al-Assad alongside the Sunni community. Another argument regularly recurs to justify these departures: the desire to live their religion without hindrance. Violence and participation in combat are never presented as initial motivations. When mentioned, they are collateral actions of an engagement that is primarily 'religious', 'communal', or 'humanitarian'. Some eventually acknowledge that the logic inherent to the battlefield has ultimately overshadowed the initial motivations: 'Everyone has their own view of radicality. It's a question in itself! Before leaving, I didn't have that impression. But there, there's a group effect. It's like in prison; there are stronger moments,' declared the defendant to the presiding judge in 2017. 'But you knew the group's purpose you were joining?' retorted the presiding judge. 'You know it's illegal? You said so in a discussion. You said you would be arrested.' 'Yes, it's true,' acknowledged the defendant. 'For me, it was to fight the Syrian regime and... no, I won't say it!' 'Yes, yes, go ahead,' insisted the presiding judge. 'In 2012,' continued the defendant, 'France was at the forefront, and it made me proud of my country. At first, everyone under the same banner, resistance, but then...' Facing this posture and an increasingly

[31] Audience statement, defendant, 16th Chamber of the Paris Criminal Court, October 2017.

heated exchange, the lawyer intervened: 'Today, it's a terrorist group; we will see it in other trials...' 'Not for me ... [silence] at the time' concluded the defendant.[32] This exchange shows the difficulty in reconstructing the steps that led the accused to join armed groups and take up arms, particularly in relation to the initial idea of wanting to help the Syrian people against the regime, the motivation of many of the accused.[33]

Another theme discussed at the trials was the relationship of the defendants with their own country, France. Questioned about their desire to leave France, other types of claims appear: 'When I saw sisters being attacked because they wore the veil, it drove me crazy. I started looking online. And then there were all those statements about us. I didn't feel good. We are rejected, with all the racism... That's also why I didn't want to stay here anymore,' declared a defendant.[34]

While in some cases the courtroom has proved to be a place where the narrative is 'co-constructed' through an exchange that is gradually built up, in other cases we have observed rather a political confrontation: 'You say you are against democracy ... Are you for Sharia?' asked the presiding judge during a 2019 trial. 'Yes,' the defendant replied. 'So how do you manage since there is no Sharia in France?' the presiding judge continued. 'I am against democracy; I do not agree with its values. I will never impose anything. We are in France, they have their rules.' 'Who are "they"?' the presiding judge asked. 'Of course, I am French (silence)... but I am against, I mean against the values of the constitution and democracy.' 'What does it mean to be against democracy? To be against a fair trial? Against having a lawyer?' the presiding judge asked. 'No, of course not,' the defendant replied. The presiding judge continued: 'Against civil marriage too?' 'It's not possible to do both ... because marriage is in the name of the Republic. For me, it's not possible!'[35]

Finally, another recurring topic since 2015 is the prison conditions for defendants. Some defendants weigh their brief stay in Syria against

[32] Audience statement, defendant, 16th Chamber of the Paris Criminal Court, September 2017.

[33] Koehler, 2016; Jayakumar, 2019; Conti, 2023.

[34] Audience statement, defendant, 16th Chamber of the Paris Criminal Court, October 2018.

[35] Audience statement, presiding judge, 16th Chamber of the Paris Criminal Court, October 2019.

the prospect of long detention, perceived as unjustified and destructive. One of them stated in 2017, at the announcement of the prosecutor's requisition for a ten-year imprisonment, the maximum sentence: 'What's more dangerous? Three months spent in Syria or eight years in detention?' This person discreetly whispered to family members, 'What are we planning for those who stay more than three months in Syria? The guillotine?' For defendants still anchored in their engagement, this sense of injustice tends to reinforce their confrontation with the penitentiary institution, in an environment where 'terrorists are stigmatised by authorities and other inmates'.[36] Prison conditions, the stigma faced by those accused or convicted of terrorism, and the relationships that form among them in prison are frequently discussed. However, the focus tends to shift toward other aspects of prison life, primarily aimed at assessing dangerousness. Penitentiary reports and psychological analyses often bring the issue of dangerousness to the forefront during debates. It is not uncommon for the names of individuals convicted in other cases to surface, highlighting connections made in prison. Judgments for phone possession and SMS exchanges involve defendants who did not seem to know each other before their detention. Press articles sometimes detail these relationships, which can also come up at the trial. The stories of previous trials are known to the defendants. Within the prison system, solidarity among convicts tends to be formed, positioning them in opposition to the penitentiary administration and, more broadly, the state.

3.1.6 International Crimes v. *War on Terror* Legal Paradigm

These prosecutions have been systematically investigated by the counter-terrorism investigation unit and not the war crimes and crimes against humanity unit. The practice has remained generally unchanged, even in 2019 when the two units were merged into one investigation structure (the National Antiterrorism Prosecution Service, 'PNAT') in charge of investigating both counter-terrorism and international crimes.[37] As a result, these trials do not render accountability for international crimes

[36] Audience statement, defence lawyer, 16th Chamber of the Paris Criminal Court, September 2017.

[37] Being an exception, the Lafarge case may illustrate well this tendency. The Franco-Swiss Lafarge company, in order to maintain the functioning of its cement factory in Syria within an ISIL-controlled zone, was 'paying for passes issued by the jihadist organisation and buying raw materials necessary for cement production such as oil

that may have occurred in Syria by French citizens. Proceedings are focused on the prosecution of AMT. Being defined very broadly and requiring relatively little burden of evidence, investigative judges affirm that, this way, it can be prosecuted more easily than war crimes, for which the investigative judge has to go on site to collect evidence and hear testimonies. While more and more resources have been attributed to counter-terrorism investigations, the investigation of international crimes has become, during this period, quite marginalised; when international crime investigations are opened, investigated, and prosecuted, they concern foreigners based on universal jurisdiction and not French defendants. Even in cases directly linked to the armed conflict in Syria, and despite the fact that the geopolitical context is clearly present in the courtrooms and in the decisions of the judges, the French legal system refers to neither international humanitarian law nor international criminal law frameworks. Instead, administrative and criminal law is continually expanded to encompass the commission or prevention of all kinds of acts, with a widening spectrum of acts and punishments. As most, if not all, prosecutions are done under the security prism of France, no accountability is provided for grave IHL and international human rights law violations committed in Syria or Iraq. This policy remains problematic on several levels. First and foremost, it denies victims justice for the specific crimes committed against them. By prosecuting individuals primarily for membership in a terrorist group and the potential danger they may represent in France, the direct harm inflicted on victims is overlooked, leaving their suffering unacknowledged and unaddressed. This contrasts with the experience of the victims of attacks on French soil, as will become even more evident in the 'third generation' of trials. Second, the gravity of the acts committed varies widely – some individuals were involved in marginal activities, while others perpetrated severe

and pozzolana in areas under ISIS control'. While of the civil party claimed that 'by having business relations with the terrorist group ISIS in Syria, this company may have taken part in the financing of the group, being therefore complicit in war crimes and crimes against humanity', the investigation at first was not opened within the war crimes unit; instead, a joint investigation was initiated in the financial investigative division. Only later, following of the insistence of an NGO and its well-known lawyers, an investigating judge of the war crimes unit joined this investigation. See Sherpa and the European Center for Constitutional and Human Rights, 2017. However, on december 2024 only the financing of terrorism charge was put on trial. The charge of complicity to crimes against humanity is still under investigation, and will probably not be prosecuted.

international crimes – yet all are prosecuted under the same broad offence. This approach fails to address the unique circumstances and severity of each crime. Lastly, from a rehabilitation perspective, understanding the nature of the acts committed is essential, not just for the victims' sense of justice but also for the reintegration of defendants. Prosecuting and detaining individuals under one sweeping category risks undermining both justice and the long-term effectiveness of efforts to combat radicalisation.

It was not until late 2024, that for the first time, three French nationals, including one woman, are due to be prosecuted for genocide of the Yezidis and for enslaving women and children from this community in Syria.[38] Beyond this case, it was primarily around the AMT that the 16th Chamber operated, prompting us to question the genesis and function of this particular crime.

3.2 ELEMENTS OF THE CRIME OF AMT: A LEGAL ANALYSIS

The three core requirements necessary for a conviction based on AMT as defined in Article 421-2-1 of the Criminal Code are: (1) The existence of a *group* with a terrorist *aim*; (2) An individual act of participation in the group (without necessarily contributing to the terrorist act itself); and (3) The individual *intention* to participate in the group while being *conscious* of its terrorist aim.

3.2.1 The First Element: A Group with a Terrorist Aim

When it comes to the first element, the existence of a group with a terrorist aim, both notions of a 'group' and a 'terrorist aim' have been defined gradually but still remain ambiguous. Beyond the fact that a 'group' must comprise at least two individuals, the precise degree of organisation necessary remains unclear. While the Court of Cassation (France's Supreme Criminal Court) has asserted that the notion of terrorism 'implies a minimum of organisation',[39] it has also ruled that AMT does not presuppose 'a structured organisation among its members'.[40] Defence lawyers have highlighted that this ambiguity has allowed the prosecution of vast networks of suspects only very loosely related to one another. Comparable uncertainties persist with respect to

[38] Dubois, 2024. [39] Court of Cassation, 1995. [40] Court of Cassation, 2015.

the conceptualisation of the 'terrorist aim' that such a group must pursue. The only indication given, from the point of view of a definition, is that it must seek to 'trouble public order through intimidation and terror' as stipulated in Article 421-1 of the Criminal Code, with the Court of Cassation noting that 'parliament and the Constitutional Court have left it to the judicial authority to interpret the outline of the notions of "intimidation" and "terror"'.[41]

In the context of prosecution before the 16th Chamber, French persons who joined an armed group in Syria or Iraq have almost always been prosecuted for AMT. In 2018, the 16th Trial Chamber made a clear distinction between jihadist groups, which are recognised terrorist organisations and those which are not, even if they all aim to apply Sharia law.[42] For instance, the court acquitted a person charged with AMT for joining the armed group Ahrar al-Sham, noting that it was not a terrorist group as 'the group Kataeb Ahrar al-Sham appeared at the end of 2011, to overthrow the government of Bashar al-Assad and replace it with an Islamic emirate; it did not claim responsibility for suicide attacks or abuses committed against the civilian population'.[43] The court further noted that the United Nations has not recognised this group as a terrorist organisation and concluded that Ahrar al-Sham is not a group 'that can be qualified as terrorist'.[44]

In another similar case heard in December 2018, the accused openly recounted how he acquired military training with Ahrar al-Sham in Syria and was willing to fight against al-Assad's government. If such an account had been provided in the context of a different armed group, the act could have amounted to a crime according to French law. In this case, however, it was not, as the al-Sham group was not recognised as a terrorist group despite this being requested by the prosecution. The judge, moreover, criticised the prosecution's request

[41] Court of Cassation, 2017.

[42] 'The question that arises is whether or not, beyond his jihadist conception, which embraces diverse conceptions and which is not necessarily synonymous with terrorist involvement, such as his willingness to have Sharia law governing that country and to take up arms to ensure such an objective, X has actually carried out [terrorist] infractions... In other words, did X join a terrorist organisation, or at least, an organisation that conducts operations that amount to acts of terrorism?' Paris Court of First Instance, 16th Criminal Chamber, 28 September 2018, Case No. 13099000941, judgment, p. 22. On file with author.

[43] Ibid. [44] Ibid, p. 23.

and clarified that it is not up to the court to take such a political decision, pointing out the relativism of the term 'terrorist group':

> An entity is not terrorist in essence; it is a relative qualification, which may vary according to the countries or international organisations called upon to decide on this point, and for the same country or international organisation, the qualification may vary from one period to another. . . . It is easy to understand that if the court follows the prosecution's request to recognise the terrorist character of the group Ahrar al-Sham, while ignoring the positions of certain Western countries, which, according to the prosecution, supported this group for realpolitik purposes, the court would venture into the sphere of geopolitical debate that cannot be its own. It appears to the court that it is not within the jurisdiction of the judicial authority to order or recognise that a group constitutes a terrorist group and that if it did, the court would encroach on the powers of the legislative and executive branches.[45]

The court, however, did not avoid ruling on the question.[46] It decided that al-Sham was not a terrorist organisation, addressing in detail the different arguments of the prosecution. One of the prosecution's arguments was that al-Sham's members are allegedly responsible for numerous crimes against humanity, as affirmed by the submission of reports by Human Rights Watch and the Independent International Commission of Inquiry on the Syrian Arab Republic. The court distinguished the crime of terrorism from crimes against humanity and pointed out that an armed group, which commits crimes against humanity, is not necessarily a terrorist group. The court further affirmed that commanders of armed forces may be found responsible for war crimes and crimes against humanity for the acts of their subordinates through the international criminal law doctrine of command responsibility. In contrast, regular fighters (such as the accused), who did not themselves contribute to the committing of any of those illegal acts, cannot be held criminally liable.[47] This may seem puzzling to anyone

[45] Paris Court of First Instance, 16th Criminal Chamber, 12 December 2018, Case No. 14108000203, judgment, p. 14. On file with author.

[46] For a discussion on avoidance doctrines, see Benvenisti, 1993; Weill, 2014, pp. 13–67.

[47] Weill, 2014, p. 15. See also:

> The fact of participating in an insurrection or an armed conflict, which is, by its nature, disorganizing, prejudicial to public order, and likely to cause death and misfortune, cannot in itself be regarded as a terrorist act... such an engagement

reading this judgment: joining a group which is listed as a terrorist group, even if no further act is committed by the individual, is a crime under French law, while joining an armed group, whose members commit war crimes and crimes against humanity, is not, as long as it is not defined as a terror group. This shows the absurd result that can emerge while articulating French law and international criminal law, in light of geopolitical considerations.

The prosecution appealed these two decisions handed down by the same judge. It seems that the appeal came about as a result of a policy concern: the prosecution would otherwise have to close numerous investigations, as it is not always possible to prove which exact armed group the accused belonged to. In June 2020, the Court of Appeal agreed with the public prosecutor's position. In their appeal to the Supreme Court, the defence lawyers maintained that the position of the public prosecutor's office contradicts the position of the State, which has never recognised this group as a terror group.[48] On 14 April 2021, the Court of Cassation approved the decision of the Court of Appeal: while the State has not recognised al-Sham as a terror group, the highest court, along with the State prosecutor, did.

3.2.2 Second Element: Act of Participation

The second element of AMT is the individual's act of participation. Although the Court of Cassation has stressed that individuals need to 'provide effective support' to be convicted for AMT,[49] it seems that the notion of effective support was broadly interpreted to enable convictions for what might be seen as minor and ineffective contributions to a terrorist organisation.[50] In the case of foreign fighters, individuals have

can only be reprehensible if it is done within a group that is itself a terrorist group or if it is accompanied by specific acts of terrorism allegedly committed by a French citizen. Weill, 2014, p. 20.

[48] Court of Cassation, Criminal Division, 14 April 2021, Memorandum in support of appeal No. 20-83.420:

> In May 2016, France used its right of veto at the UN Security Council in order to oppose the classification of the Ahrar Al-Sham group as a terrorist organisation. [. . .] France, through its representatives to international organisations, has expressly opposed the classification of the said group as a terrorist organisation [. . .] the acts committed by the Ahrar Al-Sham group in Syria were acts of war, not terrorism. (Loose translation.)

[49] Court of Cassation, Criminal Chamber, 21 May 2014, Decision No. 13-83.758. https://tinyurl.com/yy3zlym7.

[50] International Commission of Jurists, 2010, p. 2; Human Rights Watch, 2008.

been convicted for AMT solely for joining a terrorist group in Syria and receiving training, whether they participated in combat or not.[51] For women, the act of participation includes domestic tasks such as cooking and taking care of children.[52]

3.2.3 Third Element: Intention to Participate in a Group and Being Aware of the Terrorist Aim

Being 'independent of the crimes prepared or committed by any of its members', the offence of AMT is based on an 'adhesion to a collective project of trouble to public order through intimidation'.[53] The proof of participation in an AMT rests not on the individual's personal terrorist intentions: The required *means rea* only requires that the collective association has a terrorist aim, which is known to the individual, and that he joined the association intentionally.[54] In the case of Abdulkaher Merah and Fettah Malki, the Assize Court went one step further.[55] Malki admitted that he had sold a weapon to Mohamed Merah, the brother of Abdulkader Merah, who committed the first jihadist attack on French soil in 2012 against Jewish children and French soldiers. Malki was accused and convicted of AMT despite the fact that he denied being aware of Merah's intention to commit a terrorist act. According to Malki, he sold the weapon, on foot of Merah's request, and he was going to commit a robbery. The investigative judge noted that the elements in the file could not establish that Malki knew about a concrete plan and that this kind of weapon could

51 See, among many others, Paris Court of First Instance, 16th Criminal Chamber, 28 September 2018, Case No. 13099000941, Judgment, p. 2.

52 See Chapter 2.

53 Court of Cassation, Criminal Chamber, 10 January 2017, Decision No. 16-84.596. https://tinyurl.com/bdy2y7ep.

54 As stipulated by the Court of Cassation (21 May 2014) in its Decision No. 13-83.758. In practice, however, evidence of a minor action showing that the suspect had knowledge of the terrorist activity concerned will suffice. See Foley, 2013, p. 203.

55 Specially Composed Assize Court, *Public Prosecutor v. Merah*, 2 November 2017, Case No. P/12079000/4. https://www.dalloz-actualite.fr/sites/dalloz-actualite.fr/files/resources/2017/11/motivation.pdf. For background on the attack in Toulouse in 2012, which was the first jihadist attack on French soil, see: www.bbc.com/news/world-europe-17456541. The author of the crimes was killed by a police assault. The prosecution was against the brother of the author of the killings (he was accused of complicity) and against the person who sold him the weapon (accused of AMT).

indeed be used for 'regular criminality'.[56] However, according to the prosecution, Malki should have known that there was potential for Merah to commit a terrorist act: 'The prosecution never argued that Malki knew that Merah was going to attack soldiers and Jews, but he knew the terrorist potential of the two brothers ... in fact, it is not necessary to share a terrorist ideology to be prosecuted for criminal association ...[;] just knowing that the activities were potentially terrorist in nature'.[57] The court followed this reasoning in its judgment, stating: 'this court was not convinced by the explanations of Fettah Malki that, when he entrusted the weapon and the protective jacket [to Merah], he was unaware of Mohamed Merah's radical Islamism'.[58] According to the court's assumption that Malki could not possibly ignore Merah's process of radicalisation since they had been friends since childhood, selling Merah a weapon – even if Malki thought that it was for an ordinary criminal purpose – made Malki criminally responsible for being part of Merah's conspiracy, which aimed at waging armed jihad, since he should have known that Merah could potentially use the weapon to commit a terrorist act. This decision was handed down even though nothing pointed to the assumption that Malki actually knew about Merah's intention to commit a terrorist act. Quite the contrary, in fact: Merah was the first person to ever commit a jihadist terrorist attack on French soil. Even the security services, which had monitored him for years and which testified during the trial, described Merah in their notes as a curious person who liked to travel, who they wanted to recruit as an informant.[59] Other policemen described him as a lone wolf and were surprised by the attack. Despite the fact that this particular decision was appealed and, on 18 April 2019, Malki was found not guilty of AMT, the practice has evolved to shift the burden of proof to 'should have known'. Most of the following cases will focus on whether an accused should have known about radicalisation and not if he actually knew.

[56] Paris Appeals Court, Appeal on Indictment, First Investigation Chamber, 17 June 2016, Case No. 2016/0184, pp. 26–27. On file with author.

[57] Closing statement of the prosecutor before the court, in Piquet and Licourt, 2017.

[58] Closing statement of the prosecutor before the court, in Piquet and Licourt, 2017.

[59] The testimonies were given before the Court on 16 October 2017. They are not available, as in France there are no official transcripts of the proceedings. For a media report, see Durand-Souffland, 2017.

3.3 THE GHOSTS' TRIALS

'So, this indictment mentions many people who are not here, either because they are still in Syria . . . or because they have already appeared before this court. But we are used to ghosts in this chamber! There are always absentees.'[60] Later in the judgement, it will be stated: 'At the call of the case, the president noted the absence of X and read out the indictment.'

The image of a 'ghost' has become a common feature in terrorist trials, due to trials conducted *in absentia*. Even when armed groups or media reports declare an individual dead in combat, investigative judges still issue arrest warrants. This is because, as they explain, 'an official proof of death, coming from a country at war with which French authorities have cut all diplomatic relations, cannot be provided.'[61] Due to this 'absence of irrefutable proof of death' and prior incidents where jihadists presumed dead later attempted to return clandestinely to France, the policy has evolved to prosecute the 'presumed dead' in court and to consider them as fugitives. Stemming from a long history in French criminal law, the prosecution *in absentia* is allowed, when the police cannot arrest the accused or they did not appear within ten days from being notified at their home of the indictment decision. If, in the future, the convict appears, he is entitled to a re-trial.[62]

Among these 'ghosts', some particularly catch our attention – those tried by the criminal court on the first Tuesday of each month, starting in February 2017. The 'short Tuesday circuits' had in common the judgment of men who had left and were presumed dead in the Iraqi–Syrian zone. Faced with the massification of procedures and the fear of seeing those who faked their disappearance return, counter-terrorism justice has implemented new judgment procedures, leading once again to a redefinition of counter-terrorism procedures and the creation of

60 Audience statement, presiding judge, 16th Chamber of the Paris Criminal Court, May 2017.

61 Paris Appeal Court, Order for referral to the Correctional Court, 3 May 2017, Case File No. 1309900941, pp. 15 and 43. On file with author. See also Mégie, 2021.

62 See article Article 379-3 of the criminal code: 'If a lawyer is present to defend the interests of the accused, the proceedings are conducted in accordance with the regular provisions... In the absence of a lawyer to defend the interests of the accused, the court rules on the charge after hearing the civil party or his lawyer and the public prosecutor.'

unprecedented judicial situations: '*Now we judge the dead!*'[63] As early as September 2016, in the context of the 'state of emergency', a consultation within the Presidency of the Paris Court was launched in order to craft a new expedited procedure for prosecutions and judgments, called the 'short circuit', in response to the increase in 'terrorist' prosecutions, which had previously been relatively low in number. This *ad hoc* procedure illustrates the ongoing evolution in managing counterterrorism cases, presented as a mere 'specificity', with the stated goal of improving efficiency by speeding up the flow of cases. This phenomenon is not unique to this kind of litigation and reflects one of the major developments in contemporary justice, which seeks to manage the volume of criminal cases in an efficient manner:

> We have many cases open for investigation, but many concern only one or two individuals, with very few facts to investigate. Sometimes it's for consulting websites, preparing for departures. There are also those whose deaths in Syria and Iraq are more than likely. The case files and therefore the workload become untenable, with cases often being time-consuming for little result,'[64] stated an investigating magistrate during an interview in 2017.[65]

Box 3.1 Ethnographic Journal, February 2017

On 7 February 2017, there was a crowd in front of the doors of the 16th Criminal Chamber. This date, announced and relayed in certain media and on the website of the judicial press, was no surprise. Upon arriving at the criminal court, we faced metal barriers that organised the queues, with one side for those with passes and the other for the 'public', consisting of a few curious individuals, students, and researchers.

There were many journalists, around fifteen in the room, as many as the gendarmes, distributed between the interior and the entry control area. Accessing the room without special authorisation is a challenge for unaccredited researchers. This external bustle is mirrored inside the room. Much smaller than the large 16.1 chamber, the 16.2 chamber and its six benches, each accommodating a

[63] Interview, presiding judge, Paris, November 2018.
[64] Interview with an investigating magistrate in 2017, in Besnier et al., 2019, p. 68.
[65] Interview, investigating judge, November 2017.

maximum of five people, were already fully occupied by journalists and lawyers. When the first members of the public arrived, only the folding chairs lined against the back wall were left.

Many lawyers occupied the benches to observe the debate, including the bar association president himself, accompanying his 'young colleagues', some from the training conference. These lawyers, parties to the trials or 'attentive' observers, had a clearly stated goal that day: 'to ensure that the rights of the defence are upheld in this new short circuit procedure'. The public prosecutor's office, represented by anti-terrorist magistrates, was also present, with four representatives standing against the woodwork separating the two entrances to the room.

When the court entered, its president did not seem surprised by the crowd that stood up as required by ritual. We later learned from her that while she noticed 'a room with many people', she had not been aware of the presence of all these judicial authorities. 'We see some faces, but we are focused on those in front of us. But it doesn't surprise me. I suspected that everyone would scrutinise ... we couldn't mess up (laughs)!'

The room of the 'short circuit trials' has usually been empty. Sometimes, on the courtroom benches, there are family members, who learn during the trial about their children's or siblings' journey thousands of kilometres away from home, a journey that led to their probable death. However, most often these families are absent as they are very rarely informed of the trial, as we gradually understood. Since the end of 2019, some families, although exceptionally, began to be summoned as witnesses.

> My brother's apartment has long been rented out; he left there four years ago. So, we didn't receive the summons ... we changed addresses, but they didn't try to find us, huh! [...] I testified at the trial by chance. I accompanied my father, who was the only one to receive a letter barely a week before the trial. They even misspelled my name.[66]

In the cases of the 'presumed dead', families almost systematically expressed an incomprehension and often an 'anger' that they share towards the ISIL recruiters but also towards the judicial authority, which they feel stigmatises their responsibility and their pain. Having met her after the trial of her son, the mother of this 'presumed dead'

[66] Interview, Families (Sister), June 2018.

person explained to us several months after the trial: 'I suffered during this trial; I learned things, confirmations, but also huge surprises about his departure… But I never had access to my son's file. I don't understand why! […] I'm not a terrorist.'[67]

This feeling is most often of being sidelined: 'I am his family, and I'm not allowed to know. I'm not allowed to know anything about his story. The trial was one of the only means'.[68] Other elements are also mentioned, such as the fact that death certificates are not issued, leaving the families of these 'presumed dead' in insoluble notarial and inheritance situations. The 'presumed dead' declared guilty of terrorism drag their families (wives, children, or parents) into highly uncertain legal conditions, experienced as a new condemnation. Moreover, this is compounded by the feeling of social condemnation as 'parents of a terrorist'.

In some trials, critical discourses regarding security authorities and their inaction in preventing departures to Syria between 2013 and 2015 were heard:

> But we would have at least wanted an appointment with the investigating judge. For them to tell us what your son did! We were ready to listen, but nothing. We are neither heard nor understood! […] When his grandfather reported his disappearance to the gendarmerie, and when we talked about his journey. Then everything changed, he went from being missing to something else entirely… We saw everyone, DGSI, Ministry of Foreign Affairs. Then in a search at the house and we discovered the plane ticket, and then we thought, damn! […] And we told the police that he is in Syria. That they need to go get him! We said it, but they told us, 'deal with it, we're doing nothing!' Well, they didn't say it like that, but it was just the same.[69]

Thus, the routinisation of terrorist trials has also imposed itself on the trials of the 'presumed dead', despite their uniqueness – no defendant and no lawyer. Historically, the rules governing judgments *in absentia* in criminal cases have been based on a written procedure known as 'contumace', authorising the Assize Court to rule without a jury and denying the presence of a lawyer. In 2001, the European Court of Human Rights (ECHR) ruled on this matter, deeming the refusal of defence representation excessive from the point of view of its

[67] Interview, Families (Mother), June 2017.
[68] Interview, Families (Sister), June 2018.
[69] Audience statement, Mother, Paris Criminal Court, January 2020.

jurisprudence on fair trials in violation of Article 6 of the Convention.[70] Following the condemnation of France, the procedural framework was reformed in 2004: it is now possible for a lawyer to act as counsel for the absent. Yet, while the court is obliged to hear a lawyer who comes forward to defend the accused, there is still no obligation to ensure representation. Without being entitled to legal aid, as is the case in almost all of the other terror cases, the absent accused almost always remains without legal representation. Furthermore, families cannot engage a lawyer, as only the 'presumed dead' can be a party to the trial.

In the cases observed, we have never seen a lawyer appearing at the start of a criminal trial. In this context, the absence of an adversarial debate in the Criminal Court is a *de facto* situation similar to that which led to France's condemnation by the ECHR. This constant absence of lawyers for the 'presumed dead' has been challenged only twice during our trial observation since 2017. 'Madam President, as a lawyer and in light of my professional oath, it is difficult for me today to plead for my client without mentioning the situation of one of the 'presumed dead' defendants.'[71] The defence lawyer, accustomed to terrorism litigation since 2015, asked the president of the 16th Chamber if he could exceptionally become the lawyer for the 'presumed dead' individual who is not seated next to his client. The president accepted this proposal and the lawyer, without directly knowing the personal file of this 'presumed dead' person, took a few minutes to question the procedure. On appeal, this possibility was quickly refused: 'It was strange to do that, but if the president accepted it in this trial, I quickly understood when we went on appeal that this time the president would not accept. He made it clear immediately!'[72]

The second case dates from January 2020. In this trial, the Special Assize Court of Paris had to judge twenty-four people accused, among whom nineteen were absent, of which eighteen were 'presumed dead'. The last absent person was considered detained in a Kurdish-controlled camp in northern Syria. From the first day of this trial, a lawyer intervened as counsel for one of the 'presumed dead'. This unprecedented request was accepted by the president based on the default criminal procedures. Only one of the people 'presumed dead' was

[70] European Court of Human Rights, 2001.

[71] Audience statement, defence lawyer, 16th Chamber of the Paris Criminal Court, March 2017.

[72] Interview, defence lawyer, March 2017.

defended, the lawyer not taking on the other cases. This presence led to tensions among the defence lawyers when 'there was a difference of opinion' during the debate to define the responsibilities of those present and those absent. The unprecedented intervention of a defence lawyer must certainly be understood through the activism of the family of the 'presumed dead' person and their legal, social, and media resources. The parents of the young man considered 'presumed dead' since 2015 are indeed among the main figures in families who have sought to publicise their children's departure and to engage against ISIL propaganda. Another family was present at this trial, but they were unable to secure a lawyer to defend their son and brother, who were 'presumed dead'.

3.4 PUNISHING THE 'ENEMIES OF FRANCE'

In January 2017, during the primetime TV news, François Fillon, a well know politician, politicised the judicial response to the 'jihadist networks', referencing a recently pronounced judgment, and accused the justice system of being too lenient towards jihadists:

> A jihadist has just been sentenced to seven years in prison, seven years in prison for waging war against us. He will likely be out in three and a half years at most. He can start again. I want French jihadists to be eliminated, those who went there to be stripped of their nationality, so they don't come back [...].

The returnee in question spent a few months in Syria with a lot of doubt surrounding his participation in the fighting. This case, cited as an example of leniency, actually illustrated the tightening of sentences against returnees and the establishment of increasingly severe penalty and detention management policies. 'The way to prosecute people who left or attempted to leave is quite clear at the prosecution level. If we decide the sentencing scale in court, we have collective discussions with other counter-terrorism prosecutors. We discuss this sentencing scale in meetings to propose a coherent approach'.[73]

Traditionally, French counter-terrorism criminal legislation relied on a combination of sweeping legal prerogatives and relatively lenient punishment. While many suspects were caught in the wide net cast

[73] Interview with a former Counter-terrorism Prosecutor in 2017, in Besnier et al., 2019, p. 130.

by AMT, their prison sentences were comparatively light.[74] Initially, AMT had been defined in the criminal code as an offence (délit) bearing up to ten years' imprisonment and has fallen solely within the competence of the 16th Criminal Chamber. Its scope, however, has been gradually harshened. In 2004, for the first time in the history of French legislation, AMT was made a felony (crime) through a distinction that was made between the prosecution of ordinary participants, which remained defined as an offence punishable by ten years' imprisonment, and the leaders of the group, who could incur twenty years' imprisonment. Once this barrier was overcome, the escalation of sentences followed rapidly. Only two years later, in 2006, the punishment for mere participation in a group with a criminal aim (such as an attack on persons or destruction of property with an explosive, which could affect lives) was raised to twenty years, and thirty years for the leaders. This increasingly harsh process reached its peak in July 2016, with the punishment set at thirty years for participation and life imprisonment for directing the group.

In practice, until 2016, returnees were systematically prosecuted before the 16th Chamber of the lower court, with a scale of sentences gradually set by the judges. During the initial period of jihadist prosecution, the bench developed a range of penalties through case law, which varied depending on the nature of the offence. For those who had been integrated into a terrorist organisation abroad, particularly Daesh, and who were usually prosecuted *in absentia*, the sentences ranged from six to ten years imprisonment. Returnees faced prison sentences of six to nine years, depending on the length of their stay in the Iraqi–Syrian conflict zone and the severity of their acts. Individuals who had joined a terrorist armed group in France and were about to travel faced sentences of four to six years. Finally, those who had provided logistical support to persons traveling to Syria or Iraq to join terrorist armed groups received sentences of two to four years imprisonment.[75]

In addition to this range of sentencing, terrorism convictions are almost automatically accompanied by a safety period of two-thirds of the sentence, preventing parole. This choice, requested by the prosecution and confirmed by the judges, led some lawyers to focus their defence strategy on the duration of the safety period rather than on the conviction.

[74] Foley, 2013. Table 6A.6 in Annex 6A'.

[75] Mercier, 2016, p. 14.

> I will ask you not to respond to the public prosecutor's requisition, which, as always, demands a two-thirds safety period! This automaticity is really problematic because we all know ... there is no more sentence adjustment for those charged with terrorism. It serves no purpose other than to make any possibility of reintegration increasingly difficult.[76]

Interestingly, the public prosecutor systematically appeals judgments that fall short of the requisitions, even in cases in which the sentence was only one year lower than requested (nine years and not ten). Such a strategy had a significant consequence for the Court of Appeal, which has seen a sharp increase in terrorism-related cases.[77] As discussed in the next chapter, in April 2016, the prosecution policy has changed radically, and most of the cases will be referred from that jurisdiction to the Assize Court, seeking higher sentencing.

3.4.1 Hybridisation of the Criminal and Administrative Law

In parallel with criminal legislation adjustments and trials, a raft of administrative law and measures on surveillance and control have been introduced, granting increased power to the Ministry of the Interior and security agencies.[78] A two-year state of emergency was declared immediately after the November 2015 terror attacks in Paris,[79] granting the executive extensive extraordinary powers, such as house arrests, night raids, and the closure of religious sites. Those reforms should be seen against the backdrop of the string of attacks that have hit France, which have placed tremendous public pressure on the counter-terrorism judicial actors: 'We had the understandable yet dangerous temptation to lock everybody up!'[80]

76 Audience statement, Defence Lawyer, March 2017.

77 For a table of conviction punishment and appeals, Table 6A.6 in Annex 6A'.

78 For French and comparative literature in this context, see Delmas-Marty, 2010; Guittet, 2018, p. 130; Cassia, 2016; Hennette-Vauchez, 2022b; Ojanen, 2013; Masferrer, 2012.

79 The state of emergency was declared after the terror attacks of 14 November 2015 and lasted until 30 October 2017. The longest in French history, it was prolonged six times and further amended. Before that, a state of emergency had been declared in France three times in the context of the Algerian war, in 1984 in New Caledonia, and in 2005 for five weeks following violent events in the suburban areas of Paris. The prerogatives of the government under a state of emergency are set out in the Law No. 55-385 on State of Emergency (3 April 1955).

80 Interview with a French counter-terrorism investigating judge, Paris, February 2017. On file with author.

These *ad hoc* administrative powers have become gradually permanent. When the state of emergency ended, five new chapters (out of a total of ten) were introduced into the 2012 Law on Internal Security under the section 'Fight against Terrorism'. A significant number of the state of emergency prerogatives were carried over into regular law through this amendment, most notably in Chapter 8 of the Law on Internal Security, entitled 'Individual Measures of Administrative Control and Supervision'.

The proliferation of administrative prerogatives not only confers more power on the executive authorities to limit individual rights, but also transfers the competence of judicial review to administrative judges,[81] who are structurally less impartial and independent than ordinary criminal judges (who are trained at law school and the French National School for the Judiciary). Administrative judges have very different professional backgrounds. They are not required to hold a law degree. Many of them are graduates of the prestigious National School of Administration, which is difficult to get into and trains many of the future French political elite. Others may be recruited after obtaining work experience in the administration. As for the Conseil d'État (Council of State), the highest administrative jurisdiction, the government nominates a significant portion of its administrator-judges. These educational and professional networks are likely to create a culture of proximity between the government and administrative judges, which results in a general benevolence on the part of administrative judges when assessing the legality of a measure put in place by State institutions.[82] Further, their procedure differs considerably from criminal courts. For example, administrative courts rely on notes blanches (white notes) as evidence. These take the form of anonymous documents provided by the security and surveillance services of the Ministry of the Interior. They transform intelligence into evidence but provide no information vis-à-vis the sources of that information, and are undated and unsigned. While 'white notes' are not admissible before the criminal courts, their use has come to be legitimised in administrative courts,[83] attributing them a presumption of

[81] See official data in French National Assembly, 2015.

[82] For a fascinating socio-legal study on the Conseil d'État, see Latour, 2020.

[83] The legality of the white notes was first approved by the Council of State in 1991 and 2003. It was confirmed again by Council of State Case No. 394991 of 11 December 2015, where the Council upheld that there is no legislative provision

truth.[84] As long as the white notes 'are not seriously contested by the appellant', they are accepted[85] and thus the burden of proof is *de facto* transferred to the individual, who has to convince the court that he is not dangerous – an uneasy task in light of a general hostility and prejudice against the appearance and religious practices of Muslims, which has been greatly reinforced in post-terror-attack Paris. Studying the administrative courts' decisions at lower levels during the state of emergency, it was found that the administrative judges exercised only a 'façade of control'; in half of the cases, the judges based their decisions only on the white notes of the intelligence services.[86] Even if the Council of State has at times played its role of guardian of civil liberties and cancelled specific abusive house arrests, it has predominantly upheld and legitimised administrative decisions linked to the state of emergency and has generally supported and facilitated the State's actions.

By broadening the scope of the administrative procedures, the frontier between the traditional roles of ordinary and administrative judges has been blurred, and they have become complementary to each other: when the criminal system cannot operate because of a lack of evidence, the administrative framework takes over; when a convict ends a prison sentence, administrative law will provide an option for follow-up surveillance. It also functions the other way around: when an administrative order is violated, a judge in criminal cases has the power to restrict one's liberty more effectively. Individuals' dangerousness has

or principle that prevents the administrative judge from considering facts provided by the white notes if they were submitted to an adversarial process and were not seriously disputed by the applicant.

[84] As the president of the litigation section at the Conseil d'État: 'We start from the principle that the intelligence services work honestly, and they don't exaggerate the content of the white notes'. Stirn, 2016. According to an administrative judge, '[J]udicial review] is not easy to do... you have to determine the dangerousness of a person according to an uncertain factual basis, based on fears, on a number of assumptions... The decision of the administrative police, by construction, is prospective.' Cited in Odinet, 2017. For background, see Alonso, 2016.

[85] Hennette-Vauchez and Slama, 2017.

[86] Hennette-Vauchez et al., 2018. According to State statistics, the jurisprudence of the Council of State, the highest administrative jurisdiction on house arrest, represented 75% of decisions concerning the State of Emergency. Out of eighty-two decisions, sixteen reached total or partial satisfaction. As for administrative courts at a lower level, it was reported by the Ministry of the Interior that, from November 2015 until February 2016, 400 persons were placed under house arrest. Out of them, 179 persons had recourse to an administrative judge to review the decision; only twelve procedures ended in favour of the appellant, revoking the house arrest.

been assessed regularly in both the administrative and criminal justice frameworks. As a result, domestic legal boundaries have been transformed and a process of hybridisation of criminal and administrative legal doctrines and approaches has been normalised. This transformation, introduced in law, has quickly impacted other domains, such as the repression of political protest. When we weaken the foundations of democratic societies and are prepared to reduce freedoms, leading to a transformation of the balance of power between individuals and the state, beyond terrorism, the inevitable result of such a policy is its slide into other fields of action such as the repression of political opposition and social movements. Indeed, this is one of the main manifested results that can be observed in France.[87]

[87] See for example, UN Office of the High Commissioner for Human Rights, 2019; Guittet et al., 2021.

CHAPTER FOUR

THE SECOND GENERATION OF JIHADIST TRIALS

The Slow Justice of the French Assize Court (2017–2019)

In April 2016, in the aftermath of the 2015 terrorist attacks, a more severe criminal prosecution policy was put in place, and terrorism cases involving those returning from the Iraqi–Syrian front were systematically transferred to the Special Assize Court. Previously heard at the 16th Chamber of the lower court, the Assize Court now had the authority to impose much longer prison sentences for these cases. These are the 'second generation' trials. From 2017 to 2019, we closely followed all of the first thirteen trials that had been transferred.[1] Most of these cases dealt with 'returnees', often without victims/civil parties, and sometimes even without the defendants themselves, who were presumed dead. They also included a second type of trials in which terror acts were committed. The Cannes-Torcy and Merah cases were the two first two jihadist trials, and they involved a number of victims and media coverage. These prepared the big terrorism trials, most notably the Bataclan trial.

The Assize Court has the authority to impose the most severe punishments. However, appearing before the Assize Court entails a prolonged judicial process that is unique to this jurisdiction. This chapter examines the tensions and dynamics that arose following the 2016 change in prosecution policy and the transfer of cases to the Assize Court. Beyond judicial disagreements, unexpected outcomes

[1] See list in Annex 4A.

emerged as the court came to know the accused more closely, revealing a more complex reality.

4.1 CRIME AND PUNISHMENT: THE 2016 NEW PROSECUTION POLICY

Up to 2016, as discussed in the previous chapter, association of wrongdoing in relation to a terrorist enterprise (AMT) was prosecuted essentially as a correctionnel offence, which carried a maximum sentence of up to ten years' imprisonment.[2] In April 2016, however, this prosecution policy changed radically. From the perspective of the authorities, prosecuting very diverse profiles under AMT, with the ceiling of a sentence of up to ten years' imprisonment, led to a situation in which the degree of punishment did not sufficiently correspond to the differences in the gravity of the behaviour. The public prosecutor, François Molins, the 'State's public voice' during these years, then announced that it was decided to qualify the 'joining of a jihadist terrorist group on the Iraqi–Syrian front' as a felony ('criminal'), in view of committing crimes of attack on persons, instead of prosecuting such acts as an AMT offence as had been done up to then. From January 2015 – and the Charlie Hebdo terror attacks – onwards, the assumption is that joining a terrorist group means adhering to, and knowingly participating in, an organisation that commits terrorist felonies against persons.[3] This means that sentences can be increased from up to ten years' imprisonment to thirty years' or life imprisonment, and the jurisdiction of the courts change; people who return from Syria or Iraq are now tried by the Assize Court.

Traditionally, French counter-terrorism criminal legislation relied upon a combination of broad legal prerogatives and low-intensity punishment: while many suspects were caught in the wide net cast by AMT, their prison sentences were comparatively light. Prosecution for AMT before the Assize Court was extremely rare, as evidenced in Tables 6A.6, Annex 6A. However, the new prosecution policy has distorted this balance by introducing a new practice of requesting heavy sentences for relatively minor acts, which necessitate little evidence, and for which a defence is difficult to establish. Further, this

[2] For the range of the range of penalties imposed see Mercier, 2016, p. 14.

[3] Le Monde, 2016

prosecution policy has been applied retroactively to cases already under investigation:

> Some cases involving returnees from Syria, which were initially handled as *correctional* matters (i.e. under the jurisdiction of lower courts), have been reclassified as *criminal* through supplementary criminalization. This means that those involved had to be informed that they were no longer facing a ten-year sentence but thirty years or life imprisonment. Even if they are 'presumed terrorists', it is not easy to announce this at the end of an investigation! However, there have only been a few such cases. Nowadays, the criminalization of cases is done from the outset.[4]

Interestingly, the Prosecution office took this decision autonomously after the French National Assembly had explicitly rejected suggestions to elevate 'activity on the battlefields of Iraq and Syria with jihadist armed groups' to the status of felony two months earlier.[5] In practice, however, the prosecution can still decide whether to prosecute a 'returnee' as a felony or an offence, as 'the prosecution retains a pragmatic appreciation',[6] which may raise questions concerning the equality of treatment. Moreover, it has been observed that the 'criminal' or 'correctional' classification of AMT in the investigation phase seems to be determined by the ideology and personal situation of the individuals involved rather than by the nature of the acts planned. While jihadist AMTs, especially those involving returnees, are classified as criminal investigations under the jurisdiction of the Assize court, AMTs involving acts related to extreme right- or extreme left-wing

[4] Interview with an investigative judge (9 November 2017), reproduced in Besnier et al., 2019, p. 183.

[5] Capdeville and Popelin, 2016:

> This change in the scale of sentences would undoubtedly upset the balance established by the legislator to this day. Such a criminalisation would have the effect of having these offences tried by the Paris Special Assize Court, with the risk of overcrowding the counter-terrorism justice system and a loss of flexibility for the judges. For these reasons, my opinion is unfavourable. The Commission rejects the amendment.

[6] See Catherine Champrenault, Attorney-General of the Court of Appeal of Paris, in a recent interview by Jacquin et al., 2018. See also Mercier, 2016, p. 15. As of 1 December 2016, the prosecution had opened 183 criminal inquiries (i.e. inquiries on the grounds of a crime rather than a délit) under the future competence of the Special Assize Court, targeting 483 individuals for AMT in relation to the ongoing jihadist violence in Iraq and Syria. This represents a massive increase over the case numbers of previous years.

ideologies are classified as *correctionnel* offenses.[7] This raises complex issues related to the methods used to establish an individual's ideology, level of radicalization, and degree of dangerousness. It also highlights the bias in differentiating between various types of terrorism.

4.1.1 The Initial Resistance of the Investigating Judges

The change in the prosecution policy had, at first, triggered disagreements and resistance between the various judicial corps. A legal battle against the prosecution policy between the various branches of the judiciary followed, until its validation by the highest criminal court, the Court of Cassation, in July 2016.[8] These disagreements are well illustrated by one of the first trials heard before the Assize Court following this new prosecution policy, the Q and D case, which is important because of the jurisprudence that it produced.

Q and D, two Toulouse returnees, were accused of travelling to Syria in the summer of 2013 to take part in training and fighting alongside terrorist groups. The investigation in this case started as an AMT offence (up to ten years' imprisonment), and the case was designated for hearing before the 16th Chamber. However, on 27 January 2016, the public prosecutor requested that the indictment be prequalified as an AMT felony. As the prosecution did not presented any new facts, the investigating judge from the anti-terrorism division rejected this request:

> the mere fact of holding a decapitated head . . . even if this shocking act in itself demonstrates their involvement in the AMT offence, does not in itself constitute preparation for a crime against persons. The investigation has not shown that Q or D, once they had returned from their Syrian journey, had made plans for such an action on the national territory or anywhere else.[9]

Appealed by the public prosecutor, the Appeals Chamber ruled in a similar way.[10] Following those two rejections, the prosecutor referred the case to the Court of Cassation, the highest criminal court in France, arguing that, since the jihadist movements operating in Syria plan to

7 Alix and Cahn, 2023.

8 Court of Cassation, Criminal Chamber, 12 July 2016, Appeal No. 16-82.692, §4.

9 Counter Terrorism Investigating Chamber, rejection order for further investigative measure, 1 February 2016, pp. 3–4. Available in Besnier et al., 2019, p. 72.

10 Paris Court of Appeal, Pôle 7, Investigating Chamber, Order refusing a request for an investigative measure, 15 April 2016, p. 7. Available in Besnier et al., 2019, p. 51.

commit felonies, belonging to one of these organisations is an AMT felony.[11] The Court of Cassation validated the prosecution's opinion: membership of a group whose purpose is the preparation of felonies can be classified as an AMT in the form of a felony, without the need to demonstrate any effective participation in the execution of the crimes or their preparation.[12] By overturning and annulling lower decisions, and by aligning itself with the innovative position of the prosecutor, the Court of Cassation has produced a decisive case law that legitimates the prosecution policy despite the rejection of this position by parliamentarians a few months earlier[13] and despite the fact that it was against the opinion of experienced counter-terrorism investigative judges who carry out their work on a daily basis and in close contact with the persons under investigation. As critics of the law have pointed out, a legal decision necessarily implies a political choice, and supreme courts may function as political actors legitimising the policies of the state.[14] Except in manifestly erroneous cases, any ruling by the highest courts can, in theory, be decided in favour of either side by introducing an interpretation based on a desired political objective. This case illustrates how French Supreme Court judges made their decisions in favour of the State position within public and political debates that were largely focused on repression and punishment.

This new legal order, designed by the state prosecution and security agencies has been imposed from the top down in conjunction with the

[11] Brief filed at the Court of Cassation on 22 April 2016 by Catherine Champrenault, Public Prosecutor of the Paris Court of Appeal, in support of her appeal made on 19 April 2016 against a judgment delivered on 15 April 2016 by the Investigating Chamber of the Paris Court of Appeal (ch. 7/1) in proceedings No. 2016/915 against Q., D. Available in Besnier et al., 2019, p. 51.

[12] The Court ruled that there is no need to prove that the person accused of criminal AMT actively participated in the preparation or the realisation of the crime itself, only that he was a part of that group. AMT as a criminal offence is 'an independent offence and is distinct from the crimes prepared or committed by some of its perpetrators and from the crimes characterised by certain facts that concretise it' (Loose translation.) Court of Cassation, Criminal Chamber, 10 January 2017, Decision No. 16-84.596.

[13] See note 87 in Chapter 3.

[14] 'The political jurist begins with what any fool could plainly see if his eyes were not clouded by centuries of legal learning, that judges and courts are an integral part of government and politics, would be meaningless and functionless outside of government and politics and are, therefore, first and foremost political actors and agencies.' Shapiro and Stone Sweet, 2002, p. 22; See also Cotterrell, 1984; Shamir, 1990; Kennedy, 1997; Weill, 2014.

Figure 4.1 Voltaire Courtroom, Palais de Justice. Drawing credit: Benoit Peyrucq.

highest criminal court. However, discord continues to exist among the different actors, despite this jurisprudence. Furthermore, as we will see in the following part, the prosecution policy can be undermined, challenged, and nuanced at the level of the trial court, in light of continued resistance by the judges, who are rendering decisions in individual cases on a daily basis.

4.1.2 The Slow Justice of the Assize Trial Judges: Unintended Results

The Assize Court tries the perpetrators of the most serious offences and has the authority to apply the most severe punishments. However, appearing before the Assize Court also means being heard by non-specialised judges for a long period of time in a procedure that is unique to this jurisdiction. The slow justice[15] process has two main features: the *oral* nature of the proceedings and the *investigation of personalities*. This process creates a unique space in which the accused can (and is expected to) express themselves, and, through exchanges with various

[15] As indicated in the Introduction, the term 'Slow Justice' (akin to 'Slow Food') is used here means to say that terror trials in the Assize Courts are lengthy, with notable space for expressing opinions, and with efficiency seemingly not prioritised.

actors, the court seeks to unravel the processes that led young people to commit or participate in violent acts. The fact-finding process, which is the second phase of the trial, is the product of a long, gradual, and collective process. While the courtroom interaction may be a 'dialogue of the deaf,' with the two sides – the State and the defendants – unable to understand each other, the long duration of the trial can also transform it into a space that allows the various actors to adapt and learn: During the extended hearings, the sides learn to communicate, confront each other, and may end with finding a common language. It is precisely in this exchange of words and glances, in the prolonged and forced dialogue between worlds that seem completely opposed, that the complex reasons for the 'why' and the 'how' of these young French people, who have either fallen into or merely flirted with jihadist ideology – sometimes briefly, sometimes for long enough to meet death – begin to emerge.

Inquiring into the personality of the accused is an important phase of the hearing, to which a considerable amount of time is dedicated in court. It provides the public with unique access to personal stories and trajectories; indeed, one of the few places where the word of the accused is heard publicly is the courtroom. The willingness to understand the facts in the context of the personality of the accused is a feature of hearings in France.[16] The presiding judge can choose the order of proceedings, but this phase is usually held at the beginning of the trial, before the examination of the facts. This is a lengthy process; half of the hearing time can be dedicated to this phase. In the trials that we observed, this phase lasted, on average, a day per person: 'I always start with the personality of the accused because I need to have a more complete understanding of their way of being to be ready to question them about the facts. Personality investigations are valuable for gaining a fuller knowledge of the accused because the judge is supposed to question close relatives, friends, and employers'.[17]

During this phase, the path of the accused is closely examined. In linking the individual to their social and familial context, an intimate space is created in which the accused can directly describe their world: their family, childhood, and aspirations, as well as wounds that have marked their lives. After an in-depth interrogation from the

16 See Garapon and Papadopoulos, 2003.

17 Interview with the President of the specially constituted Assize Court (July 2017) Cannes-Torcy trial, reproduced in Besnier et al., 2019, p. 177.

judges, the accused and the witnesses answer questions from the public prosecutor as well as the lawyers for the civil party and the defence. We noticed that the judges familiarise themselves with the complex sociological and geopolitical context, which they discover during the proceedings. The questions posed by the various actors in the courtroom attempt to clarify the individual trajectories, with a particular focus on the link between conversion to Islam, religious practice, radicalisation, and jihad,[18] as many of the defendants in the terrorism trials were revealed to be non-practising before their radicalisation, and sometimes totally ignorant of Islam.[19]

In the case of Cannes-Torcy,[20] the first three weeks were devoted to the personalities of the twenty defendants, half of whom converted to Islam. Some of them described a regular childhoods, playing football in the suburb of Torcy. One of the accused came from a Parisian bourgeois neighbourhood. So why did they follow their leader into the violence of radicalism? This is what the court tries to figure out without always getting clear answers in establishing a shared narrative to explain why and how these very different, yet seemingly 'ordinary,' young individuals rapidly progressed through the stages of radicalization, becoming a terrorist jihadist group within just a few months.[21] While looking into the personality of the accused, the judge also questions witnesses such as their parents and relatives to better understand the family, social, and professional environment of the accused and how this relates to their process of radicalisation. In this case, the public prosecutors questioned the parents in a reproachful tone: 'Sir, were you not aware of your son's radicalisation?' Some parents, overwhelmed with shame, did not attend the trial. Sometimes they even provided medical certificates to avoid having to testify. Others were always present. The continued presence of the parents of the accused during the trial, on

[18] Some of the recurring questions asked were, for example: 'In what family context did you grow up?'; 'At what age did you convert?'; 'Which mosque did you attend?'; 'Did you have a religious marriage or a civil marriage?'; 'What countries did you go to?'; 'Why did you travel to the Middle East?'; 'Did you impose certain behaviours on your family members?'; 'Is it possible for you to practise your religion in France?'; 'Do you force your wife to wear a veil?'; 'Do you see Sharia law as superior to the law of the state?'; 'Has there been a failure to integrate in school?'

[19] Roy, 2016; Khosrokhavar, 2021.

[20] For more discussion on this case, including the facts, see in Annex 4A.1 to this chapter, in page.

[21] Conti, 2021.

the bench near us, carried a strong emotional charge. They were there to understand what made their child turn violent, but they were also there to support them and to show that they were not being abandoned. The father of the main defendant, who referred to this leader of the terrorist group in question as 'my kiddo', described him as 'such a nice boy, always helpful, very sensitive and emotional', creating a real discrepancy between the person accused of terrorism in the box and the *child* described by the family. Family testimonies often embarrassed the accused in front of their fellow gang members, as seen by the fact that they hid their faces in their hands or bent their heads. These moments, when the intimate lives and vulnerabilities of these young people were revealed in the courtroom, were particularly difficult for some of them. They found themselves caught between feelings of shame and shyness, in complete contradiction with their ideological and/or warlike attitudes and discourse.

The long duration of the Assize Court proceedings can, in certain situations, illuminate the course of the case, including for the accused themselves. In the Cannes-Torcy case, we heard twenty defendants, all from very different origins and social backgrounds. We heard their parents, and we learned of their backgrounds and the facts in great detail. According to the assisting judge of this case, the lengthy duration of the trial allows for the evolution of their testimonies: 'We have time to get to know everyone. Our perception of the accused has refined; the trial has humanised them. The final words of the accused moved us.'[22] According to the presiding judge in this case:

> The testimonies of the imam from Torcy and the rector of the mosque from Cannes were also significant. Additionally, some spontaneous statements made by the accused during the proceedings allowed for a better understanding of their attitudes and were useful during the deliberations. I noticed an evolution in the behaviour of the accused during the trial. Those who did not stand up when the court entered at the beginning of the trial started to do so after a week. Furthermore, I observed that some accused individuals changed their statements during the trial to align more closely with the truth as reflected in the case file.[23]

[22] Interview with assisting judge, (July 2017), reproduced in Besnier et al., 2019, p. 101.

[23] Interview with the president of the specially constituted Assize Court (July 2017) Cannes-Torcy trial, reproduced in Besnier et al., 2019, p. 179.

Our observations throughout this first trial, which lasted two months and involved many defendants, showed that the changes observed were not limited to the defendants but extended to all the actors involved. While witnessing these situations, the accused are no longer seen as only a faceless 'enemy'. What has become evident is that their trajectories are complex: sometimes 'almost nothing'[24] can lead to their radicalisation. This is the case with a different case, the case against O., a young foreign fighter from the Paris suburbs, who explained to the court how, after breaking up with his girlfriend, he was hesitating between going as a backpacker to Barcelona or to Syria.[25] When the presiding judge questioned him about the reasons for his departure, he responded: 'Even I find it hard to explain … I left on a whim … overnight,' on an impulse after an argument with his girlfriend. 'I needed a change. I watched videos on YouTube, I saw the situation in Syria, and I wanted to do something for humanitarian reasons. I wanted to contribute to Assad's downfall.' According to his lawyer, it was vital for him to be able to speak in court for his own rehabilitation. He had, for the first time, the space to deliver his version of the facts freely in the presence of his family.[26]

Due to the significant increase in the range of punishments, from ten years to twenty years up to life imprisonment, for group leaders, the criteria by which the sentence is requested by the prosecution and finally imposed by the court is not always clear, especially since the assessment of dangerousness and the level of radicalisation of the accused person are the main criteria used. The tendency to act in a repressive way is manifested through the prosecution's systematic request for the maximum level of punishment. Yet, unexpectedly, in the first cases heard before the Assize Court, when the benches lacked specialisation, we observed a resistance to this tendency on the part of the trial judges: The court handed down lighter sentences than those requested by the prosecution, and even rendered several acquittals.[27] An assessor judge, interviewed at the end of the Cannes-Torcy trial on 12 July 2017, provided the following explanation:

> The criteria for deliberation are the following: punishment according to the severity of the facts (not all had participated in the actions in the

[24] Conti, 2024. [25] For more on this case, see in the Annex 4A to this chapter.
[26] See Besnier et al., 2019, p. 33.
[27] For the level of punishment in the 13 first cases observed see table in Annex 6A.

> same way, with varying degrees of involvement); their young age at the time of the actions was considered; their role in the group, whether they were leaders or not and what is most beneficial for society. After examining all these criteria, we concluded that the sentences handed down made more sense. We give them a chance to make it, a hope, but it's a gamble... the fact that they have not been detained until the end of the proceedings indicates that the investigating judge did not consider them dangerous enough to keep in pre-trial detention. There is continuity in our decision.[28]

As our data show, the public prosecutor's office demands high sentences and systematically appeals decisions that are lower than it requests. At the same time, the trial judges did not follow these requests and imposes a level of punishment – around ten years, which is the level of punishment at the 16th Chamber. This undermines the rationale of the prosecution policy, and it seems that the trial judges have joined the investigating judges in resisting the imposed policy. The judges of the Assize Court seem to be guided by the prospects of rehabilitating the convicted person beyond the concern for prevention and suppression. The lengthy duration of the Assize Court proceedings favours the process of individualisation and understanding the defendants' trajectories and has an impact on the severity of the sentence.[29] It seems to us that non-specialised judges not only use an anti-terrorist analysis perspective but also make their judgment through the lens of ordinary delinquency with rehabilitation approaches in mind. This indicates that the judges of the Assize Court confirm their independence from the prosecution policy; it also shows that the prosecution has been 'over-charging' and requesting heavy punishments in a rather harsh manner.

28 Interview with an assisting judge, 12 July 2017.

29 For example, in the case of Q and D (April 2018) discussed above, the prosecutor requested 20 years' imprisonment. The court sentenced each of the accused to 15 years' imprisonment. On appeal, filed by the state, the court went even further and imposed ten years' imprisonment for each one. In the case of G and B, tried in March 2018 in the first instance, the prosecution requested 20 years' imprisonment for each of the accused, but the court imposed sentences of 12 and 14 years respectively. On appeal, in November 2019, the Assize Court handed down lesser sentences than the trial court: 11 and 13 years respectively. In another similar case, the case of O., where the version of the accused was very well articulated, the Court sentenced him to ten years' imprisonment, and 12 years on appeal (instead of the 20 requested).

4.1.3 The Push Back: Specialising the Benches

This tendency, however, did not last long. In terrorism cases, as already mentioned, Assize court benches are composed only by professional judges and no jury. In the first phase, in each trial, the court had a different bench composition, with different presidents and assisting judges. The assisting judges were selected from among a list of volunteered magistrates, most of whom had no experience in terrorism. They could come from family courts, sentence courts, the investigation chambers for crimes against humanity, or in financial offenses. Not only did the assisting judges lack special knowledge on terrorism, but as jury members, they also did not have access to the file before the trial; only the President did. This effectively positioned them as juries, discovering both the facts and the accused, alongside us and the public.

One way of structurally ensuring that judges will follow the prosecution's demands more effectively has been to specialise the benches. Indeed, as the literature shows, the more specialised the chambers, the higher the sanction.[30] From 2019 onwards, there has been a tendency towards specialisation in the composition of the bench, with the increasingly permanent presence of certain judges. In this period, they were also granted access to the file. By the end of 2019, out of nineteen presidents at the Paris Assize Court, six of them had volunteered to preside over the terrorism bench. A list of assisting judges specially dedicated to these trials has been created. Among them are judges who have served at the 16th Chamber of the lower criminal court, specialising in terrorism cases. The exponential increase in the number of cases to be judged has meant that judges sit regularly, even daily. This configuration led to specialisation in the Assize Courts, resulted in a tendency to routinise the practice, which led, as is generally the case in mass litigation before special courts, to gradually impose a higher level of punishment and closer to the Prosecution demands – as it has been the case since 2020. This confirms the fear, already expressed in the 1980s, that specialisation, along with the routinization it entails, risks leading to a less collaborative process in the search for truth and, consequently, to a more punitive form of justice.

[30] Ni Aoláin, and Gross, 2013.

4.2 THE PREVENTION SHIFT: RADICALISATION AND DANGEROUSNESS AS CENTRAL PARADIGMS

During the trial, apart from the facts, judges are required to assess the potential dangerousness of the accused and their radicalisation process – both for establishing the incrimination (AMT) and for defining the level of punishment. The changing role of French judges, from one of establishing facts to one of predicting behaviour, as clearly articulated by the French vice counter-terrorism prosecutor Camille Hennetier,[31] seems to indicate that we are moving away from the criminal judges' field of competence. This is what defence lawyers are denouncing, including Bendavid, who, in a petition before the Constituional Court, pleaded the following: 'How could the court judge the future, let alone the future of a human conscience? [. . .] Will he desist? Will he act? We do not know [. . .] The judge does not possess such resources. And yet, it is expected that he will punish, and punish severely.'[32] This concern is stressed not only by defence lawyers, but also by other actors, such as Antoine Garapon, a former magistrate and Michel Rosenfeld, a scholar, who emphasise: 'The fight against terrorism, by asking justice to punish before the crime is committed, disrupts the foundations of classical criminal law: it replaces the classical idea of prevention with the more uncertain one of pre-emption [. . .] The suspect becomes a more important figure than the perpetrator, and the logic of intelligence gathering replaces the logic of proof.' 'Suspicion prevails over judicial logic and requirements (presumption of innocence, administration of evidence, procedural guarantees. . .). [. . .] Pre-emption is triggered by an interpretation of signs to establish correlations'.[33]

The *prevention shift*[34] and the issue of 'potential dangerousness' were present at most of the trials that we followed. To assess these questions

[31] See above.

[32] Constitutional Court, M. *Amadou* S., Decision No. 2017-625, Appeal for Judicial Review (QPC), 7 April 2017. www.conseil-constitutionnel.fr/decision/2017/2017625QPC.htm

[33] Garapon and Rosenfeld, 2016, pp. 128–129; Monod, 2016, p. 177.

[34] In the aftermath of the Bataclan attacks in November 2015, the 'Action Plan against Radicalisation and Terrorism' introduced new objectives: 'to detect radicalisation trajectories and terrorist networks as early as possible'. The emphasis was on detecting individuals 'on the path to radicalisation'. This considerably broadened its scope, as it no longer concerned only jihadists or 'radicals', but also people 'in the process of being radicalised' or potentially radicalised. This reflects a shift, where the cursor of the 'dreaded evil' is positioned further upstream. See De Galembert, 2016.

and to establish the level of *radicalization*, the presiding judge is increasingly interrogating new actors such as psychologists, Penitentiary Integration and Probation Officers (CPIP), as well as reports produced by various services, starting with evaluation reports from the QERs.[35] For example, at the trial of O., on the third day of the hearing, a psychologist testified based on reports written after meetings with the accused in prison.[36] The president questioned this witness about the dangerousness of the accused, and the psychologist replied that he was not able to answer such a question, showing the difficulty, or even the impossibility to 'establish' such thing. Finally, the psychologist gave a response – 'I would say "immature"' – and also asserted that the accused did not express self-criticism when it came to his actions and said that he was afraid of reprisals. After this testimony, the accused spontaneously took the floor and asked: 'This person saw me twice, each time for ninety minutes. How can he reach all of these conclusions? How can he be so sure of my profile?' The presiding judge replied: 'That's the work of an expert.' These considerations were later reproduced in the sentencing.[37] This case is emblematic of the difficulty judges face in assessing the dangerousness and level of radicalization of defendants. Furthermore, it highlights the importance of exchanges during the trial in addressing these questions, particularly the defendants' statements.

A similar pattern was also observed in the 16th Chamber, as discussed in Chapter 3, where the specialisation of the judges on this bench was reflected in the repetitive structure of the hearing, which combined a chronological approach to the facts with questions on the degree of radicalisation and the consideration of the dangerousness of future defendants. Indeed, a prosecution based on AMT, which is the most frequently used incrimination, symbolises this paradigm shift towards prevention. Other practices, such as the systematic recourse to prolonged pre-trial detention and the trials of the 'presumed dead', are another expression of

[35] On the QER, see above, p. 77.

[36] For more discussion on this case, see in the Annex 4A to this chapter.

[37] See the decision of the Paris Assize Court Special Sitting in the Case of O., 22 November 2018:

> To set the penalty, the Assize Court took into consideration the following elements ... an influenceable and immature personality capable of a certain ambivalence; disciplinary incidents in custody despite generally appropriate behaviour; a lack of proselytising in custody; the recommendation by the prison authorities at the end of his 'radicalisation evaluation' to place him in ordinary detention; and the uncertainty about his potential dangerousness.

the dangerousness assumption. In the cases observed, from the prosecution side, we can see a prevalence of safety measures with no other concern than defending the society, which has become the main, if not the only, concern in the fight against radicalisation and violent extremism. Under these conditions, it is difficult to envisage any kind of reintegration. Radicalisation is another name for dangerousness. We are witnessing a regime centred on the police, the intelligence services, the administration, and the prisons, which shows the achievement of the 'preventive shift'.

4.2.1 The Presumption of Innocence v. *taqiya*

One issue in jihadist trials is the clash between the presumption of innocence and the *taqiya* (dissimulation, a practice of concealing or denying one's faith to avoid persecution).[38] In many trials, the prosecution has advanced this argument as follows: even if there is no material evidence against the person, a case against them can still be built around the concept of *taqiya*. Up against this argument, any defence then becomes impossible. During the Merah trial, the prosecution referred to this practice on numerous occasions. This line of argument was highly criticised by the defence:

> If the two brothers do not visit each other in the two weeks preceding the crime, it is a matter of dissimulation; if they visit each other repeatedly, it's evidence of complicity. If he wears his watch on his right hand, it's suspicious; if he puts it on his left hand, it's *taqiya*. How can you defend a client with that approach? If he doesn't visit his sick brother in hospital, it's suspicious; if he does, it's also suspicious. ... There is no evidence of preparation of a crime, nothing before, nothing after ... [The prosecutor] is proposing the theory of *taqiya*. Did you see [the defendant and his brother who committed the murders] together? No. So it's *taqiya*. You don't know what they said, but that must mean it's criminal.[39]

[38] Accoding to Bartolomeo Conti,

> Concealment is common to anybody involved in illegal and clandestine activities but takes on another dimension in radical Islam with the concept of *Taqiya*, now part of everyday language and symbolising the culture of suspicion. *Taqiya* is the idea that the 'real radical' is not the one who shows but who hides this, who puts his religiosity 'on hold', for strategic reasons. *Taqiya* reflects the idea of betrayal and the enemy within. The spectrum of those under suspicion is widening to such an extent that any prisoner, whether Muslim or not, practising or not, may end up being subject to surveillance, in what could be defined as an escalation of suspicion Conti, 2021.

[39] Field note, 31 October 2017. See also Mucchielli, 2017. Indeed, one of the incriminating reasons mentioned in the decision was 'the discovery in a multimedia player

The following exchange took place between the defence lawyer – who in the summer of 2020 was nominated to be France's Minister of Justice – and the investigating judge, called to take the stand by the defence:

DEFENCE LAWYER: You say that they saw each other on the 11th?

INVESTIGATING JUDGE: The testimonies, it is true, are divergent on this point.

DEFENCE LAWYER: We can say anything, in that case. We can even say that watching a football match is *taqiya*!

INVESTIGATING JUDGE: We can interpret the facts in this way.

DEFENCE LAWYER: When a trial is based on interpretation, it's scary . . .

Another important consequence that arises from the setting of suspicion is pre-trial detention and the associated solitary confinement that became a consistent reality during our observations. In the context of terrorist attacks, the fear of action by those who are under judicial control has become recurrent for some investigating judges. The supposed dangerousness of persons prosecuted for terrorism generates this risk, and the desire is to limit it as much as possible. During our observations, we noted that most of the accused were in pre-trial detention, often in solitary confinement for three or four years before appearing before the court. For these defendants, the practices are far more restrictive than those for other crimes, which also raises concerns about detention conditions.

4.3 THE ROLE OF CRIMINAL COURTS IN THE CONTEXT OF THE WAR ON TERROR

This chapter has shown contradicting tendencies. The imposition of the prosecution policy involves a clash of positions within the judicial profession. This struggle around the prosecution policy demonstrates that 'justice' does not speak with one voice; on the contrary, it is made up of different actors with different professional practices, interests, and their own personal way of doing things. The 2016 prosecution policy,

of 17 audio files . . . [which] revealed . . . the teaching of various techniques used by Al Qaida to train mujahid to dissimulate before committing the crime'. See Specially Composed Assize Court, *Public Prosecutor v. Merah*, Case No. P/12079000/4, 2017. www.dalloz-actualite.fr/sites/dalloz-actualite.fr/files/resources/2017/11/motivation.pdf.

which was put in place despite its rejection by parliamentarians a few months earlier, has introduced a new practice of imposing very severe punishments for relatively minor acts. At first, the investigating judges opposed this approach until the Court of Cassation, in line with the state, imposed the policy from the top down. Bound by this jurisprudence, the cases had to be prosecuted as AMT felonies and had to be heard before the Assize Court. However, we saw that, although the prosecution requested maximum punishment, the trial judges were guided by additional concerns beyond security and prevention, because of the long and individualised nature of Assize Court criminal procedure, and did not accede to the requests of the prosecution. By imposing a punishment not much heavier than that of a lower criminal court, they openly resisted the prosecution policy, along with the investigative judges.

Based on this empirical study, it is proposed that lower criminal courts, acting within a transnational context, can offer more robust resistance to states' policies than the Supreme Courts. This is because of the routine of their work and the banality of their function, and the direct interaction with the accused persons, coupled with the judges' own notions of judicial independence and professional criminal justice ethos. Unlike the Supreme Courts, whose role is more visible and thus under the constant scrutiny of the political branches of the state, lower courts can operate in a more distant, independent space. Supreme Court jurisprudence is doctrinal in nature, often decided without hearing the specific facts or the sides of the case directly. In a lower court, however, the situation is radically different. Lower judges work on a case-by-case basis through the establishment of the facts, where the accused is fully present, leaving room for a shared narrative to emerge. In doing so, they have room for dissociating themselves from doctrine or jurisprudence; in this space – in an ordinary courtroom, far away from the centre of power and the media – they can resist state policy and promote other values such as stronger criminal rehabilitation approaches. Lower judges may have an important role to play here; under certain conditions, it is those judges who can develop an alternative approach to the preventive doctrine.

4.3.1 Trust and Truth: Fassin's 'Moral Economy' and Its Expression in Terrorism Courts

Here, a central question arises: how does the climate of suspicion influence the fact-finding process, given this paradigm shift towards prevention, which requires the judges to determine future acts? Can this exercise be even possible within a criminal procedure still bound by the legal framework of 'fair trial'?

In the public debates about terrorism, fuelled by security concerns, a suspicious mindset, preoccupied with managing a dangerous population, is set against the need to uphold democratic principles such as the rule of law in the act of trying an accused person (including most notably the presumption of innocence, the establishment of facts based on evidence, and conviction beyond reasonable doubt). As found by Fassin and Kobelinsky in the context of the migration courts in France, we can clearly see that, in terrorism courts too, the act of trying an accused person involves a contradiction between 'the principle of justice and the feeling of mistrust'.[40] These two sets of opposing values and goals, which are reflected within the moral economy of terrorism,[41] determine the operations of the court's actors: on the one hand, the objective of prevention, framed by a prevailing climate of suspicion and, on the other hand, the criminal justice procedure, still committed to the principles of a fair trial and the independence of the judges, both of which are anchored by criminal judges through their professional ethos. During the ethnography, it became apparent how judges position themselves both in relation to their attempts to handle their own personal and societal feelings of suspicion towards those accused of terrorism, and, on the other hand, a professional concern to produce a fair criminal court decision.

This contradiction leaves the observers (and the accused and/or their lawyers and families) with mixed feelings: although the process is often carried out with attention and openness, offering an important space for expression and nuance, the impossibility of this preventive task, in which the judges are asked to assess dangerousness and radicalization, renders the process profoundly unjust and arbitrary. Despite the judges' firm commitment to conducting a fair criminal justice trial (in a more or less sensitive way, depending on the presiding judge's own personality), profound injustice can result, due to the climate of suspicion and the preventive role imposed on judges.

[40] Fassin and Kobelinsky, 2012, p. 657.

[41] According to Didier Fassin, the moral economy of a societal issue is characterised by 'the production, circulation and appropriation of norms and values, sensibilities and emotions that account for how it is treated at a given moment, both in the public sphere and in private actions'. See Fassin, 2009.

4A Annex: Ethnographic Accounts

4A.1 THE TRIAL OF THE 'CANNES-TORCY' NETWORK (2017)

The 'Cannes-Torcy' network was the first jihadist-related case to be tried by the Paris Assize Court. The events occurred in September and October 2012, six months after Mohamed Merah's attack, which marked the beginning of jihadist-linked attacks in France. After the cell was dismantled in October 2012, judicial authorities, particularly the Public Prosecutor François Molins, described this group as 'the most dangerous uncovered in France since 1996', referring to the Algerian GIA attacks in the 1990s.

This trial was notable for its length, six weeks, as it involved nineteen defendants. The case was tried in its entirety in the first instance as no appeals were filed by the defendants. We attended all fifty-five days of the proceedings, witnessing the entire trial. We held regular meetings every Friday afternoon to share our perspectives on what we had seen, heard, and felt during the debates: the testimonies, the defendants' statements, the conduct of the trial by the president, the prosecutors' interventions, and the observations of the defence and civil party lawyers. At the end of the trial, we supplemented our notes with interviews conducted with judicial actors: the president, an assessor, a prosecutor, a civil party lawyer, two defence lawyers, and the parents of a defendant.

Despite seventy accreditations granted by the public prosecutor's office before the trial, only one journalist attended the entire trial. Journalists were present in large numbers at the beginning and end of the trial. During the proceedings, the journalist and public benches were mostly empty except for the occasional visit by some students. Most of the time, we were alone alongside the father of the main defendant, J. B., who attended the entire trial. His son was the number 2 in the Cannes-Torcy cell, the 'faithful lieutenant' of J. L.-S., the spiritual leader of the network who was killed while shooting at police officers during his arrest. J. B. was prosecuted for throwing a grenade in a kosher grocery store in Sarcelles. Among the twenty defendants, he received the heaviest sentence: twenty-eight years of criminal imprisonment.

4A.1.1 Summary of Facts

On 19 September 2012, the day Charlie Hebdo published new caricatures of the prophet Muhammad, a grenade attack was carried out against the Naouri grocery store in Sarcelles (Val-d'Oise), resulting in minor injuries to one person and broken windows. Investigators quickly identified a group of young individuals who had converted to Islam and were recently radicalised, revolving around J. L.-S., whose fingerprints were found on the grenade. J. L.-S., a former drug trafficker, regularly travelled between Cannes, Torcy, and Strasbourg. On 6 October 2012, during his arrest, he fired at intervening forces before being killed by police. The investigation revealed a violent, highly radicalised man with deep-seated anti-Semitic views, invoking the example of the Toulouse and Montauban attacks by Mohamed Merah. He had gathered childhood friends and people he met at mosques in Torcy and Cannes. In the summer of 2012, six people from Torcy travelled from the Paris suburbs to Cannes in a camper van, meeting ten members of the Cannes group led by J. L.-S., their leader. According to the investigating judge, this was a 'founding moment' that prepared for the Sarcelles attack, future terrorist acts on French soil, and planned departures to Syria. They discussed religion, jihad, displayed weapons, referenced the Toulouse and Montauban attacks, adhered to the same ideology, and targeted the same groups: Jews and military personnel. During the trial, there were recurring references to the Toulouse terrorist, establishing him as a model in the jihadist movement. His assassinations marked the beginning of the wave of attacks in France in the name of Islamist jihad from 2012 onwards. A month after the failed kosher grocery attack, the same individuals planned to destroy a McDonald's in Lognes, Seine-et-Marne (Paris region), on 3 October 2012. The attack was aborted. The dismantling of the group prevented two additional criminal plots. The first involved an attack on a military camp in Canjuers, Var (southern France), on 19 June 2013. The attack was thwarted thanks to the partner of one of the defendants, who when making a complaint about domestic violence, informed authorities of the planned attack. The second plot was organised in Syria for 2014 by returning jihadists. The entire network was dismantled between 6 June and 17 June 2013.

The investigation lasted three years, starting in October 2012 with the first arrests following the events, and concluding in December 2015 with the indictment order by the investigating judges, who referred the defendants to the Assize Court. The investigation resulted in eighty-five volumes addressing the investigation, the defendants' personalities, and their behaviour in detention. The indictment comprised 358 pages, describing the progress of the investigation since the events in novel-like detail. The pedagogical presentation is illustrated with numerous colour photos of the defendants, locations, recovered items, and maps. This legal document belongs to the case file and is not public, but we obtained it through lawyers and journalists. Although the oral nature of the debates remains a fundamental principle in Assize Courts, as convictions must be based on the adversarial exchanges during the trial, Assize Court judges in terrorism cases have had access to the case file since the law of 23 March 2019. During the 'Cannes-Torcy' network trial, judges did not yet have access to the case file, a shortcoming noted by some of them. This gap observed in early terrorism trials led to a law granting all judges access to the case file, not just the president, before the trial and up to the deliberation.

4A.1.2 The Defendants: From 'Investigating Their Personality' to 'Their Last Words'

Among the twenty defendants, aged twenty-three to thirty-three, ten were in custody and placed in the dock, seven were free under judicial supervision, and three were subject to arrest warrants, one of whom was on the run, and two suspected of remaining in Syria. Two defendants were prosecuted for the kosher grocery store attack in Sarcelles, Val-d'Oise, facing the maximum penalty of life imprisonment. All of the other defendants faced twenty years of criminal imprisonment for conspiracy in connection with a terrorist enterprise (acts committed before 2016). Additionally, some had travelled to Syria and returned to France, intending to commit attacks. The profile of the defendants included elements that would become a new subject for Assize Courts.

Examining the defendants' 'personalities' lasted three weeks at the beginning of the trial. The president started with this topic to gain a more comprehensive understanding of the defendants' backgrounds before addressing the facts. When parents attended the trial, they bore the guilt for their child's alleged actions but also provided moral support. The constant presence of Mr B. (the father of the main accused) throughout the trial was noted by the judges. It took courage to stay at the trial as the father of the main defendant prosecuted for throwing the grenade in the kosher grocery store in Sarcelles, but he was there to understand: 'I had never been to a court. When he was arrested in 2012, it was a shock. I discovered a whole new world. Prison visits. Lawyers. I knew nothing about it. I had to go online to learn. We were a normal family. I worked all my life as a taxi driver.' Then Mr B. expressed his guilt:

> Of course, I worked a lot, finished late, but it was for him! But I managed the football club, you know. His whole childhood, his teenage years, I coached him and his friends from the neighbourhood every weekend. I attended all the matches for years. Yes, we divorced, his mother and I. But it went quite well. And many children have divorced parents, right?

For five years after their son's incarceration, Mr and Mrs B. had visited him three times a week:

> He has changed institutions several times, it's complicated logistically. But he is our son. We are not going to leave him. He wouldn't hold up. What do you expect? Isolation is hard; it drives you crazy. Fortunately, now I'm retired. It's easier to organise. As long as I'm standing, I'll visit him in prison. But we're not eternal, his parents. Who will take care of him when we're no longer here?

The continuous presence of the accused's parents conveyed a strong emotional charge. They were there to understand what drove their child to violence, but they were also there to support them and to show the judges that they came from ordinary middle-class families.

A new question arose during the trial: when should religion be addressed? At the time of the facts or at the personality stage? The president addressed it along with the facts, but the lawyers recommended addressing it along with the discussions on personality.

Indeed, religion concerned both aspects, but the separation between personality and facts forced a choice of theme and reduced the relevance of the exchanges. The inability to discuss the accused's 'radicalisation' during the personality examination was regrettable, according to an assessor: 'The facts are too closely linked to the personality to separate them. They should be treated concurrently for each of the accused.' According to the same assessor, 'it took a month to understand certain things' because the facts, and therefore the radicalisation, were addressed three weeks after the personality. Also, when religion is addressed with the facts, the lawyers see it as an incriminating element. The defence would prefer it to be addressed with the personality. The debates raised the following difficulty: questions regarding conversion, religion, and radicalisation are intertwined and pertain to both personality and facts. The separation between personality and facts, a classic in common law cases, poses a problem when addressing radicalisation in terrorism cases. This dichotomy should be reconsidered in terrorism cases where the issues of conversion and radicalisation are central.

As the interrogation proceeded, the questions attempted to refine the distinction between conversion to Islam, religious practice, radicalisation, and jihad. The recurring questions to understand the conversion to Islam and then the commitment to armed struggle were as follows:

> What kind of family environment did you grow up in? When did you convert to Islam? At what age did you convert? Which mosque did you attend? Did you have a religious marriage? A civil marriage? To which countries did you travel? Why did you travel to the Middle East? Did you impose certain behaviours on your family members (dietary habits, clothing)? Do you force your wife to wear the veil? Do you see Sharia law as being superior to state law? Was there a failure of integration at school? Where have you worked? Do you think it is possible to live your religion in France?

In this trial, non-specialised judges familiarised themselves with the complex sociological and geopolitical context that they discovered during the debates.

The interrogations were conducted with the underlying question of danger and recidivism. Where did these defendants stand in their religious practice, in their radicalisation, in their relationship with death? The forms of adherence were varied, and the acts committed were diverse: knives, explosives, trucks. The latent question that underpinned the debates is to understand what these young people were capable of doing. The question of danger is difficult to grasp because, in jihadist doctrine, there is the idea of dissimulation (taqiya) to better strike the enemy. It is therefore difficult to evaluate this danger, which is a very new and evolving matter. Seen as a major element of jihadist strategy, the concept of taqiya prevents any attempt at repentance by the defendants, becoming, as one lawyer points out, 'a permanent incriminating element'. Beyond the issue posed by the use of the vocabulary of armed jihad by judicial authorities or lawyers, this problem of dissimulation perfectly illustrates the risk of making a judgement solely based on ideological speeches and postures during the hearings, as a judge noted: 'It is only the factual elements present in the file and debated during the hearing that allow us to do the work of justice!' According to a prosecutor, this trial demonstrated that the notion of taqiya needs to be explored from a socio-anthropological angle, which is a major implicit key to understanding for professionals and can introduce a presumption of guilt. At the request of a defence lawyer, a rare occurrence, a specialised sociologist came to testify at the end of the hearing. The absence of a clear claim for armed struggle during the hearing placed the justice system in a difficult situation. Was the non-claim or even the repentance of the defendants genuine? Or was it part of a desire to escape conviction and resume armed struggle as soon as they were released? It is in these conditions that taqiya constitutes an element of the debates.

In this trial, the imam of Torcy and the rector of the Cannes mosque testified. The defence called an expert at the end of the hearing. Generally, in the observed hearings, there were no testimonies from context experts (cultural experts) such as sociologists, historians, or specialists in Syria, Islam, the Islamic State, or radicalisation. Cultural experts would have provided valuable insights to the non-specialised judges confronting these issues for the first time.

The gendarmes had difficulty maintaining silence in the dock after four years of isolation for the suspects. During court recesses, the accused exchanged documents, displayed relaxed postures, and talked among themselves. Nonetheless, the accused always addressed the president and assessors respectfully, without challenging the ritual of the debates. They explained their commitments and convictions with apparent sincerity in some cases. When questioned about the Charlie Hebdo attack, one of them stated, 'I don't approve, but I don't condemn. It was to be expected; you don't attack the prophet without risk.' Sometimes their remarks were threatening: 'I do not recognise the laws of the Republic,' or regarding handling weapons, 'I like violence, I like action.'[42] We noted an evolution towards more conciliatory postures from some of the accused, who modified their statements to align more closely with the case content. Freedom of expression, facilitated by the

[42] Salas, 2018, pp. 193–195.

president's management of the debates, led to spontaneous testimonies that provided better understanding of their attitudes in relation to the accusations.

From the public benches, we observed some of the accused sometimes disappearing under the dock to pray. At the start of the hearing, some of the accused did not stand when the judges entered the room. The prosecutor pointed out this disrespectful behaviour to the court and lawyers. The main accused explained that standing was 'committing shirk', meaning showing respect to an authority other than their god. This accused person then found a compromise, not sitting down when entering the dock, so as not to have to stand up as a sign of deference. Generally, there was an evolution: those who did not stand at the beginning of the trial began to do so after a week. The relaxed atmosphere during court recesses allowed for the debates to be conducted smoothly, without major tension. The president took into account that the accused were observing Ramadan. The hearing time was slightly shortened to avoid fainting and in response to the defence lawyers' comments in this regard.

The accused felt heard, as they expressed in their final statements. Their words and behaviour evolved thanks to the length of the trial. According to an assessor we interviewed (interview on 12 July 2017): 'Our perception of the accused has become more nuanced; the trial humanised them, and their last words touched us.' One of the accused declared from the dock:

> [. . .] My lawyer opened a door for me; I could talk about my plans. The sentence requested by the prosecutor is the majority of my son's life; my project is him! I need to serve a good sentence [. . .] Thank you for giving me the floor; I have learned many things about myself and about you. . . as you can see. Know that I love life! I won't bother you any longer.

Another one of the accused said:

> I think I will be nostalgic about this trial and this story. . . it taught me many things! (Silence) Lots of discussions from people who are interested in the person. . . we could get past the image of the terrorist. We all have hope. . . I hope you will be fair in your decision [. . .] tomorrow we close the book, and whatever book is opened, I will not forget this one. . .

The accused apologised to the judges for their behaviour in the dock: 'We sometimes laughed, chatted, it wasn't out of disrespect towards you,' insisted one of them. In the same vein, we heard these words: 'I apologise for my behaviour; it wasn't disrespectful, but we are like that! Even regarding Islam, we don't always behave well.' Only K. P., ostracised by the rest of the group for denouncing some of his co-defendants, had a word for the victims of the grenade attack on the Sarcelles grocery store: 'I regret what happened; I never wanted to harm anyone. I commit to paying compensation to the victims.' Finally, the main suspect concluded with these words: 'I feel like I'm facing walls. Imposing a draconian sentence on a person makes them a dissident, a hater,' he sighed between sobs. He was referring to the life sentence requested against him. Finally, the last words of one of the accused were: 'I thank the judges for listening to my story. For the first time, someone took the time to listen to me.' These final statements oscillated between prepared speeches and tones of sincerity, and their emotional impact was real.

4A.1.3 The Atmosphere of the Trial

On 20 January 2017, Jean-Baptiste Jacquin, in an article in Le Monde entitled 'Terrorism: the Fear of Judges', draws the reader's attention to the fear gripping judges:

> For the past few months, some of those handling these cases have requested that their names no longer be mentioned in written or broadcasted court reports by journalists. Judges from the anti-terrorism section of the Paris public prosecutor's office, who present the case before the specialised terrorism court, communicated this directly to journalists or through the Judicial Press Association in early January. Some trial judges also wonder if they should remain anonymous, shielded by their robes

These fears manifested during the trial when judges requested protection for their movements. This protection was granted before the hearing, but only for the prosecutors.

4A.1.3.1 Minute of Silence

On 20 April 2017, the evening of the first day of the trial of the Cannes-Torcy network, prosecuted for several attempted and planned attacks (the first jihadist assize trial), a police officer was killed on the Champs-Élysées by a French jihadist. This attack, which was claimed by Islamic State, put a strain on the procedure when the civil party's lawyers requested a minute's silence at the opening of the trial. There was no precedence for this demand. The defence lawyers, many of whom had relatively limited experience with terrorism cases, expressed strong objections in court: 'This is exploitation! If there is another murder on Monday, will we stop earlier? This minute should not be observed in this courtroom! We are being held hostage by this request from the civil party . . . if we refuse, we will be accused of not supporting the police. It is unbearable!'[43]

The court decided to allow the request, which led to unrest in court: while those involved in the proceedings and the audience stood and observed the silence for a minute, one defence lawyer chose to leave the room while two other lawyers remained seated with three of the accused. Later, tensions rose when civil party lawyers questioned to what extent the accused had 'respected' the minute's silence while the defence highlighted the 'instrumentalisation' of this disruption in court. According to the presiding judge, interviewed after the end of the trial,

> the court, caught off guard, was somewhat stuck, which is why it agreed to this unexpected ritual with the consent of all of the judges. This minute's silence was highly controversial, but if it had not been granted, the court would have faced criticism from the other side. The collective emotion disrupted the judicial ritual. However, no defence lawyer requested that the incident be recorded and the minute's silence took place before the debate, which had not yet started.[44]

During the same trial, other attacks took place: in Manchester on 22 May 2017, at London Bridge on 3 June 2017, and in Paris, in front of Notre-Dame Cathedral on 6 June 2017.[45] These attacks were on everyone's mind when the hearing resumed. Despite the fact that the trial is overseen by professional judges, and without jurors who could potentially be swayed by accompanying media reports and external events during the proceedings, many defence lawyers urged the judges to 'maintain their professional perspective and allow justice to be administered according to the law... and nothing but the law!'[46]

[43] Audience statement, defence lawyer, Paris Assize Court, 20 April 2017.

[44] Interview with the President of the specially constituted Assize Court, Cannes-Torcy trial, reproduced Besnier et al., 2019, p. 91.

[45] The judicial ritual was also disrupted on another trial on 3 October 2019. An attack was carried out at the Paris Police Prefecture, just meters from the assize court. The hearing was suspended for several hours, with an announcement over the loudspeaker informing all parties and the public of the ongoing attack.

[46] Audience statement, President, Paris Assize Court, 19 October 2020.

4A.1.3.2 The Heatwave

In late June 2017, France experienced an unprecedented heatwave. The heat in the courtroom gradually rose, reaching around thirty-five degrees Celsius by the end of the trial. The president of the Paris Court of First Instance allowed the legal professionals to remove their robes. On that day, we were on the last day of the defence's closing arguments. The judges entered without their robes, to everyone's surprise. The prosecutors and lawyers kept their robes on as a silent protest. The Assize Court judges put their robes back on the next day to deliver the verdict. A lot of ink was written on this episode. Symbols are very strong in the Assize Court, and this behaviour shocked many, appearing to some as a break from judicial rituals.

4A.1.3.3 Food in the Dock

It was around 10 pm on Thursday, 22 June, when the accused returned to the courtroom to hear the Assize Court's verdict. The ten accused appearing in detention had not eaten since 5 am due to Ramadan. In the room, those who were not under arrest and appearing freely finished eating the food they had started in the witness room, where the president asked them to wait for the verdict. Their families had brought them the food. Those appearing freely handed food to those in the dock, including a pizza that was passed around, sparking the attorney general's anger. The accused had gone without food for a whole day in a heatwave, waiting to find out how long they would spend in prison. These unusual conditions in an Assize Court were meant to be adapted to the accused.

4A.1.4 The Deliberations

The deliberations lasted twelve hours. The five judges, armed with their notes from the trial, answered seventy questions regarding the twenty accused. Voting on questions of guilt requires a majority of three out of five. The accused in the dock had been held in isolation for four and a half years (from October 2012 to April 2017). The prosecution's demands were severe, up to life imprisonment for the main accused. The court handed down sentences ranging from one to twenty-eight years in prison without safety periods and three acquittals. None of the accused under judicial supervision returned to prison.

According to lawyer Elise Arfi: 'These are clear-sighted decisions; the court was able to differentiate based on the profiles of the accused.

A dividing line emerges between those who appeared freely and all walked out free, and the detainees, among whom two were nonetheless released.' She added: 'The accused are very young; five years after the events, some have found work, and others have started families. Imprisoning them would have destroyed everything and exposed them to radicalisation. As for the sentences, they are severe but less harsh than the demands and not accompanied by safety measures.'

The verdict was accepted by all; there were no appeals from the public prosecutor or the defendants. It is interesting to note that this is the only case where the public prosecutor's office did not appeal, whereas in all other criminal and correctional cases, the prosecutor's office systematically appeals when the requested sentence is not upheld.

4A.2 THE TRIAL OF 'RETURNEE O' (2017)

This case, involving a returning individual from the suburb Créteil, revealed the significance of the temporality of the debates. O. was accused of AMT. He was prosecuted for travelling to Syria in 2014, joining the Islamic State of Iraq and the Levant (ISIL), undergoing military and religious training, agreeing to carry out a suicide bombing in Lebanon, and upon his return from Lebanon, proposing to take action in France. According to his defence lawyer, it was fundamental for him to be able to speak for the first time, which proved to be very important for his own rehabilitation. She was not assigned by the Parisian bar, as in most terrorist trials, nor was she an expert in terrorism, and it was her first time pleading before a specially-composed Assize Court. Initially, she regretted that this case was not being dealt with in a first instance court setting. However, she acknowledged the benefit of the oral nature of the Assize Court. According to her, it was crucial that her client could express himself freely, and the Assize Court hearing provided him with this opportunity for the first time. The time in court allowed the accused to reconstruct the facts and his journey in quite a detailed and intimate manner. After three days of hearings, the accused thus disclosed the facts to his family, who discovered them for the first time. During the trial, through a coherent narrative where the accused delivered a long testimony, another reality was unveiled. The oral nature of the debates restored a voice absent from the previous phases of the judicial process that started in the investigation.

During the trial, through a coherent narrative where the accused delivered a lengthy testimony, another reality was unveiled. As later confirmed by his lawyer, he finally recounted his journey: initially leaving alone for Turkey – an uncertain departure – and a chance encounter at the airport that led him to Syria with the intention of joining ISIL. However, upon arrival, he was suspected of being a spy working for the West. He had to answer for this under the risk of execution by ISIL authorities, who eventually believed him. Once cleared, he was immediately integrated into military training for fifteen days. He discovered a reality vastly different from the videos he had seen, which shattered his illusions and horrified him. Fearing for his life amidst real violence, he decided to return to France, but knew he had to use cunning to do so. According to his account, he pretended to volunteer for a suicide attack in Beirut, Lebanon, to retrieve his confiscated passport and facilitate his escape to France. Upon his return in June 2014, to avoid suspicion from ISIL and to protect himself, he remained in contact with members of the terrorist organisation for a few days, claiming to be on a fictitious mission in France. He justified his departure by the extensive questioning he faced in Beirut, stating he could also act in France while fearing possible reprisals.

When questioned by the Assize Court president about the reasons for his departure, he responded, 'Even I find it difficult to explain... I left on a whim... overnight,' following a conflict with his girlfriend. 'I needed a change. I watched videos on YouTube, saw the situation in Syria, and wanted to do something for humanitarian reasons. I wanted to contribute to Assad's downfall.' His employer, the director of a restaurant, attested in his testimony that he was also very surprised. According to the employer, the accused showed no signs of radicalisation and was always very diligent in his work. The president sought to understand: 'You went to a country at war. What kind of group did you think you were joining? If you had no religious conviction, why didn't you join the Free Syrian Army?' The accused replied that he had no specific idea before arriving, did not understand the situation well on the ground, and considered all groups more or less equivalent. He was led to ISIL by an unexpected encounter and stated he could have joined any other group, including UNICEF. The president further questioned, 'But within two days of your arrival, you were already a member of ISIL.' The accused confirmed that indeed, the recruitment was swift, even though ISIL members suspected him of being a spy. He then explained the research he had carried out on jihadist websites and others as simply wanting to stay informed about the situation. He stated that if he had genuinely intended to commit an attack in

France, he would have done so and not simply returned to his mother's home.

Thus, the version of events presented by the accused differs significantly from that of the prosecution and is relatively underrepresented in the court decision. However, since no transcript is available, this version of the accused can only be conveyed through our observations. Indeed, the oral nature of the debates restores a voice absent from earlier phases of the trial. It is a lengthy moment where the accused has the first opportunity to deliver his truth to convince the judges, in the presence of his family. The oral procedure has the advantage of offering the public and researchers unique access to the stories and personal trajectories that led to their involvement in terrorism-related acts. We regret that this orality leaves no trace, that the wealth of interaction in the audience is not even the subject of a recording.

The court argues in a very detailed manner, which is quite rare for a sentencing statement,[47] the elements that lead it to impose a 'reduced' sanction compared to the prosecutor's requisitions and societal expectations in this type of case. The criteria considered relate to the gravity of the facts, the personality of the accused, his past experiences, as well as his family context, his demeanour during the trial, throughout his detention, and finally, an assessment of his potential dangerousness.

4A.2.1 Social Media

On 18 November 2018, one day before the trial began, facts from the investigation file were disseminated on Twitter by the think tank CAT

[47] Since the decision of the Constituional Court on 3 March 2018, the sentencing in Assize Court decisions has been required to be justified. This principle of individualising penalties, derived from Article 8 of the French Declaration of Human Rights (1789), mandates that a criminal sanction can only be applied if expressly pronounced by the judge, taking into account the specific circumstances of each case. These constitutional requirements necessitate the justification of judgments and sentencing decisions, both for guilt and for penalties. The Constituional Court ruled that by not requiring the Assize Court to justify the choice of penalty, the legislature had disregarded the requirements derived from Articles 7, 8, and 9 of the Declaration of 1789. Therefore, the second paragraph of Article 365-1 of the Code of Criminal Procedure was declared unconstitutional. The article was later amended: see Art. 365-1 of the Code of Criminal Procedure: 'The motivation also consists in setting out the main elements that convinced the Assize Court in the choice of penalty, in light of the elements presented during the deliberation provided for in Article 362' (loose translation)

(Centre for the Analysis of Terrorism), along with a photo of the accused.[48] CAT defines itself on its website as 'a research centre aiming to become the leading European think tank in the field of terrorism analysis'. Marc Trévidic, a former investigating judge at the Paris High Court's anti-terrorism division, is among its honorary committee members.

The photo depicted a man with a menacing look quite different from the face that would be seen in court. The two-page document entitled 'Focus on plots to attack the Shiite community in France and Lebanon', which described various travels and actions, directly mentioned the accused. For instance, it stated that the accused was initially recruited as a fighter, and quoted him as saying he was ready to carry out a terrorist attack 'in any location chosen by the command'. Under the subtitle 'Failures in Lebanon', it mentioned that the accused recorded a series of farewell messages to his family, including telling his sister that he couldn't 'turn back'. CAT does not disclose its sources of information, and its descriptions are presented as factual reality before the trial has actually established the facts. While CAT's narrative pre-empts that of the judges, it is likely based on elements from the secret case file, but in a biased manner. The way CAT, with its declared security-oriented stance and without ever having met the accused, presents the information differs significantly from the story revealed by the accused during the trial, thus creating a gap between what emerged in court and the version given publicly by CAT outside the courtroom. Revealing such information during the trial impacts not only the procedure itself – the accused's right to a defence and presumption of innocence, and the truth-seeking process – but also influences public perception. The accused's version of events during the trial was radically different from CAT's assertion; he said that he sought to escape ISIL and return to France by falsely volunteering for an attack in Lebanon. Yet, without any available transcript and with the decision itself being difficult to access, even for researchers, it is the public version that will be widely disseminated – completely sidelining the accused's version, which risks becoming non-existent.

48 CAT [@CAT_Centre] (2018). https://twitter.com/CAT_Centre/status/1064217207192907776. Reposted on the account of Jean-Charles Brisard, President of the CAT (23,505 subscribers at 1 July 2019).

Court decision (related to sentencing), 29 November 2017, Paris Assize Court:[49] To determine the penalty, the Assize Court took into consideration the following elements: regarding the facts, their objective severity with on-site military engagement of short duration (six weeks) and the accused's involvement in a terrorist plot from which he withdrew at the last moment, thus mitigating his criminal determination. Regarding the personality:

- A personal history marked by several traumatic events: born prematurely, several accidents, including a serious knife injury, disrupting his educational path (interrupted vocational training in carpentry) with significant physical and psychological consequences;
- A supportive family environment is expected to facilitate his rehabilitation;
- No prior involvement in proven delinquency before the events, with only one conviction related to traffic offences;
- A stance during the procedure and at trial that does not reveal a significant awareness of the gravity of the facts;
- A lack of critical distance from the facts;
- An impressionable and immature personality capable, however, of some ambivalence;
- Disciplinary incidents during detention despite overall appropriate behaviour;
- No proselytism during detention.

[49] The decision is available in Besnier et al., 2019, p. 289.

CHAPTER FIVE

THE 'TRIALS FOR HISTORY'

A New Paradigm for the Prosecution of Mass Crimes?

> *Then came the moment when the cartoons were projected. It was a moment where everyone was brought together: civil parties, defence, defendants, and victims. Everyone burst out laughing while looking at the cartoons. Apart from being a key moment for the audience, it was also a moment of great humanity*
>
> Defence lawyer, The Charlie Hebdo case[1]

The January 2015 attacks were a series of Islamist terrorist attacks that took place between 7th and 9th January 2015, in Paris and its suburbs.[2] They primarily struck the editorial team of *Charlie Hebdo*, where twelve members of the satirical newspaper were murdered, and through them, the freedom of expression they represented. For the first time, journalists were not killed in war zones but in France, at the offices of their own newspaper. This was followed by an attack on a Jewish grocery store that targeted freedom of belief and thought in a state that defines itself through secularism. And lastly, police officers were killed on the outskirts of Paris. It was not random victims who were targeted but symbols of the State. The civic and secular foundations of democracy were attacked. Secular because the diversity of beliefs is guaranteed in France through the neutrality of the state; civic because freedom of expression has been a condition for exercising citizens' rights since the French Revolution.[3] Hundreds of 'republican marches' were held in response to these two massacres, where two slogans prevailed: 'Je suis Charlie' and 'Freedom of Expression'. A few months later, on 13 November 2015, terrorist attacks hit the *Stade de France*, cafés, and the Bataclan concert hall in Paris, resulting in 130 deaths and hundreds of injuries, and a major shock for French society.[4] These attacks can be seen as France's 9/11 and a turning point in its

[1] Reported in Les Cahiers de la Justice, 2021, p. 246. [2] For more info see p.
[3] See Article 11 of the 1789 French Declaration of the Rights of Man and the Citizen.
[4] Truc, 2016.

counterterrorism policy.[5] A series of legal and administrative measures was instituted, including an unprecedented state of emergency due to its two-year duration and the powers granted to the administration. This legal framework granted enhanced security prerogatives driven by preventive and surveillance logic, which were gradually incorporated into common law.

It is within this period of social anxiety that these two cases – the Charlie Hebdo and Bataclan terror attacks – were investigated. In 2020, five years after the facts, these so-called Trials for history started to arrive in the courtrooms, with an explicit socio-political role.[6] The French President asserted it was the response of the French nation to the 'barbarians'.[7] With their long duration, high media coverage, transnational reach, and, above all, the participation of a significant number of victims as civil parties, these trials mark the 'third generation' of jihadist terrorism trials in France. They mark a peak in terms of performance. It was as if all the expertise accumulated, as discussed in previous chapters, and in conjunction with previous French 'historic trials', such as the Barbie and Papon trials,[8] was to put in place these trials.

Although criminal trials are primarily designed to repress individual acts, a new role has emerged with the third generation of jihadist trials. They have become a 'forum', giving voice to different actors to reconstruct a socio-historical phenomenon in all its complexity, as we have

[5] Hennette-Vauchez, 2021. For the impact of the 'War on Terror' on other democratic contexts see Abel, 2019; Vedaschi and Scheppele, 2021.

[6] Lindeperg, 2023; Hayaert, 2023, p. 121; Rousso, 2016; Arendt, 1963; McEvoy et al., 2022; Heller and Simpson, 2013; Jackson, 2023. In the context of the prosecution of terrorism, specific challenges are at stake: Saul, 2020.

[7] Emmanuel Macron, 11 March 2023, on the national day of homage to the victims of terrorism:

> Faced with the fury of the murderers, we have put at the heart of our response what these ideologues of hatred loathe: the rule of law, the guarantee of freedoms, appeasement through the force of our laws... Despite all the obstacles and constraints, these trials were held in dignity, with the highest standards of humanity and truth. They allowed the necessary words to emerge... This is the most resounding victory for our values, that of human justice in the face of barbarism. The trial of November 13 was, by its scope and the magnitude of what was said, an important moment for you and for the entire Nation. It will remain an exceptional milestone commensurate with the event in the history of our republican justice. 'Tribute of the President of the Republic to the Victims of Acts of Terrorism', 11 March 2023, available at www.elysee.fr/front/pdf/elysee-module-20957-fr.pdf.

[8] Sadat, 1994.

seen with truth commissions in post-conflict countries.[9] These trials have become a space where the defendants recount their path to radicalisation, the victims relate their trauma and expectations, the experts situate the phenomenon in a political, social, and medical context, and the police and security services expose their work and their difficulties. The rich narratives exposed by the different stakeholders, and most notably by hundreds of victims, are at the centre of this organic process, which is being constantly developed by the actors themselves. The trial was strictly framed by criminal law procedure and prosecution policy, but this framework was partly circumvented, enriched, and even subverted during the trial.

This chapter discusses the Charlie Hebdo and Bataclan trials and the emergence of a hybrid procedure, which introduced important elements of restorative justice.

Box 5.1 The Charlie Hebdo and Related Attacks Committed in January 2015

The January 2015 attacks in France were a series of Islamist terrorist attacks that took place between 7 and 9 January 2015, in the Île-de-France region. These attacks targeted the editorial office of the satirical newspaper *Charlie Hebdo*, customers at a kosher supermarket, and police officers in Montrouge on the outskirts of Paris. The events began on Wednesday, 7 January 2015, with the attack on *Charlie Hebdo* at the newspaper's Paris headquarters. Two French jihadists, the Kouachi brothers, murdered eleven people – including eight *Charlie Hebdo* staff members – and injured eleven others before killing a wounded police officer, Ahmed Merabet, during their escape. Among the victims were famous journalists Cabu, Charb, Tignous, and Wolinski. Two days later, the Kouachi brothers were killed by the police after a standoff at a printing facility in the northeast of Paris. The attack was claimed by Al-Qaeda in the Arabian Peninsula (AQAP), based in Yemen. In a coordinated attack with the *Charlie Hebdo* attackers, on 8 January 2015, Amedy

[9] Truth commissions are *ad hoc* institutions created in nearly fifty countries affected by mass violence over the past forty years. Members are drawn from civil society and include academics, clergy, psychologists, etc., whose proceedings are detached from the judicial system. They are tasked with establishing the facts, hearing the victims, and proposing reparation measures to effect a 'reconciliation' of the country. See Lefranc, 2022a; Hayner, 2002; Wiebelhaus-Brahm, 2010.

Coulibaly, a Frenchman associated with the Kouachi brothers, murdered municipal police officer Clarissa Jean-Philippe and critically injured a municipal employee in Montrouge. The next day, Coulibaly took hostages at a kosher supermarket in Paris, killing four people. Coulibaly was ultimately killed in a police assault. He claimed to act on behalf of the jihadist group Islamic State (ISIS).

The trial in numbers: Duration: ten weeks, fifty-seven days of hearing days. Case File: 171 volumes of procedure. Participants: fourteen defendants: eleven present, three judged *in abstensia* (presumed dead in Syria); 200 civil parties; 144 witnesses; fourteen experts; ninety-four lawyers; ninety accredited journalists (of which twenty-seven foreign media).

The Bataclan and Related Attacks Committed on 13 November 2015

On 13 November 2015, in Paris and Saint-Denis, three terrorist commandos carried out three series of attacks within minutes of each other. Three sites were targeted: the Stade de France (two explosions at 9:19 pm and 9:22 pm), several café terraces in the tenth and eleventh quarter (targeted between 9:24 pm and 9:40 pm), and the Bataclan concert hall, where the attack began at 9:40 pm. At the Bataclan, 1,500 spectators had gathered for a concert by the American rock band Eagles of Death Metal. In total, six coordinated attacks were carried out by three heavily armed commandos composed of nine men. Salah Abdeslam was the only surviving member who fled the scene that night. He was arrested on 18 March 2016, in Belgium. Three investigating judges conducted the inquiry over five years in France and abroad, enabling the reconstruction of the organisation of the attacks, from Syria to French soil via Belgium. The case file comprises 472 volumes, amounting to one million pages. These attacks caused 132 deaths, over 400 injuries, and left numerous survivors traumatised.

More than 2,300 individuals registered as civil parties in the trial. Twenty people were referred to the specially composed Paris criminal court by an indictment order dated 13 July 2020, and an amended order dated 21 October 2020. Eleven of the defendants were in custody during the hearings, three were not detained until the end of the proceedings, and six were the subjects of arrest warrants (five presumed dead in Syria, and one was in detention in Turkey). Salah Abdeslam, the sole surviving assailant, was joined by accomplices and logisticians implicated to varying degrees, including for forged documents and other support activities.

The trial in numbers: Duration: ten months of trial, 140 days of hearings (four weeks interrupted due to COVID-19). Investigation file: 542 volumes. Twenty defendants, of which eleven in custody, three appeared free, and six were tried in absentia, five of which are presumed dead in Syria, and one was detained in Turkey, which refused extradition; over 2,300 civil parties and 330 lawyers; 141 journalists, including fifty-eight foreign media.

5.1 THE CHARLIE HEBDO TRIAL

The Charlie Hebdo trial began on 2 September 2020, during the COVID period, and lasted two and a half months. The first major trial has a specific context and legal history, as these attacks had previous echoes in court. In 2006, the newspaper reprinted the cartoons of Muhammad that had been published by the Danish newspaper *Jyllands-Posten*. In response, the Paris Mosque filed a lawsuit, which was dismissed by the courts on the grounds that criticism of religion does not constitute a punishable act when it comes from a satirical newspaper, which is protected by freedom of expression:

> Considering that Charlie Hebdo is a satirical magazine containing numerous caricatures, and that nobody is obliged to buy or read it, in contrast to other media such as posters displayed on public thoroughfares; Considering that all caricatures can be interpreted as portraits that ignore the conventions of good taste for the purpose of parody by adopting a burlesque or grotesque style; that exaggeration functions like a form of wit enabling the caricaturist to circumvent censorship and to use irony as an instrument of social and political criticism that encourages critical thinking and debate; Considering that the literary genre of caricature, although deliberately provocative, is for that reason entitled to freedom of expression and communication of thoughts and opinions; that, precisely because of the excessiveness of its intentionally irreverent content, the exaggeration and subjectivity inherent to caricature must be taken into account when analysing the meaning and implications of contentious drawings, even though the right to criticism and humour is not entirely unrestricted.[10]

This attack brought together the two obsessions of jihadists: freedom of expression and the Jews. This trial is primarily characterised by the

[10] Judgment of the Paris Tribunal (17th chamber) dated 22 March 2007. See Viennot, 2015.

rhetorical inclusion of a historical dimension by the civil parties, intended to highlight a conflict of values. During the 2020 Charlie Hebdo trial, the journalists of *Charlie Hebdo* continued to uphold the values of freedom of expression and secularism on behalf of those who are no longer here. This central issue for democracy was a focus of the pleadings of *Charlie Hebdo*'s civil parties during the trial, particularly by lawyer Richard Malka,[11] who framed the caricatures of *Charlie Hebdo* as part of a tradition of freedom of expression in France since 1789 and the terrorist attack as a major threat to republican values. In the name of this freedom, albeit interpreted in a libertarian manner, *Charlie Hebdo* claims an old tradition. They were, however, accused of abusing it, by those who saw their acts as a manifestation of Islamophobia. Some within the French intelligentsia (especially the radical left) place *Charlie Hebdo* among those who reject immigrants, particularly Muslims. Others believe that 'adding fuel to the fire' should be avoided since believers are entitled to respect for their religion.

The day before the trial began, *Charlie Hebdo* was criticised for republishing the caricatures. For the lawyer of *Charlie Hebdo*, Malka, the defence of democracy – and this trial symbolises it – requires the sanctity of freedom of expression. In a secular society, only publications that personally stigmatise members of a religious community can be punished, not those that target religion in general or its symbols: 'To renounce the free criticism of religions, to renounce the caricatures of Muhammad, would be to renounce our history, the *Encyclopédie*, the Revolution, and the great laws of the Republic, critical thinking, and a world governed by the laws of men rather than those of God.'[12]

The second expectation, raised by the lawyers representing the Jewish community, concerns the freedom of thought and belief, which the law establishes but leaves to the judiciary to defend. In a country marked by the Dreyfus Affair and the anti-Jewish laws of the Vichy regime, the fight against anti-Semitism is a constant challenge. This is especially sensitive in France, which hosts the largest Jewish community in Europe (around 450,000 members), alongside the largest Muslim community in Western Europe (around five million members), tied to the painful history of decolonisation. The testimonies of the victims of the Jewish grocery store were framed within the broader history of anti-Semitism in France, and

[11] His plea was published under the title 'The Right to Annoy God', Grasset, 2021.
[12] His plea was published under the title 'The Right to Annoy God', Grasset, 2021, p. 48.

the court explicitly acknowledged the anti-Semitic dimension of the Hyper Cacher attack in its ruling.[13]

As researchers, we did not anticipate how deeply the victims' testimonies would reveal a post-war atmosphere. 'It was a scene of war!' This phrase was repeated a thousand times in the courtroom by witnesses on the stand. These hearings echoed the war in its speeches and references, as a monstrous event that still haunts them. It was as if the violence of the bullets, the smell of blood, and the smoke-filled room from the gunfire tore through the courtroom. When the *Charlie Hebdo* cartoonist, Coco, recounted how she begged her executioners for her life, she re-created the scene, crouching with her hands over her head, in the position of a condemned prisoner. 'I thought I would die, executed', she testified. Jewish witnesses, facing deadly anti-Semitism, used a different lexicon in relation to the attack on the Hyper Cacher in Vincennes. As 'survivors' or 'escapees', they spoke on behalf of those no longer there. They placed themselves within the legacy of our responses to the mass crimes of the twentieth century, with multiple references to the history of the Holocaust. The reading of victims' names at the beginning of the trial was done in the spirit of the day of remembrance for Holocaust victims. While civil parties referenced anti-Semitic crimes, Black victims, such as police officer Clarissa Jean-Philippe, killed in Paris, invoked the history of colonialism as a descendant of slaves. These groups of victims from the Jewish and Black communities heavily influenced the debates.

The place reserved for the victims, the centrality of suffering and emotions, and the fact that the crimes were framed as part of a French ethos opposing freedom and obscurantism, have created a particular atmosphere that has financially shaped the entire trial.

5.1.1 Two Parallel Hearings: Victims and Defendants

Victims play an important and proactive role, which aligns with the objective of restorative justice. This is particularly important in the

[13] Court decision, 16 December 2020:

> Coulibaly was accused of targeting the Jewish community by attacking the Hyper Cacher grocery store on a Friday afternoon, just before the start of Shabbat, taking customers hostage, asking for their identity to verify if they were Jewish, and executing some of them for that reason alone … the hostage-taking of Hyper Cacher customers was undeniably anti-Semitic, as was the murder of four of them and the attempted murder of the store manager. Only a procedural issue related to the timing of the law's application prevented the aggravating circumstance of belonging to a specific religion from being applied to the crime of hostage-taking.

context of jihadist cases in France, where victims and perpetrators, living in the same society, must, accordingly, 'build an ethics of living together that will need to be found even as the domestic terrorist threat remains and is likely to persist for a long time'.[14] However, in this kind of trial with strong political and societal resonance, where the presumption of innocence is likely to be weakened a priori, the principle of equality of arms and the rights of the defence must be protected. In this case, it was decided by the presiding judge that the trial will start with the depositions of dozens of the victims and civil parties.[15] This format will be followed in the later 'Trials for history' – the Bataclan and Nice trials. However, for defence lawyer Marie Dosé, the interventions of the dozen civil parties' lawyers and the prosecutor before the turn of the defence took up too much space at the trial, to the point where, when the defence finally spoke, 'it seemed that it was too late'.[16]

What we will retain from the Charlie Hebdo trial are two parallel processes, barely connected, experienced during the hearing. On the one hand, there was the victims' voice, a grave and painful voice, rarely heard before, where the victims reconstructed the horror of the attacks. During the first month of the hearing, more than 100 civil parties shared in great detail and with much emotion their post-traumatic suffering. On the other hand, we witnessed a criminal trial, which did not include any of the principal authors of the crimes. They were killed during the police assault. On the contrary, the trial involved accused persons with marginal responsibility that was cruelly distant from the facts recounted by the victims. The defendants present in court were only marginalised criminals, drugs and arms traffickers, mostly unemployed, connected by life's coincidences. Most of the defendants (who, unlike most jihadist trials, were not radicalised) acknowledged their actions as common law offences – illegal arms or car trafficking – and all denied having any knowledge of the terrorist plot by the main perpetrators, and barely knew or did not know them at all. What perhaps distinguishes mass crime trials from the Charlie Hebdo trial is this gap, this tenuous link between the charges against these distant defendants and the suffering of the victims. A gap that widens even more in the absence of the main perpetrators and in the face of legal qualifications that in no way reflect the horror experienced by the victims and their families.

[14] Hubrecht, 2019. [15] See discussion in p. xxx.
[16] Field notes, December 2020.

Most of the defendants were charged with AMT. As discussed in the previous chapters, in these cases, the defendant's background is closely examined, thus individualising the judicial process. This trend was confirmed during this trial. Apart from a significant divergence between the sentences requested by the prosecution and those imposed by the judges, seven of the fourteen defendants were not even found guilty of terrorism.[17] Even more surprising was the fact that the public prosecutor did not appeal, as it had systematically done until then. This clearly demonstrates a tendency to broaden the scope of AMT during the investigation phase and the 'over charging' of the investigating judges during the state of emergency period and beyond.

Furthermore, as essential as it is to ensure that victims have effective access to justice, the experience of the January 2015 attacks trial shows that there is a significant risk of creating false expectations for both civil parties and society as a whole. This discrepancy also invites the defence to denounce a spectacle trial that undermines the presumption of innocence and the right to a fair trial. In the end, it is all parties – civil parties and defendants – who fall victim to the excesses and dysfunctions of anti-terrorist justice. The penal policy of the public prosecutor's office, by continually expanding the scope of AMT and preventive justice, sends individuals to a court of assize, some of whom have little (or no) connection to the original terrorist project, to face victims who are deeply wounded and seeking truth – a truth that, to be affirmed, requires a common ground. Yet, during the Charlie Hebdo trial, incomprehension was often seen in the eyes of the defendants – a misunderstanding that was at times disconcerting for both the victims and the accused, as spectators of a trial out of sync.[18]

As in François Boucq's drawing, published in Charlie Hebdo, the judge moves forward on a tightrope, keeping his balance despite the leaning motion that threatens to precipitate his fall. The pleadings of the civil parties, with their broad perspective, highlighted the underlying political stakes of this trial. It is notable that the role of the judiciary as the 'last bulwark' of democracy was underscored by a newspaper not usually inclined to show leniency toward institutions.[19] Yet, this trial also showed the limits of such justice, from the perspective of those who have found themselves caught on the accused benches, supposed to carry the responsibility for such an ethos.

[17] See Annex 6A.3. [18] Weill and Sulzer, 2021. [19] Riss, 2020.

Figure 5.1 Drawing by François Boucq, published in *Charlie Hebdo*, as part of the newspaper's regular trial coverage.

In the Bataclan trial, which began a few months later, unlike the Charlie Hebdo trial, several defendants were charged with a high level of responsibility as key figures in the terror group, including Salah Abdeslam, a member of the commando who survived the attack.[20]

5.2 THE BATACLAN TRIAL

The Bataclan trial represents forms of justice that seek alternatives to mere repression and penal retribution. Instead of solely punishing individuals, these approaches emphasise collective reflection on the crime's meaning, reparation, and reconstitution of the social bond.[21] These objectives were explicitly claimed during the trials, representing a hybridisation of criminal and restorative justice. Like other examples of transitional justice mechanisms, it is emblematic of efforts to build

[20] Salah Absdeslam was arrested a few months after the attack on 18 March 2016, in Belgium. He will be tried in France and, later also in Belgium, for his involvement in the March 2016 attacks in the airport in Brussels, along with 4 other defendants: Mohamed Abrini, Osama Krayem, , Sofien Ayari, Ali El Haddad Asufi.

[21] This part is based on an article written by Sharon Weill and Sandrine Lefranc published in the *Leiden Journal of International Law* (2025).

justice 'for the victim'. But this trial was not conducted as an independent process outside the framework of the criminal justice system, as truth commissions are, nor was it conducted by an *ad hoc* mechanism as the *Jurisdicción especial para la paz* (Special Jurisdiction for Peace) in Colombia.[22] It was an integral part of the criminal justice system. This trial thus appears as an experiment that renews penal law 'from within', opening an avenue to reflect on the lessons that can be learned within the wider field of transitional/transformative justice.[23]

The Bataclan trial was exceptional in several respects: its long duration over ten months; the intensive participation of victims – consisting of over 2,300 civil parties and their 330 lawyers; the high level of responsibility of some of the accused; the investigative file of a million (!) pages and a 500-page indictment resulting from over five years of investigation. Hundreds of professionals were involved in the daily work on the case. To accommodate a large audience – including journalists, lawyers, victims, security professionals, and researchers – a temporary courtroom was built within the courthouse. There was a dedicated video infrastructure, and the general public had access to other courtrooms designated for public broadcasting. Civil parties could follow the trial via a web radio. Security was significantly reinforced, with 1,000 police officers assigned to ensure safety, and access was controlled. Remarkably, the trial took place in the city centre, while tourists continued to visit the chapel in the courthouse courtyard and enjoy coffee unaware that the trial was in progress. At the same time, it was framed within the regular criminal procedure and was anchored within the court routine.

In the continuity of the Charlie Hebdo trial, the first five weeks of the trial were devoted to the victims/civil parties, which were given a central

22 The Colombian *ad hoc* mechanism was created following the peace agreement with the FARC and the State of Colombia in 2016 and operated with the financial support of the international community since 2019. For a review of its first years of work see: Ambos and Peters, 2022. With a specially composed restorative mechanism, the court has started legal procedures of 11 'macro cases', involving hundreds of thousands of victims. As a civil law country, the centrality of the victims within the legal procedure was a part of its legal culture, but this mechanism went a few steps further in its restorative approach. The court recognized as a civil party the territories where native communities live and were displaced. See Huneeus and Rueda-Saiz, 2021.

23 For the advocates of 'transformative justice', 'transitional justice' often perpetuates existing power dynamics. Transformative justice aims to instigate more radical changes, emphasising a broader approach to justice from 'below', looking into deeper social and structural dimensions, and promoting the rights and interests of marginalized communities. See Gready and Robins, 2014.

role. Civil parties' lawyers are granted extensive rights such as the right to access the investigation file, the right to summon witnesses and request specific investigative measures, the opportunity to question the accused and witnesses during the trial, the ability to present oral depositions, and to submit their view on the guilt or innocence of the accused.[24] In contrast to international criminal trials held before *ad hoc*/hybrid tribunals originating in civil systems, such as in Cambodia or Senegal,[25] victims were not compelled to be represented by victims' associations. Each victim/civil party had the freedom to select their own lawyer and decide whether to be represented by a victims' association. Legal aid, estimated at fifty million euros, was fully funded by the state.[26] The request to be recognised as a civil party can be made at any time from the start of the investigation until the end of the trial. As a result, out of 2,300 registered civil parties, represented by over 330 lawyers, 397 victims provided deposition before the Court, averaging twelve to eighteen testimonies per day. This marked a shift from a criminal justice system that only examines the responsibility of a few defendants to a restorative justice system that listens to several hundred victims.

5.2.1 The Sociology of the Victims and Legal Constructions

Despite the diversity of their experiences, the sociological profiles of the victims were relatively homogeneous, significantly influencing the trial's atmosphere. They set its tone. They were mostly young people who went out on a Friday night in east Paris, a left-wing part of town, just as they did many other weekends, to hang out in bars and watch a heavy metal concert. Tattoos and black t-shirts paying tribute to one rock band, or another, replaced the usual formal dress code and helped ease the rigorous ritual associated with criminal proceedings.[27] A large proportion of them are university graduates,[28] holding common values of freedom, critical

[24] Victims' reparations are guaranteed through the 'The Victims of Terrorism and Other Offenses Guarantee Fund'. It is funded by a 6.5 Euro tax (as of 2024) collected through mandatory house insurance. For more details see Chapter 1.

[25] Werner and Marchand, 2020, p. 125; Trujillo, 2022.; Sperfeldt, 2022.

[26] Legal aid is granted for the representation of each civil party at a rate of 1,000 euros per day. Several lawyers represented large groups of clients, numbering in several dozens, leading to criticism of the imbalance in the payment of legal aid to defence lawyers.

[27] Laugerud and Langballe describe the PCs' respect for judicial formality in the Breivik trial, their fear of becoming emotional: Laugerud and Langballe, 2017.

[28] 80% of the 180 respondents to the research group questionnaire. Antichan et al., 2023.

spirit, and hedonism. They often display their critical position towards the state and a French society considered conservative and closed.

Yet, this community of victims was challenged during the trial. This reminds us that the individual and collective victim is always constructed; individuals are not victims, they become one, in the course of interactions with labelling institutions and other victims.[29] The court was a privileged agent both of the ratification of established public hierarchies (between Bataclan and the rest) and of their re-examination, based in particular on the proposals of the Prosecution and their contestation. Divisions emerged when judges applied legal boundaries that are otherwise questionable. To be legally recognised as a civil party, victims need to prove a *direct* link between the crime and the harm. The Public Prosecutor's Office had frequently recalled since the trial opening that a distinction should be made between the status of civil party and that of victim, using mainly a criterion of being directly exposed to the crime. The French Supreme Court introduced a distinction between a 'direct victim' – *targeted* by the terrorists – and an 'unfortunate witness'.[30] These legal categories created moments of tension and uneasiness in the courtroom when lawyers asked the judges to grant their clients the legal status of civil parties. In court, we heard the case of a person who came down from his flat to assist the injured after he had heard the shooting. The judges did not grant him civil party status. Such exclusions fuelled a feeling of illegitimacy, creating a violent dichotomy between legal and sociological definitions of 'victim'. 'It is clearly hyper-violent to be challenged in this way', confided a victim who was recognised as a civil party.[31] There were also divisions among the civil parties themselves. The relatives of the dead did not have the same views as the survivors. The latter were distinguished according to the seriousness of their injury and its physical or psychological nature.

29 Hacking, 1991.

30 While ruling on the inadmissibility of providing the status of civil party to a person who, while witnessing the killing on the terrace, fled for their life, the French Supreme Court states that this passer-by 'did not find himself in the path of the terrorist shots, which were aimed at the "La Belle Équipe" restaurant, but was an *unfortunate witness* to these facts', Decision of the French Cassation Court, Criminal Chamber, 15 February 2022. In general, as noted by Alix, the conditions for admissibility of civil party actions have been slightly broadened to include 'victims by implication', certain legal entities, and relatives of non-deceased victims. See Alix, 2020.

31 Antichan et al., 2021.

5.2.1.1 *The Courtroom as a Space to Express Emotions*

The victims' depositions triggered intense emotional moments, normally excluded or regulated by the judicial procedure. Aligned with forms of justice, which seek to return control 'stolen' by professionals to the parties involved,[32] the Bataclan trial also places significant emphasis on emotions, in contrast to the cold, impersonal authority of conventional law, which relies on legal rhetoric, justified to maintain neutrality and impartiality.[33]

Testimonies were largely devoted to describing the suffering endured during and since the attack, and the difficult mourning of loved ones was at the centre of the narratives. The restorative ambition endorsed by the court tended to transform it into a therapeutic space. Testimonies often took the form of homage to the dead: photographs of the dead at different moments in their lives, praise for the dead person, and accounts of the burial ceremonies. All these elements are unusual in a court of law. The criminal justice system broke with the principle of strict neutrality by showing great benevolence, as evidenced by the presiding judge's frequent warm words towards the victims. The coldness of the judicial procedure was abandoned, opening the door to emotions,[34] and tears flowed abundantly. In later discussions we had, judges affirmed that they were crying. One said she was happy that she had to wear an anti-COVID mask, so no one could see her tears.[35]

Even if these testimonies did not contribute significantly to the factual reconstruction of the events, they did allow the civil parties, after six years, to complete the puzzle: the course of their evening, the identity of the people killed next to them, or of those who reached out to them.

The accumulation of these individual stories formed a collective narrative of shared trauma. A sensitive question timidly raised by one witness sometimes turned into a shared inquiry, illustrating a language that, as the hearings progressed, became a common thread among the community of victims. While not all victims were present every day, several hundred listened to the hearings via a web radio station. This

32 Christie, 1977; Braithwaite, 2004; Olson and Dzur, 2004.

33 Bourdieu, 1987; Dahlberg, 2009; Bergman Blix and Wettergren, 2018; Tornqvist, 2022.

34 See Bergman Blix and Wettergren, 2018; Maroney, 2019; Roach Anleu and Mack, 2021.

35 This was told to us during a conference that we organised at the **National School for the Judiciary** a few months after the end of the trial.

remote listening fostered cross-referencing effects and mimicry: the words spoken by some were echoed and occasionally quoted by others

The 126-page verdict, which provided very limited insight into the hearings, nonetheless recognised the traumatic state of the civil parties. The heavy sentences are justified by the suffering of these 'innocent victims'.

> The testimonies of 397 civil parties, whether injured, shocked or mourning the loss of a loved one, as well as police officers, first responders to the crime scenes, such as the doctors and the special police forces, highlighted both the horror of the crime scenes discovered, comparable to scenes of war with dramatic ballistic injuries, and the immensity of the psychological damage persisting more than six years after the events, which may have contributed to the suicide of two of the civil parties after the events.[36]

5.2.1.2 *A Forum of Exchanges between the Victims and the Accused*

The participation of victims in the trial is often analysed as an opportunity for confrontation and empowerment of the victims in the face of diminished perpetrators.[37] However, beyond being a platform for dialogue among victims, the trial also evolved into a potential meeting place for the accused.

Civil parties tried to engage in a dialogue, with a view to rehumanising those who 'are not monsters', while one might have expected, from the perspective of a 'repressive' trial in the sense of Durkheim, they designate monsters and barbarians. Sometimes, victims chose to address a question directly to the accused, which led to spontaneous exchanges between the parties. The defendants, often binational, appeared less as an 'enemy within'. They were rather perceived by many as young people from the suburbs, children, or grandchildren of North African immigrants, who have not found their place in society and whom the state failed to educate.[38] The prevalence of the failed education and integration issues in the civil parties' depositions is striking. The values of secularism and tolerance were prominent among the civil parties, shaping their

[36] Verdict, at 101. [37] See Laugerud and Langballe, 2017.

[38] '(The terrorist) addresses us like a buddy. I come from the suburbs, we could have played soccer together' (a survivor among the Bataclan hostages, 19 October). A survivor of the restaurant 'Petit Cambodge' attack spoke of the resemblance between a killer and one of his friends (30 September). A man wounded at the Stade de France made a similar comment, after having specified that he is himself a practicing Muslim: 'The guys in the box are the same as in the suburbs, and our thoughts are with their parents' (26 September). Field notes.

inclination to challenge a narrow religious interpretation of the terrorist acts they endured. While the trial took place within the realm of criminal justice, there were alternative narratives to that of criminal repression.

A few defendants spoke of how difficult it was to listen to the victims' testimonies. They noted that most of them had been imprisoned for several years in complete isolation and now suddenly they found themselves in a courtroom every day, sharing seats with their co-accused, talking with their lawyers, and listening to six to seven hours a day of victims' testimonies. When the defendants were questioned later in the proceedings, they went on to say that they had decided to talk because of a look in a grieving mother's eyes, or because of a specific question raised by a victim. This was the case with Sofien Ayari, who remained mostly silent but attempted to explain why he had travelled to Syria.[39] The defendants' last words were addressed to the victims. They expressed their remorse, offered their 'apologies' – including Abdeslam, the only surviving direct participant in the attacks, who regretted having used words that were 'a bit harsh' like telling a Muslim victim she had been hit without being targeted – or condemned the attacks, wishing that the victims are able to 'turn the page, rebuild their lives' (Mohamed Abrini) or 'overcome the difficulties they face every day' (Sofien Ayari).[40]

Several civil parties even wished to exchange directly with the three defendants, who were not detained until the end of the proceedings. These three defendants came in and out of the courtroom, like the public, and in the breaks, they were smoking cigarettes on the same

[39] In his words:

> I didn't want to speak out, I thought it was pointless, and I changed my mind. There were the five weeks of testimonies and the question of this mother who had lost her daughter. She looked like my mother. She said [about the defendants]: 'When they were 2 years old, I could have taken those little ones in my arms. But what made them turn out like that?' So the least I can do is answer that question. I thought I owed her that (cited in Besnier, 2023, p. 106).

[40] This was reported in the verdict, but in a very limited way:

> Indeed, during the debates, he (Abdeslam) asserted and claimed his status as a fighter for the Islamic State, asserted that the acts committed in the name of the Islamic State were legitimate, declared that he assumed responsibility for his actions while minimising his involvement, thereby demonstrating the absence of any awareness of the seriousness of the facts, the absence of regrets and of any questioning, even if he was able to express that he had been touched by the testimonies of the civil parties (Verdict, at 122).

Figure 5.2 The Bataclan trial courtroom, as viewed from the bench reserved to the researchers. Drawing by Benoit Peyrucq.

stairways. One civil party, who had a conversation with them in the courthouse yard during a break, told us how significant it was for him, as he had previously considered the defendants only as being terrorists. This kind of interaction can be transformative. One of the victim associations even organised a visit to the Bataclan with these defendants. As long as the rights of the defence and the presumption of innocence are respected, this experience demonstrates that a justice approach embracing large-scale participation of victims can function effectively, suggesting that courts need not fear being overwhelmed by an influx of victims.

5.2.2 What Role for the Social Sciences?

The 'right to truth' has found a form of legal consecration at the international level. As in post-conflict societies, the victims in the Bataclan trial are driven by the same quest for truth, where understanding the political and social motivations of the accused is essential for their rehabilitation.[41]

In seeking to understand, the civil parties called to the bar many *witnesses of context* – including members of the political establishment and security agencies, as well as sociologists, academics, and experts – to provide an informed background on radicalisation, transnational

[41] Naftali, 2016; see Antichan et al., 2021; Salas and Weill, 2021.

jihadism, the war in Syria, and security policies. Thus, the role of the civil parties was not limited to the initial space dedicated to their own stories. They further shaped the trial through the witnesses they invited, creating a new and unprecedented aspect to the trial, which allowed experts to provide insights into the socio-political context in which the attacks occurred and to respond to the questions posed by the parties.

The former President of the French Republic, the minister of the interior, the head of security services, the prosecutor general, a social worker, and social sciences academics were all called to testify by the civil parties. While none of them could provide direct testimony about the defendants' actions, they were able to shed light on the socio-political context before and after the attacks. The court's decision to allow the testimony of political figures and experts in the quest for the 'truth' is one more illustration of the trial's similarity to truth commissions, which attempt to explain the dynamics of violence.[42] These trials did not only try suspected terrorists, they also shed light on the workings of the state – in the same way that truth commissions often expose the involvement of the entire state's apparatus in repression (in South Africa or post-communist Europe, for example).

5.2.2.1 *Revealing Truth or Obscuring Failures?*

A court called upon to rule on the guilt of the individuals being tried cannot rule or allow the debate to focus on other facts, such as security failures.[43] It was the victims who wanted, and obtained, this question to be asked, by summoning senior officials who undertook to justify their results. The defence lawyers seized this opportunity to reintroduce the

[42] While the defence objected to their testimonies on the basis that this would turn the judicial proceedings into a political trial, the judges decided to allow these witnesses of context to testify before the court. The objection was based on Article 331 of the French Criminal Code of Procedure that requests that: 'Witnesses testify only as to the facts with which the accused is charged, or as to the character and character of the accused.'

[43] The failures of the security services were examined by a parliamentary commission of inquiry, which issued a report in the summer of 2016, criticising the disorganization of the services, in constant competition and reform. This commission, which was unable to interview service agents, was nevertheless weak – particularly in view of the British initiatives. About the latter, see assets.publishing.service.gov.uk/media/5a81ec68ed915d74e6234d7c/Attacks_in_London_and_Manchester_Open_Report.pdf and www.gov.uk/government/publications/mi5-and-counter-terrorism-policing-implementation-report-2017-terrorist-attacks.

question of the foreign policy pursued by France. By bringing and questioning witnesses of context, the parties sought to expand the boundaries of the typical context presented in terrorism trials, which had previously been dominated by the perspectives of the police and security agencies invited by the prosecutor. These had often presented a constructed top-down analysis, while using graphic power points to describe the hierarchy and networks of various jihadist groups, along with their connections with armed groups in Syria. In contrast, the Bataclan trial attempted, through a different use of expertise, to explore not only the functioning but also the dysfunctions of the security services. In this context, Bernard Bajolet, former head of the French foreign intelligence service (*Direction générale de la sécurité extérieure*), acknowledged the error of his service in failing to consider the announcement of the preparation of the attacks by a close associate of its organiser, Abdelhamid Abaaoud. He said he was stunned by the scale of the attack. He even confessed to 'a sense of failure'.

> Abaaoud has been on the radar since October 2013, but for us, he is a jihadist like any other. It becomes clear when we see him dragging corpses around, in March 2014 (referring to ISIS videos)… At that time, we employed minimal means to locate Abaaoud. We were not successful.[44]

This questioning into the responsibilities of the state was conducted by civil parties. While the police and the health services were almost unanimously praised, the disorganisation of the state when confronted with the attacks was strongly criticised.

Whether it was a move towards politicising the trial or introducing a political component into the trial, the testimony of former President Hollande merits a closer look. The initial objection of the defence lawyers to the President's testimony, the contradictory debate on the question, and the deliberation time for the judges to decide on the matter, resulted in a delay of three hours, while the former President waited in the witness room. When he finally entered the courtroom, his first words were:

-'Bonjour, Mr President.'
-'Bonjour, Mr President' replied the judge.

On this November afternoon, the court was transformed into a democratic forum with the opportunity to exchange highly critical views.

[44] Field notes, 16 November 2021; ten lawyers questioned him following this testimony.

Encircled by a room full of lawyers, victims, and journalists, the testimony of the former President lasted for four hours. Dozens of victims' and defence lawyers had the extraordinary opportunity, one by one, to ask their questions, any question, without censorship or guidance, and they received immediate answers from the former head of state. Different themes emerged from the questioning. The first centred on the failure of the state's security policy: What had been done to protect the population and how effective was information gathering in the face of the threat of attacks in France? The adequacy of surveillance conducted by French and Belgian intelligence was questioned.[45] The second theme of inquiry revolved around geopolitics. It raised questions such as why France decided to intervene in Syria or Iraq, knowing that such military involvement could result in terrorist attacks. It also questioned how a democratic state like France could maintain a 'killing list' in Syria. Thirdly, and perhaps most intriguingly, questions by a defence lawyers sought to explore how it was possible for a generation of young people to become so vulnerable that they embraced such violent propaganda and ideology. It also questioned what mistakes the state may have made in this regard. While the questions were challenging, provocative, and thought-provoking, the former President remained in his official role, and most of his answers were predictable, excluding any attribution of responsibility to the education, security, or any state services.

5.2.2.2 The Elephant in the (Court) Room

What has become of the 'Educative State' since it was unable to prevent radicalisation? This question was largely evacuated by the Court.[46] Indeed, the main absence at the trial was the establishment

[45] Do you think that there were holes in the intelligence system? – There is necessarily a failure when there is an attack. How many attacks are prevented thanks to the services? Attacks that could have resulted in particularly atrocious figures... The terrorists were trained to kill, came to kill. I have been demanding of the services. I want you to know that all these services did everything they could.

At times, doubts arise: 'Have we done enough? Do we ever do enough? We had already put in a lot of resources as early as 2012...' (Field notes, 10 November 2021).

[46] The notion of 'Educative State' originates in the French revolution: The revolutionaries envisioned of an educational state capable of taking in charge the children. See Canivez, 1995.

of social linkages with experiences of social exclusion, racism, post-colonialism, and radicalisation, all of which have been well identified by leading sociologists in academic literature.[47]

While radicalisation was presented almost solely through the prism of individual pathways, ideology, propaganda, and wrong choices, the expertise provided ignored the important role of existing social structures. Having historians and/or sociologists highlighting these social factors would have triggered a deeper understanding than what was provided by the political echelon present at the trial.

The only exception to this absence was testimony from a social worker specialised in radicalisation and worked for many years in poor neighbourhoods in Belgium. As noted by the presiding judge this was of major importance for their understanding:

> With his testimony, he enlightened us all – the court, the defence lawyers, the civil parties. ... For him, it was a phenomenon of hyper-violence seeking justification and legitimisation, which they found in the form of radical Islamism, even though they knew nothing of the Coran. He gave us explanation ... which was very interesting because it went beyond a strictly religious explanation (Presiding judge).[48]

The absence of further expertise, most notably academic, is related to the organic formation of the trial. Sociologists such as Professor Gilles Kepel, and his student Dr. Hugo Micheron, were invited by the civil parties, but they would deliver just another version of the security approach. Unfortunately, other sociologists with different viewpoints, more social and structural, who were invited by the defence lawyers, refused to come. The position of social scientists in relation to their participation in trials is not a new debate.[49] In this trial, their refusals were based on different arguments. Olivier Roy's position is that he is studying a general social phenomenon, and, therefore, he is not able to provide testimony in a trial involving the criminal responsibility of individuals he does not know.[50] This stance is evidently rooted in a very stringent interpretation of what constitutes a criminal procedure.

47 Ali-Adraoui and Roy, 2018; Truong, 2017; Khosrokhavar, 2018; Conti, 2023.
48 Verbatim of the round table at Sciences Po Paris on the 18 November 2022 (program available at www.sciencespo.fr/centre-etudes-europeennes/fr/node/38357.html).
49 Atlani-Duault and Dufoix, 2014. See also Hagedorn, 2022; Caldwell, 2012.
50 Olivier Roy's talk in two conferences organised at Sciences Po, Paris (November 2021 and November 2022).

Refusals are also motivated by the fear of personal attacks within the academic community, of being the 'sociologists of terrorists', too quick to 'excuse' excluded people who have become radicals.[51] Farhad Khosrokhavar, a sociologist who has spent years conducting numerous interviews with jihadists in prison, would have been able to provide the court with a more nuanced approach. His refusal to testify was related to his view that his voice would not be heard. Although it is true that the debate on this topic may indeed be considered 'closed' in various circles, including academia, where there has been in recent years a witch hunt targeting leftist academics as '*islamo-gauchistes*',[52] and accusing them of sympathising with terrorism, the situation in the trial was quite different. This was due to the openness of the judges to listening and the sociological makeup of the victims, as described previously. Moreover, it appears that there might be a misunderstanding regarding the role of expert witnesses in civil law trials. In contrast to the common law system, when an expert witness is summoned in a civil law trial, they are considered the witness of the court itself rather than a witness for a specific party, regardless of who calls them. The court typically does not know who specifically called the witness.

To leave the selection of expertise, the invitation of the parties is problematic in different regards. In mass crime trials, which have broader objectives than the repression of individual illegal acts, it seems essential to have sociological, historical, and political perspectives to understand the geopolitical context as well as the more local social structures that frame the crimes, facilitating the deciphering of the evidence and the identification of broader responsibilities, so that appropriate remedies, rehabilitation, and reparations can be provided. An interesting example of such practice is the Special jurisdiction (*Jurisdicción especial para la paz*) established in Bogotá, where no less than 100 social scientists (out of a thousand of employees) were hired as an integrated part of the tribunal in an effort to reconstruct the pattern of crimes, while placing the victims at the centre of the analysis.[53] In other places, social scientists were incorporated within judicial benches, and in prosecution offices, or as experts invited by the court to give testimonies.[54]

Why should justice be reduced only to the legal profession?

[51] Lahire, 2016. [52] Marlière, 2023.

[53] Field research and interviews at the Special Jurisdiction for Peace, February 2019.

[54] Seroussi, 2018; Holden, 2019; see Lefranc, 2021, *supra* note 17.

5.2.3 Establishing Criminal Responsibility

Osama Krayem, a Swedish/Palestinian man accused of being complicit, decided after a few weeks not to participate in the trial, maintaining his right to silence and refusing to appear in court. He justified his attitude in a letter read by his lawyer: 'I saw how the proceedings were going. And I have lost hope. I think that no one is looking for the truth, no one is here to understand. This trial is an illusion. I don't think that appearing in court will change anything about its outcome…'

Out of twenty defendants, only fourteen were present in the courtroom. Those tried *in absentia* were five defendants presumed dead and one who had not been extradited from Turkey. Half of the defendants were charged with very serious crimes for playing a major role in the attacks, including direct involvement and complicity. It was not obvious that these defendants would 'play the game' and participate in this justice project. For men who certainly know they are condemned to live part of their lives in prison, alongside other jihadists, what was the point of collaborating, of answering questions, particularly, at the risk of endangering their prison reputations? Indeed, the main defendant, Salah Abdelslam, had remained silent and uncooperative with investigators for six years. In addition, many of the defendants were awaiting trial in other countries where they face very long sentences for their involvement in other attacks such as those at Brussels Airport or on the Thalys train.[55] And as foreigners, from Belgium, Pakistan, and Sweden, some of them were unfamiliar with the French legal culture. Yet, surprisingly, only two defendants disengaged from the proceedings, invoking their right to silence. The others answered the questions asked by the judges, the prosecutors, and the victims' lawyers.[56]

The extended duration of proceedings in the assize court can, in certain circumstances, shed light on the course of the case also for the accused, and evoke feelings of regret and a desire for rehabilitation. In the Bataclan trial, it allowed the defendants to hear the victims over several weeks. For Abdeslam's lawyers, this lengthy duration was

[55] Regarding these attacks see: www.nytimes.com/2023/07/25/world/europe/brussels-terror-attacks-trial-2016.html; www.nytimes.com/2015/08/23/world/europe/thalys-train-attack-france-moroccan-suspect.html.

[56] On this use of trials as platforms for propaganda or narratives of injustice, see Choblet, 2022.

fundamental because it allowed to reveal nuances, which might have otherwise been missed. The victims were able to address him directly, and the public was able to hear what he had to say and to try to understand his path to radicalisation and violence. It also allowed for unexpected developments, such as his asking for forgiveness from the victims.[57]

What emerged during the hearings was the banality, not of evil, but more modestly, of men: how, from a dreadful general portrait of jihadists, we were brought to differentiate the defendants, by being introduced to their person, their family relationships, their friendships, and their ideology (or the lack of it). How, from being a group of friends who regularly meet in a neighbourhood bar and specialised in small drug trafficking, they became part of one of the most dangerous jihadist cells in Europe and were connected to the leaders of Islamic state of Iraq and Syria (ISIS) fighters in Syria. The accused had to face their families and consider the impact of their actions on their own environment.

5.2.3.1 Reconsidering?

One of the psychiatrists with whom Abdeslam met, Dr. Daniel Zagury, who testified in court, explained that the defendant was in 'permanent oscillation between becoming the young man of Molenbeek or remaining the soldier; between openness and hardening'.[58] According to him, Abdeslam was at risk of a psychological collapse if he was to question his own radical ideology. This is because this ideology justified his actions and provided him with a righteous justification, a shield.

This shield remained present at varying degrees during the trial. At the same time, being confronted with the victims, being exposed to medical-socio-political experts, and being faced with their own family and familiar environment facilitated a space where the defendants could view their actions from a different angle. Here, the trial could contribute to the rehabilitation of the defendant and, more broadly, reconstitution of the social bond.

Many of the defendants, including those with a high level of involvement, answered most of the questions posed by the judges and

[57] Field notes based on a discussion with his defence lawyers on the court stairs, 16 June 2022.

[58] Cited in Chesnelong, 2022, indicating that it was only during the trial that Salah Abdeslam agreed to meet with the two psychiatric experts appointed by the investigating judge.

victims, when they could have kept silent. Some of the defendants expressed how the victims' testimony influenced their willingness to talk. The courtroom provided a privileged space for this exchange: during the investigation, they were confined in isolation in prison, only interacting with security agents. However, during the ten-month trial, seven hours a day, they had listened to numerous victims and witnesses. Depending on the perspectives of the experts and witnesses, there was a potential risk of creating additional distance that might have led to a disengagement from the judicial process. This risk could materialise, if the experts of context were viewing the defendants as mere sociological objects manipulated by an external ideology, or if security service agents were portraying them as faceless figures within the matrix of a power hierarchy and network. To ensure the success of this process, an additional component was necessary.

The repressive stance of the prosecution and the demand for an exemplary sentence in the context of such an attack was not surprising. Yet, the line of demarcation between individual and collective responsibility, between direct participation, complicity, and support, was not always clear. The notion of complicity was transformed to broad understanding of direct participation, up to the prosecution's advancement of the 'interchangeability doctrine'.[59] The conviction of the main accused as a co-author of all attacks committed on 13 November 2015 in the various locations is based on an unprecedented extension of the notion of a 'single crime scene'.[60] This legal approach prompted the defence to argue that the fragmented examination of the facts, where all individuals involved were intertwined, may have established the overall coherence of the investigative file but did not effectively determine the individual responsibility of each accused. This, in their view, could lead to a form of 'impressionistic justice', as advocates Marie Dosé and Christian Saint

[59] Camille Hennetier, the state prosecutor, said in her final statements: 'Salah Abdeslam is responsible as a co-author of all the attacks. He is the only survivor of the commandos. There is little doubt that the attacks were a single, coordinated, and simultaneous action by a group whose members were interchangeable.'

[60] For a legal analysis of the ruling and the failure to clearly distinguish between the categories see: Alix, 2023: 'we move from the single scene of violence – unity of time, unity of place, unity of object – to a single scene of attack by considering that several massacre scenes committed in different places can constitute a single crime scene'. Yet only few critics 'were troubled by this double qualification – single attack scene and co-action – which perhaps reflects the idea that (French) criminal law is not suited to the attribution of mass crimes committed collectively'.

Palais out it. The defence lawyers stressed that they were not pleading 'for history' but for the defence of their individual client.

Individual criminal responsibility is also the result of a social reality. If this social reality does not diminish the criminal responsibility of the defendants in a criminal trial, it can provide a contextual explanation for the victims, the society, and the defendants, a necessary element for any form of rehabilitation process. If the trial also intends to create a space for the accused to question their actions by highlighting their consequences on people's lives, then the state should also acknowledge its responsibility in enabling the evolution of this social phenomenon. The recognition of such a societal structure could allow the accused, without risking the so-called psychic collapse, to reconsider their actions. But this is only possible if their actions are understood not only as the result of their own individual and ideological choices, as strongly portrayed in the trial, but also, in part, as the result of societal realities constructed (or at least facilitated) by the state. However, this differentiated analysis of the defendants came up against the limits imposed by the legal construction of the terrorist act during the trial.

5.2.4 Verdict and Punishment[61]

> *The sentences handed down appear to the Court to be necessary to punish extremely serious offences, sufficient to protect society, prevent the commission of further offences, and restore social equilibrium.*[62]

The Bataclan trial has, in its own way, become a memorial where the victims publicly exposed their suffering and their questions. The contribution of this 'historic' trial is supposed to respond to the 'duty to remember', but its contribution to creating a narrative that can be shared by all, at least shedding some light on the structural causes of terrorism, is less certain.[63]

After 148 days of hearings and closing statements from thirty defence lawyers, the verdict against the twenty defendants was rendered in a courtroom filled to capacity. It began with the judge declaring all defendants guilty.[64] While the hearings were deemed innovative, the

61 For a list of all sentences requested and pronounced, see in Annex 6A.4.

62 Verdict, at 111.

63 Gensburger and Lefranc, 2020; Faucher-King and Truc, 2022.

64 Although a technical incident disrupted the video transmission, and the filming was cut, the judge continued to read the decision. A few days later, the judge was filmed again reading the verdict for the recording before an empty room.

126-page court decision was disappointing from many perspectives. Far from echoing the diverse voices expressed in the 'forum', the decision was largely aligned with the logic of the prosecution – in particular by relating the trajectories of all the accused to the same process of religious radicalisation. Although, this trial presented an opportunity to account for complex trajectories and motivations. It linked together individuals motivated by the terrorist project and others driven to support them out of friendship, weakness, or opportunism. The trial hearings provided rich descriptions of the relationships of mutual obligation that bound the defendants together, portraying their lives as both ordinary and self-contained, both close to and distant from those of their fellow citizens, including Muslims. However, none of this appears in the court decision. The interpretation favoured was much simpler. The story told was that of individuals driven by ideologies of hatred and a process of religious radicalization, acting 'as one'. Such a discrepancy sparked criticism, including the unusual mobilization of eleven of the defence lawyers after their clients refused to appeal:

> The fate of twenty defendants was debated in forty-eight hours. These two days of deliberations resulted in the drafting of one hundred and twenty-six pages of motivation. The question arises: was there really room for debate in such a short space of time?… Our feeling is that these ten months of hearings have served no purpose in the final decision… It must be said that nothing seems to have been called into question.[65]

During the Bataclan trial, the central debate about the meaning of punishment opposed the prosecution against the defence. In its final pleading, the Prosecutor, with a direct reference to Durkheim, stated: 'Your verdict will not aim to repair the torn curtain or restore the victims' original peace. It will not heal the wounds, visible or invisible; it will not bring the dead back to life. But at the very least, it will assure them that here, justice and the law have the final say.'[66] The court is asked by the

[65] The defence lawyers in a collective opinion piece published in daily *Le Monde*, 18 July 2023, available at www.lemonde.fr/idees/article/2022/07/18/le-proces-des-attentats-du-13-novembre-n-a-pas-ete-exemplaire-et-les-droits-de-la-defense-ont-ete-malmenes_6135154_3232.html. This echoes the analyses of unfair and rough prosecutions of accused of terrorism: the trial of anyone labeled as terrorist, Robertson reminds us, cannot, by definition, be fair, but justice needs not to be rough. Robertson, 2007. See also, for a comparison, Ni Aolain and Gross, 2013.

[66] Hearing of 10 June 2022 (Camille Hennetier, counter terrorism prosecutor).

prosecution to 'eradicate' evil. 'Do not let your hand tremble!'[67] they are urged. Citing Durkheim, the State position is that it is impossible to react with moderation when the collective sentiments have been too severely violated.[68] This is the foundation of the Prosecution's central thesis of the 'single crime scene', where, according to the prosecutors, all members of the terrorist cell had interchangeable roles.

Everything opposes the prosecution's vision of an interchangeability of roles within the terrorist cell to that of the defence, which highlights the individualization of each man. The 'single crime scene', according to the defence, is a legal fiction that cannot indiscriminately encompass all the accused. The defence favours a reintegrative approach to punishment. According to them, these men are not all criminals, as some have renounced violence. Furthermore, they are not all 'enemies of society' since some disassociate themselves from jihadism or were never fully aligned with it. The life sentence without possibility of parole requested for Salah Abdeslam was seen as a 'white death sentence' that dishonours the State that abolished capital punishment.[69]

In the face of such opposition, the task of individualization ultimately falls to the judge. Their role is to judge specific individuals, while the prosecution generally fights on the frontlines of counterterrorism. The guarantee of balance lies in the principles of a fair trial, individualised by the judges and informed by the defence's work. The moment during the hearing when these two views converge is crucial. If the accused expresses a desire to reintegrate into the community, if they detach themselves from their act and their group, they mitigate the severity of their crime.

At the highest level of severity, the corresponding punishment will be of maximum length and without leniency. The major consequence is the tendency to attribute only one meaning to such sentences: the neutralization of dangerous individuals. Indeed, life sentences have been pronounced for the principal perpetrators, but these sentences were individualised for

[67] Ibid. [68] Durkheim, 1893, p. 55.

[69] In France, life sentences typically allow for parole consideration by a review committee after 18 years (with an average of 25 years), but exceptions exist for the gravest crimes, including terrorism, after 30 years. In the Bataclan case, Salah Abdeslam was sentenced to life without parole, the harshest penalty under French law, following the prosecutor request that he remains imprisoned indefinitely. According to EU law, "Life imprisonment is compatible with the European Convention on Human Rights, as long as prisoners have some chance of being released and it is possible for their sentences to be reviewed." www.coe.int/en/web/portal/-/new-factsheet-on-life-imprisonment-and-the-echr.

others. For the principal perpetrators, the sentences are severe and non-negotiable, with the courts implicitly adopting an 'eliminative' function of punishment. In the verdict, the paragraph is titled 'General Consideration on the Extreme Gravity of the Facts'. It mentions the word 'war' five times, enumerates the number of bullets fired, as well as the number of civil parties, but most importantly, the court goes on to outline the guiding principles behind its choice of sentences.

> It must be taken into account, with regard to the circumstances in which the described crimes were committed, for each convicted individual, the degree of involvement in the acts and their more or less strong adherence to jihadist ideology... The sentences pronounced appear to the Court necessary to punish the extremely serious acts, but sufficient for the protection of society, the prevention of new offenses, and the restoration of social balance.[70]

Here, we observe a concern for individualization in terms of involvement and ideological adherence. However, the resulting conception of punishment does not mention the perspective of social reintegration. The court, like the prosecution, emphasises the protection of society and, from a Durkheimian perspective, the 'restoration of social balance'. According to the court, the punishment of Abdeslam is not disproportionate given the magnitude of the crimes. He remains, the court wrote, trapped in his ideological cage. No future prediction is possible, given the persistence of his involvement in jihadism. His dangerousness remains intact. In this regard, for the Bataclan trial, the court imposed the most radical sentences in recent judicial history (six irreducible life sentences). In comparison, it is worth recalling that for war crimes and crimes against humanity, the ICC has never handed down life sentences. Conversely, the charge of 'terrorist criminal association' was withdrawn for one defendant in the Bataclan trial. The sentences were therefore individualised after a thorough examination of each person's responsibilities, but inclusion in FIJAIT (the automated file of terrorist offenders), when imposed, requires long-term monitoring after incarceration. Behind the judgment of guilt, dangerousness remains a constant concern.

Having imposed such a punishment is not surprising, but it contrasts strongly with the atmosphere and exchanges that unfolded during the ten months of hearings. 'If no rehabilitation is envisaged, why did we need to spend ten months in court?' asked one civil party observer.

[70] Bataclan Trial, Motivation Sheet.

5A Annex

5A.1 OLIVER KEMSLEY, A CIVIL PARTY WHO CAME DAILY TO COURT WRITES ABOUT THIS EXPERIENCE

I came to Paris from London for the weekend with a flatmate. We had arrived by Eurostar at Gare du Nord in the early evening on Friday, 13 of November 2015 left our things at the rental apartment, and then headed directly to the Bataclan. An hour later, when the terrorist attack occurred, I found myself trapped on the dance floor in a sea of bodies, having to try and escape out of the main hall under a rain of bullets into an internal staircase, through a skylight onto the building roof, then hide inside an apartment directly above the concert hall for the following hours.

I decided to come back to live in Paris six years after the attack, to attend the full ten-month trial, to witness a historic trial, and to see justice prevail for the victims, perhaps gaining a sense of 'closure' with this. The last time I was in the same room as many of the people sitting around me, we were scrambling for our lives while being shot at by three gunmen with Kalashnikovs. Now, as we sat in the (relative) calmness of a huge, purpose-built courtroom inside the Palais de Justice, I had the time to take in my surroundings.

Despite it being a historic trial of grand proportions within a different legal system from the one I had known growing up in the United Kingdom, I found it strange that there appeared to be several judges and prosecutors, instead of one of each. A pack of pistol-carrying gendarmes (French military police) constantly patrolled inside the courtroom, skulking up and down the main aisle. Including the armed gendarmes who sat behind the shoulders of each defendant in the box, on some days, there were more guns in the courtroom than victims. The sheer number of lawyers surprised me too, sometimes over 200 present. I was amazed that every defendant had between two and four lawyers representing him. The French Legal Aid budget was clearly a generous one!

The media section of the courtroom was large, with around fifty journalists present daily (plus another neighbouring courtroom dedicated to the journalist overspill where they could watch the trial live feed projected onto a screen). Generally, I avoided reading any of the media coverage of the trial. The few occasions I did, however, I found several of the lawyers – and prosecutors – had done 'exclusive' interviews with various media outlets regarding themselves, their personal histories, and their 'important' role in the trial. Often accompanied by photographs of the lawyers themselves, many of the articles had a strong whiff of self-promotion. Legal duty and personal aspirations of celebrity seemed to blur.

One of the biggest surprises for me was the sheer casualness of the audience gallery. Attendees (in the majority, victims of the attacks) could come and go as they pleased during the court session. Chit-chat was permitted among those watching. Audience members could wear whatever they wanted to: from Hawaiian shirts with bermuda shorts, to t-shirts scrawled with expletives and tracksuit bottoms. There was no written or unwritten dress code like in UK courts, and this suited me just fine. The audience regularly made collective reactionary sounds: gasps, tuts, utters of 'non', or even raucous laughter. The Judge's tolerance threshold for this seemed extremely high. Only once, when there had been two rounds of rapturous applause among the gallery, did the judge actually intervene to reprimand (and this was only because of an official complaint from the defence lawyers). People often put their feet up on the bench in front. One audience member stuck up visual diagrams of the defendants every day on the wall and the bench space surrounding him. During one particularly dreary court session, I noticed the person to my right price-comparing flights to Italy on her mobile, the person in front of me sleeping, and the person to my left perusing a broadsheet newspaper. When a trial spans 150 days across ten months, allowing the audience such freedoms of relaxation made sense.

I was not prepared for how often debates between opposing lawyers (and the judge) would descend into lung-busting slinging matches. With vicious finger-pointing and theatrical arm-waving, lawyers would regularly shout over each other, and the permitted threshold for this level of tension seemed unbelievably high. A particularly vociferous day culminated in several minutes of chaotic shouting between the defence lawyers and the judge, with neither party willing to back down. The judge temporarily suspended the court. Upon our return to the courtroom, one of the forty or so defence lawyers stood up and announced that they were all exiting the courtroom in protest of what they believed to be incompetence of the Judge. Twenty minutes later, I saw a lot of them drinking in the pub across the road.

Nor had I been quite prepared for just how deferential the treatment of the defendants would be. The men in the box regularly interjected into proceedings, without genuine reprimand. I remember clearly when one defendant (the only surviving terrorist from the night of the attacks) stood up and declared calmly to the judge, 'I'm sorry, Monsieur Le President, but I think the way that you speak to women is disrespectful'. In another instance, a defendant demanded for the courtroom lighting to be adjusted to suit his tastes better, and so the judge immediately acted on the request. Midway into the trial, several of the defendants decided they weren't really in the mood for appearing in the courtroom box, and so they were permitted to stay each day in the holding cell elsewhere in the building instead, which would delay court proceedings by hours as signatures and paperwork had to be completed each time this happened.

It was highly commendable that every single victim was allowed to come and speak. I also found it extremely interesting hearing the former President and other political figures being summoned to testify, and was impressed by the way these figures could be rigorously questioned by lawyers without any apparent deference. Former prosecutors, academic experts, and even civil servants overseeing youth activities in the Brussels suburbs where some of the defendants had grown up also came to the stand. Discussions concerning radicalisation, marginalisation, and geopolitics all came to the fore. It strayed far away from the tighter, evidence-focused procedures I had generally presumed trials to be.

Given the extraordinary, 'no expense spared' budget allocated to the trial, the lack of ability of the courtroom translators was often farcical.[71] One kept translating 'le massacre' as 'moussaka'. The earpiece technology also regularly malfunctioned, so the translations would disappear altogether. As the months of the trial passed, I learned and improved my own French so that I could survive without the misfiring translations.

The day of the verdict was extremely chaotic. The courtroom was at its 500+ capacity early, and there was a mosh-pit of victims (including myself), lawyers, and journalists scrambling to gain entry at the

[71] Interprets were providing simultaneous translation for foreign civil parties.

Figure 5.3 In this drawing, Oliver Kemsley portrays Sharon Weill, one of the authors of the book, whom he met during the trial proceedings. He was invited to her class to discuss his reflections on the trial with students.[72]

courtroom doors, captured on camera by the adjacent pen of paparazzi. The quickness and the severity of the Judge's verdict were jarring, completely at odds with the in-depth, wide-reaching, and nuanced trial we had experienced. The trial had provided drama, spectacle, and an unrestricted platform for victims to have their moment to speak publicly, but there had been no real revelations into the defendants' motives nor any major shifts in their individual culpability from the start of the trial to the finish. As I exited the courtroom for the last time, I couldn't help wondering whether, given all this, the trial could have been completed in six weeks rather than ten months.

[72] For more of his sketches/drawings from the tribunal: https://photos.app.goo.gl/jo4DPTtaKLM4aSSr7 Photos from the tribunal: https://photos.app.goo.gl/NUitvi41ZFi5QDU66.

CHAPTER SIX

FINAL REFLECTIONS

In September 2021, when the Bataclan trial in Paris began, the United States was commemorating the twentieth anniversary of the September 11 attacks in New York. The proximity of these two dates invites us to reflect on the two different responses to terrorism on either side of the Atlantic. Both responses followed the most severe and unprecedented shock experienced by both societies since World War II, and yet the responses are starkly different. By examining different themes, we can see how these two countries have mobilised their judicial systems and the extent to which their trials were anchored in a geography, legal culture, and an audience. This will also allow us to see the different ways of revealing 'the truth' and ultimately 'doing justice'. The first part of the chapter examines these approaches and, more broadly, the historical role of such trials. In the second part, we reflect on the lessons that can be learned from the French Experience for the prosecution of mass crimes. Lastly, we conclude with reflections on the French judicial response to terrorism during the global war on terror.

6.1 THE 9/11 AND BATACLAN TRIALS: A TRIAL FOR HISTORY OR AN EXPERIENCE TO FORGET?

The first difference concerns the locations where the trials took place. In Paris, the trial of the November 13 attackers took place on Île de la Cité, near Notre-Dame, where justice has been rendered in France for a millennium. Located in the city centre, the trial was easily accessible, with tourists still able to visit the Sainte-Chapelle, situated in the courtyard of the *Palais de Justice*, and cafés around the courthouse, often unaware that a trial was taking place. Hundreds of professionals were involved in this legal work on a daily basis, alongside numerous accredited media outlets covering the trial with intense national and international attention. The location of the trial facilitated the access of hundreds of victims, members of the media, the general public, as well as the three defendants who were not in custody, and entered through the same entrances as the public.

A second difference concerns the ordinary versus exceptional procedure. In Paris, the judges and lawyers conducted the proceedings as they would in a regular trial.

Legal debates over charges highlighted the intensity of the adversarial proceedings. The criminal hearings ultimately reaffirmed the values of the rule of law, which may have been diluted during the administrative and police phases of the criminal trial. It was an inclusive trial, given the high number of victims and the emotional impact on the country, and everything was designed to facilitate their participation. During the civil parties' testimony phase, victims rose from their dedicated benches, approached the stand, and silently returned to their seats after testifying. The extended oral procedure of the Assize Court allowed for an in-depth exploration of the defendants' personal backgrounds, revealing moments of intimacy, and insights into their paths to radicalisation.

Nevertheless, a sense of 'justice of exception' persisted: police witnesses remained anonymous, long detentions in isolation under the state of emergency granted security forces extensive leeway, and a substantial security apparatus protected the court proceedings. However, within this secured framework, fair trial guarantees were supposed to be secured through the ordinary criminal law process. Lawyers argued 'ordinarily', with case files in hand, and without challenging the court's authority. The judicial routine and professional 'habitus' facilitated dialogue among the judges, prosecutors, and defence attorneys, demonstrating a commitment to thorough exploration. The historical significance of the trial, its collective function, helped to create a common aim for the trial to be conducted in the best possible way.

In Guantanamo, nothing appears to be 'ordinary'. On the military base of the island, the 'expeditionary judicial complex' persists over twenty years later. It remains the most visible symbol of America's response to 9/11. Among the dozens of persons still detained after two decades are five defendants from the 9/11 trial, who were arrested in 2003, charged in 2012, and are yet still in the preliminary stages of the trial.

The court, akin to a fortified camp, is set on the island's old airstrip. A special courtroom was constructed for the 9/11 trial, with benches for the five defendants positioned centrally. The courtroom was designed to maximise control: a glass barrier separates the small public gallery from the main courtroom, introducing a forty-second audio delay to allow the judge or security to censor the feed if necessary. The court's remote location from the crime scenes makes access extremely difficult – requiring Pentagon authorisation, military flights from Washington, and on-site stays for the entire duration of the hearings. The media and NGOs are housed in military tents or disused hangars, departing on a military flight back to Washington after each session.

Hearings are often cancelled for various technical, health, or legal reasons. Defence lawyers also deliberately prolong the proceedings with numerous technical motions. As one lead defence attorney stated, 'given that the electric chair awaits my client at the end of this trial, I have no interest in bringing it to a conclusion; there are so many procedural issues to resolve that the trial may never actually begin'.[1] The lengthy timeline results in high turnover among participants, further complicating the trial. Over time, media and victim interest have waned, and few Americans are even aware of the ongoing process.

The 9/11 trial is not held for the victim nor for American society in general, despite the fact that one high-level perpetrator is on trial. The main defendant, Khalid Sheikh Mohammed ('KSM'), is alleged to have been the mastermind behind 9/11. With a defendant of such significance, conducting a secretive trial is, in fact, a deprivation of citizens of access to the truth. In the collective imagination, this tribunal unfolds in a 'black hole' – the elusive Delta Camp of Guantanamo, where any visual is forbidden, rendering the entire trial not only inaccessible but surreal. In Paris, there was equally a surrealist dimension, such as posthumously trying to accuse persons who are now deceased, like Fabien Clain, whose targeted killing was carried out by French armed forces in Syria in 2019 and was widely covered by the French media.

[1] Field research notes, interview with head of defence unit at the Pentagon, 30 April 2016. Cited also in Weill and Robinson, 2020.

Yet another major difference concerns the space allocated to the defendants in both procedures. First, in Guantanamo, we do not hear them. Second, the proceedings in the context of the September 11 trial are fraught with complications: the defendants are both perpetrators of mass crimes and victims of the CIA's torture programs. Thus, over the past decade, the focus of the procedure has shifted, largely due to the defence, towards treating the accused as victims and scrutinising the role of the United States in developing torture programs worldwide, rather than delivering justice to those who suffered in the attacks.

A final difference concerns the role of political players and, ultimately, the State. In Guantanamo, exception has become the norm. The secrecy surrounding the military commissions is aimed at concealing information about the CIA's torture program and the conditions of detention that the accused have faced since their arrests in 2003. This is why the proceedings are kept far from public scrutiny, under the total control of the military and the CIA. In 2009, Barack Obama sought to close this prison and transfer the cases to New York, their natural jurisdiction. However, the only trial transferred experimentally faced numerous obstacles, including issues related to the independence of federal court judges.

In conclusion, both trials in question have been deemed historic. However, their underlying objectives differ greatly. Despite the U.S. military prosecutor's initial statement that this was 'the most important trial since Nuremberg', it appears that one of the goals in the United States is to forget this dark chapter of American justice. Thus, in the United States, memories and historical narratives are not constructed through the trial itself but through other means, such as museums and memorials. Indeed, while a trial can establish a judicial truth, the aim, in the U.S. case, is not to fulfill all of the expectations in terms of reparations and restoration. Other American institutions, beyond the trial and the judges, carry out such tasks. The spotlight is not on the military commissions at Guantanamo but rather on the reparations for damages resulting from the September 11 attacks.

Meanwhile, in Paris, the active involvement of victims, the accessibility and its public dimension, transformed much of the trial into a kind of 'truth commission', transforms much of the trial into a kind of 'truth commission', similar to those observed in Argentina or South Africa, providing victims with the opportunity to recount their experiences without time constraints, the defendants to speak, the politicians to be questioned and the experts to explain. It was a trial, where the whole country was invited to watch justice being made. For some victims, the passage of time has allowed them to begin healing from their physical and psychological wounds, with the trial serving as a means to close this chapter of their recovery. The criminal court offers a space for both direct and indirect victims to speak at the witness stand. Driven by the demands of the civil parties to attempt to understand how a crime of such magnitude could occur, high-profile security figures are called to testify, including intelligence agents, police officers, geopolitical experts, and even the former President of the Republic.

6.2 TRIALS AND MEMORY

France has decided to turn the 'historic terrorism trials' into societal moments. France has chosen to extend its major terrorism trials in both space and time. They have been called 'historic' because of the societal resonance of the attacks and the expectation for justice. Criminal trials are no longer conceived as theatre with unity of place, time, and space. Instead, they become 'augmented' judicial events with new devices. A web radio broadcasts the proceedings almost live, at the request of victim associations. Accredited journalists relay the trial in real-time via live tweeting. A broad audience was thus able to follow the proceedings through digital networks and foreign press websites. Alongside this augmented judicial space, there is a strong will to inscribe these major trials in time. Aware of this historical legacy, France chose to record audio-visual footage of the trials for judicial archives created at the initiative of former French Minister of Justice, Robert Badinter.[2] The recording reveals this desire to include terror trials as part of these 'historic' trials of the past, and therefore to extend the trial over time, but on the other hand, it also shows a certain danger in turning the Charlie Hebdo and Bataclan trials into a spectacle. The first filmed trials in Nuremberg (1945) and Jerusalem (1961) granted bold freedom to filmmakers. In contrast, France assigns a strictly archival function to filmed images, with strict rules: following the procedure, fixed cameras, no cutaway shots. By eliminating co-presence, this setup is inspired by video surveillance.[3] Originally planned for World War II crimes and crimes against humanity, the Badinter law allowed for the preservation of the so-called second purge trials: those of Nazi,

[2] Law of 11 July 1985, known as the Badinter Law.
[3] Lindeperg, 2012 and Gorce, 2023.

Klaus Barbie (1987), militia leader, Paul Touvier (1994), and Vichy official, Maurice Papon (1997–1998) and, later, the trials relating to the Tutsi genocide in Rwanda. This exception, to allow filming, has been applied for the first time to terrorism cases, starting with the Charlie Hebdo trial. Filming the trials is a notable exception to the French approach of the 'orality of the debate', where there is no transcription. However, the films are not broadcast to the public and remain in the archives for fifty years, not easily accessible to the public.

How can we understand this French reluctance to publicly broadcast the trial and to embrace transparency? This debate must be viewed through the lens of judicial culture. In countries with a Romano-Germanic tradition, criminal justice is inquisitorial, meaning that it is conducted by an investigating judge who builds their case in great secrecy. As a product of an inquisitorial system dominated by the secrecy of written proceedings, the public aspect of trials is not as common. Orality is only required in the trial hearing phase. Since one cannot follow the debates and there are no transcripts, the trial is concentrated on the verdict, which condenses and reduces judicial performativity.[4] In common law countries, by contrast, justice is understood as the result of an adversarial debate open to the public. 'Justice must not only be done, but also be seen to be done.' In the United States, trials can be filmed under the authority of the judge, and since 1991, a TV channel (*Court TV*) has been dedicated to broadcasting them. This reflects the spirit of transparent justice, as evidenced by the publication of dissenting opinions within the judgments themselves. Here, understanding the decision-making process is an integral part of the quality of the verdict. In terms of transparency, France lags behind: even the GTMO commission website provides access to thousands of documents and transcripts of the proceedings, while in France it is hardly possible, even for experienced researchers, to obtain access to much more banal and supposedly public documents. At the same time, the filmed image enters a memorial temporality, allowing it to be integrated into the future Museum and Memorial of Terrorism,

4 'The access to "images of justice" is not only perceived as a right of journalists but also as a right of citizens to be informed and to benefit from transparent justice. Spain . . . is currently the only European country that allows cameras to have full access to courtrooms, within a specific legal framework that ensures a balance between the right to information and the respect for the principle of public hearings.' For more on this constitutional jurisprudence, see Gheorghe, 2010.

scheduled to open in 2027, and to be accessible to future generation to study these trials against the ethos constructed.[5]

6.3 WHAT ARE THE LESSONS THAT CAN BE LEARNED FROM THE FRENCH EXPERIENCE FOR PROSECUTION OF MASS CRIMES?

Our premise is that the Bataclan judicial experiment, both in its innovations and its limitations, could offer a new paradigm for mass crimes prosecution, opening the door to transitional and restorative justice approaches within criminal prosecution with the following three main takeaways.

6.3.1 Active Participation of Victims and Defendants

Transitional and restorative justice mechanisms stress the importance of victims playing an active role in the justice mechanism, either individually or collectively. Beyond their own process of rehabilitation and reconstruction as active agents rather than passive victims, this role is also important for the rehabilitation of perpetrators. It allows perpetrators to connect faces and destinies to their actions, acknowledging the human repercussions of their acts. Creating a platform where the perpetrator can express themselves can help replace violence with oral expression.[6]

It appears that civil law legal traditions are often better designed to achieve these goals, as their procedures already allow for victim participation and place a strong emphasis on orality. Consider, for example, the trial in Senegal of former Chadian dictator Hissène Habré for crimes against humanity,[7] the Special Court in Cambodia,[8] and the Special Jurisdiction for Peace in Colombia. All these mechanisms allowed for important victim participation, as they originated from civil law. Victims in these trials were regrouped in associations to facilitate their representation. In contrast, in the Bataclan trial, everyone was free to choose his/her representation individually or collectively.

Victim participation is an essential component of a fair (restorative) trial. Allowing space for victims within the legal process, including

[5] See the website www.musee-memorial-terrorisme.fr.

[6] In other trials observed, defendants thank the court for being able to listen to them, to have the time to do so. See Salas and Weill, 2021.

[7] See Weill et al., 2020. [8] See Sperfeldt, 2022.

accommodating their emotions and ensuring their active legal rights, does not necessarily conflict with the rights of the defence and the presumption of innocence. It is possible, as the Bataclan trial demonstrated to some degree, to find a balance between these two fundamental aspects of justice by carefully crafting legal processes and procedures.[9] Victim participation and defence rights are complementary rather than contradictory. Nevertheless, questions remain regarding the balance between the two, with the defendants' testimony set in an atmosphere imbued with the suffering of the victims and the emotions that flow from it.

6.3.2 Narratives and Emotions: Placing People, at the Centre of the Process

The legal procedure went beyond technical exchanges among lawyers; instead, it revolved around giving voice to the central figures in the trial. A restorative process inevitably affects the language habitually used by the courts. The court managed to achieve a delicate balance between adhering to standard legal procedures and allowing space for victims' and defenders' narratives, thereby moving criminal proceedings closer to the restorative approaches observed in truth commissions or restorative justice settings that facilitate face-to-face meetings between victims and offenders. Our premise is that a trial can encompass both emotions and fairness. A trial can be both emotional and just. The emotions of victims and accused should gain their place within the justice process as they are an integral part of it.[10] Instead of attempting to conceal them by deeming them irrelevant or, worse, an obstacle to justice, it is better to allow their expression and take them into account, especially when dealing with such violent events. Emotions are a part of the reality, the *truth*, and both victims and perpetrators have a right to access (and express) that facet of the truth. This is not to suggest that the accused will not receive a fair trial in terms of establishing facts and legal responsibilities impartially. This is what judges do; they can make a distinction between relevant and irrelevant considerations while dealing with their own emotions. Yet, here, too, questions arise, particularly in relation to the risk of making emotions the basis of the

[9] See Weill and Sulzer, 2021.

[10] Their emotions, *all* their emotions. The judges have in fact favored the expression of certain emotions (traumatic suffering) to the detriment of others (anger). See Lefranc, 2022b.

sentence, to the detriment of the accused, who may be relegated to the role of guilty parties.

6.3.3 Integrating Social Scientists in the Legal Procedures to Understand the Social Context and Political Environment

It seems crucial in trials of such magnitude to include knowledge from social sciences, such as history, sociology, and criminology. If the trial aims not only to establish criminal responsibility of individuals but also situate such violence in a broader social framework – to understand its roots and structuring, and the possible roles of the state not only in managing violence, reducing and preventing it, but also in producing it – it is highly questionable whether trials should be left only to the legal discipline. A simplistic reading of actions while establishing 'legal truth'[11] could be enriched by a greater participation of social scientists. Their poor representation at the Bataclan trial can be explained by their refusal to respond to random invitations from (random) lawyers in a context where the social sciences are reductively seen as 'excusing' offenders.[12] Here again, the criminal trials of mass violence could draw inspiration from the mechanisms of transitional justice. Truth commissions, for example, include academics from the outset – historians, psychologists, sociologists – as much or even more than jurists. In the Colombian Special Jurisdiction for Peace, 100 social scientists and experts are working within the court, with the pre-trial judges, to construct the macro cases and the pattern of violence based on the victims' experiences. Why deprive the justice system of such a complementary perspective, when it must judge acts that are part of individual life histories as well as broader socio-political processes, on a national and international scale?

[11] In its decision, the court determined that Abdeslam did not detonate his explosive belt because it malfunctioned, and this was the reason for the failed detonation, rather than him being 'full of humanity', as he had claimed. However, the possibility that he simply did not want to kill himself or was afraid to do so did not appear to be considered in the court's decision.

[12] Already in 2015, two weeks after the 13 November attacks, then Prime Minister Manuel Valls declared: 'I've had enough of those who are constantly looking for excuses or cultural or sociological explanations for what happened'; and also stated later in January during a tribute to the victims of the Hyper Cacher/Charlie Hebdo attacks: 'There can be no valid explanation. Because to explain is already to try to excuse a little.'

6.3.4 Judging Terrorism in France – At the Frontiers of Ordinary Justice, Specialised Justice, and the Justice of Exception

What is the role of the French judiciary in the context of the fight against terrorism? Despite terrorism cases being prosecuted in a political context of repressive and harsh prosecution policies developed alongside the global war on terror and its transitional architecture, the routine of regular criminal procedure has enabled a certain resistance on the part of the judges to this repressive position, and with them, the resilience of the rule of law. Should we speak of an evolution towards a 'justice of exception', or have we remained within a rule-of-law framework that preserves civil liberties, the right to a fair trial, and rehabilitation objectives when sentencing? The answer is not unequivocal. In this book, we show that policies and practices that have been shaped by various actors consist of arbitrating between a logic of suspicion and prevention, and a concern for justice. It seems to us that the French justice system, in the context of the fight against terrorism, lies between three pillars: its exceptional status, the heavy tendency towards specialisation, and the routine functioning of ordinary justice. With the prosecution of major terrorist attacks, we have also witnessed the evolution of hybrid justice, where victims, defendants, political figures, and experts share the space created by this forum.

Faced with the deadliest terrorist attacks in its history, France enacted the longest state of emergency since the Algerian War. Extended five times, the country remained under this regime for more than two years. With the state of emergency, legal boundaries were blurred. Many of its liberty-restricting measures were subsequently incorporated into ordinary law, such as administrative searches, house arrests, and marginalisation of the judiciary. By authorising the executive to take measures that infringe on freedoms, the rule of law has been weakened, and the separation of powers has been threatened. In this context, the fight against terrorism is undeniably marked by a combative approach. During this period, the term 'war' recurs constantly in political discourse. We have seen how terrorism and its random violence have led to a paradigm shift in the legal system: dangerousness carries more weight than proven guilt, perceived risk more than acts committed, and prevention more than suppression. This, *a priori*, undermines the notion of criminal justice, since it is traditionally understood as intervening after the fact. When the main goal becomes anticipation, to be effective, it cannot be concerned with legal obstacles. This pre-emptive justice is based not on the act and its causes, but on an interpretation of the signs identified as being preparatory to the crime. The growing role of intelligence services, and with the constant use of AMT as the main means of incrimination, symbolises this shift. This broad incrimination net encompasses the entire range of roles within a terrorist cell. The defence contests this 'legal impressionism', which substitutes hypotheses for evidence and dilutes guilt into dangerousness. While this debate ran through all the hearings, the suspect is seen as a dangerous individual, and the sentence must be dissuasive to respond to collective concerns. The mistrust with which their statements are perceived, along with suspicions of taqiya, is indicative. Clearly, we have moved away from liberal criminal law, which is based on the principle of legality. The paradigm shift is clear: henceforth, the assessment of dangerousness matters more than legally established guilt, risk outweighs the act committed, and prevention takes precedence over punishment.

Within this climate of suspicion,[13] we have observed an increasing institutional specialisation. The French judicial system has been profoundly reformed to respond to terrorism to construct a uniform, expert, and hierarchical judicial task force. It has centralised prosecutions with the creation of the National Anti-Terrorist Prosecutor's Office (PNAT) in 2019 and has specialised more and more the trial courts, which have developed their own analytical tools (such as the categories of 'returnees' and 'presumed dead'), allowing for the profiling of individuals. In Chapter 3, we have discussed how the 16th Chamber of the lower courts has specialised and created the first case law based on constructed expertise, with defence lawyers who have de facto become specialised. Chapter 4 demonstrated that, as a push back against the initial resistance of Assize court judges to the prosecution policy, the non-specialised nature of the judges was modified, and a special list of

[13] President Macron called for the 'whole nation's' vigilance, encouraging everyone to develop a 'good listening attitude towards the other' to 'know how to detect weaknesses, deviations, whether at school, at work, in places of worship. These small moves signalling a drift away from the values of the Republics . . . these little things which become huge tragedies'. He was thus inviting everyone to take responsibility for detecting the signs of radicalisation, widening the scope of prevention to the entire population. According to Ragazzi, 'the fight against terrorism is in the hands of security professionals (intelligence, police, attorneys, judges), while policies preventing terrorism seek to mobilise society at large to counter radicalisation processes' (2016: 153).

judges was created. These judges, whom we have increasingly seen on the benches, were also granted access to case files.

With specialisation and expertise also comes rigidity. The accused are repeatedly confronted with their actions, not with their retrospective interpretations of them. Hesitations before committing the act, their claimed disengagement, or their disobedience to the cell's orders are often dismissed as 'fables' that do not convince. Their explanations during the hearing, their empathy for the victims, and even their pleas for forgiveness seem to hold little weight. The evidence gathered in the case file, articulated by police witnesses, prevails. In most of the trials, the prosecutor requested the maximum punishment and systematic appeal. The ultimate goal of this specialisation is the narrative coherence of terrorism-related jurisprudence, especially regarding sentencing. This specialised judicial system is meant to guarantee the imposition of higher sentences.

However, this tendency should be understood in a nuanced way. Despite repressive legislation and prosecution policies, the principle of a fair trial remains a reality, alongside the values of the rule of law, which had been diluted during the administrative and police phases of the criminal process. The ethnography highlighted the crucial significance of trials for the accused to narrate their stories and for the public to hear them. We witnessed the 'ordinariness' of the trials, where the defendants had the opportunity to present their voices and personal paths. The trial was the only platform where such narratives could be heard in such a meaningful manner. The defence lawyers draw out the biographies of their clients, and the testimony of their relatives and even of experts such as sociologists who stress the counterproductive effects of imprisonment. More often than not, lawyers proceed as they would in an ordinary case. The arguments focus on the weak points of the charge, namely the degree of criminal intent. The accused is no longer an enemy but a person subject to trial. The majority of the defendants want to explain and defend themselves. The major difference with previous terrorist trials in France is the absence of a rupture defence, meaning a radical challenge to the legitimacy of the court. Instead, the defence in current terrorism trials focuses primarily on challenging the charges in the indictment and the heavy sentences requested. Facing the accusation, lawyers fight on three fronts: recounting the irreducible humanity of the accused, contesting the broad incriminations, and denouncing the disproportionate sentences.

Conducting an ethnography within this court provides a rare insight into the radicalisation process of the accused individuals, as recounted by various actors. During our research, we observed that the Assise court's procedure facilitated the emergence of narratives that had an unexpected impact on the final decisions of the judges: the court came to know the accused more closely, revealing a more complex reality. It is within the inherent tension that emerges between harsh legal categories and the prosecution policy on the one hand, and the individual experiences and singular trajectories on the other hand, that the judges who form and perform justice position themselves and gradually define their own role. Chapter 4 has shown that imposing the prosecution policy involves a clash of positions within the judicial profession. This struggle around the prosecution policy demonstrates that 'justice' does not speak with one voice; on the contrary, it is made up of different actors with different professional interests and their own personal way of doing things. Judges considered those accused who they viewed as taking steps towards the construction of the truth. At the sentencing stage, they distinguish between those who distance themselves from their group and express a desire to reintegrate into the social pact. The punishment they receive may then retain a rehabilitative perspective. However, if, on the contrary, their silence or statements reflect a desire to break away, the sentence will be more severe.[14]

In the major trials, we observed how the democratic dimension of the fair trial was expressed through the judicial ritual. While trials are expected to be transparent and accessible, they heavily rely on classified information held by security agencies. The management of secrecy in these trials raises critical questions about the information disclosed and what remains hidden. We observed how trials are embedded within this paradox, being both public and secret. In this context, the role of victims/civil parties was predominant. In their quest for truth and justice, they summoned public authorities and administrations – including the President, Ministry of the Interior, Mayors, and Intelligence Services – to court, questioning and challenging them extensively, often in collaboration with defence lawyers, in open court. During these trials, decision-makers in the state were held to account for contradictions, including intelligence service failures. As discussed in Chapter 5, the criminal arena transformed into a democratic forum.

[14] See for example, Charlie Hebdo Trial, court decision, December 16, 2020.

It is rare for political or judicial leaders to answer for their actions before a court, giving these proceedings an unprecedented democratic dimension. It is as if the excessive suffering imposed on the victims has authorised them to question the decision-makers through their lawyers, even though nothing had previously predisposed them to play such an active role. Indeed, the accused are not the sole bearers of responsibility; they are embedded in broader socio-political constructions. Revealing and understanding these structures, while humanising victims, are essential steps toward their rehabilitation, a process in which criminal trials can play a central role.

6A Annex

TABLE 6A.1 Proceedings Observed in the Assize Court (2017–2019)

	Defendants	Facts/accusation	1st instance hearing	Appeal hearing
1	Four defendants S., R., K. and N.	Hostage-taking of the family of a postal worker in Seine-et-Marne in April 2013 with a view to financing an attack	13–22 February 2017 Eight days of hearings	Appeal only for N Prosecutor's appeal 27–29 March 2018 three days of hearings
2	Twenty accused Cannes-Torcy Network	Several acts, including throwing a grenade into a kosher grocery shop in Sarcelles in September 2012; and the planning of a terror attack after returning from Syria.	20 April–22 June 2017 Forty-two hearing days	None
3	Five defendants from the family G.: two parents and three children	Tried in absentia.	20 April 2017 One day of hearing	None
4	Two defendants: M., and M.	The terror attacks perpetrated by Mouhamed Merah (who was killed) in Montauban and Toulouse. Including the shooting in front of the Jewish school, resulting in four deaths on 19 March 2012. It was the first jihadist attack in France.	2 October–2 November 2017 Twenty-three hearing days	Prosecutor's appeal 25 March–18 April 2019 Nineteen hearing days
5	Two defendants: A. and B.	Two returnees from Brittany. Were in Syria from December 2013 to June 2014	19–23 March 2018 Five days of hearings	Prosecutor's appeal 12–15 November 2019 Five hearing days

6	Two defendants Q., and D.	Two returnees from Toulouse. Were in Syria in June–August 2013	3–6 April 2018 Four days of hearings	Prosecutor's appeal 2–6 December 2019 Four hearing days
7	Five women and ten men	Defendants from the Lyon suburbs. Departure to Syria during the period of 2013–2014	12–30 November 2018 Fifteen days of hearings	None
8	One defendant, O.	A returnee from Créteil Facts: May–June 2014	19–23 November 2018 Five days of hearings	Prosecutor's appeal 25–29 November 2019 Five hearing days

TABLE 6A.2 Observation of the 'The Trial for History' in specially designated courtrooms (2020–2022)

Trial	Defendants	Dates	Courtroom
The Charlie Hebdo Trial	Fourteen defendants (of which three are in *abstensia*)	2 September–13 December 2020 Three months of hearings during COVID	The New Courthouse 'Les Batignole'
The Bataclan Trial	Twenty defendants (of which six were in *abstensia*: one was detained in Turkey, and five presumed dead)	8 September 2021–27 June 2022 148 hearing days	Temporary specially built courtroom at the 'Palais de la Justice'

TABLE 6A.3 The Charlie Hebdo trial: penalties

Found responsible for terrorism related crimes:

1. Ali Riza Polat (for crimes committed in connection with a terrorist enterprise):
   Sentence requested: Life imprisonment with a twenty-two-year irreducible security period.
   First-instance sentence: Thirty years of criminal imprisonment with a two-third security period for complicity in murder related to Amedy Coulibaly and the Kouachi brothers.
   Appeal sentence: Life imprisonment with a twenty-year irreducible security period.
2. Amar Ramdani: Sentence requested: Seventeen years of criminal imprisonment with a two-third security period for participation in a criminal terrorist organisation.
   First-instance sentence: Twenty years with a two-third security period.
   Appeal sentence: Thirteen years of imprisonment with a two-third security period.
3. Nezar Mickaël Pastor Alwatik (for participation in a criminal terrorist organisation):
   Sentence requested: Twenty years of criminal imprisonment with a two-third security period.
   Sentence pronounced: Eighteen years of criminal imprisonment with a two-third security period.
4. Willy Prevost (for participation in a terrorist organisation):
   Sentence requested: Eighteen years of criminal imprisonment with a two-third security period.
   Sentence pronounced: Thirteen years of criminal imprisonment.

Tried *in abstensia* (presumed dead in Syria):

5. Hayat Boumedienne (She is the widow of Coulibaly, and was tried for participation in a terrorist organisation and financing terrorism).
   Sentence pronounced: Thirty years of criminal imprisonment with a two-third security period, and an arrest warrant maintained.
6. Mohamed Belhoucine (for complicity in murder related to a terrorist enterprise). Sentence pronounced: Life imprisonment with a two-third security period, and an arrest warrant maintained.
7. Mehdi Belhoucine: The court recalls that he 'participated in combat' there, although 'no evidence allows for certainty in considering him deceased' in Syria. However, he was already judged and sentenced for terrorist criminal association (AMT) in January 2020, he cannot be sentenced again.

Sentences pronounced for offenses not related to terrorism:

8. Christophe Raumel (for participation in a criminal organisation unrelated to terrorism):
   Sentence requested: Five years of imprisonment.
   Sentence pronounced: Four years of imprisonment.
9. Said Makhlouf:
   Sentence requested: Thirteen years for participation in a terrorist criminal organisation.
   Sentence pronounced: Eight years of imprisonment for participation in a regular criminal organisation.
10. Mohamed-Amine Farés:
    Sentence requested: Seven years for participation in a regular criminal organisation.
    Sentence pronounced: Eight years of imprisonment for participation in a criminal organisation.
11. Michel Catino (for participation in a terrorist criminal organisation):
    Sentence requested: Fifteen years with a two-third security period and a ban from French territory.
    Sentence pronounced: Five years of imprisonment for participation in a common criminal organisation.
12. Metin Karasular:
    Sentence requested: Fifteen years for participation in a terrorist criminal organisation with a two-third security period.
    Sentence pronounced: Eight years of imprisonment for participation in a regular criminal organisation.
13. Abdelaziz Abbad:
    Sentence requested: Eighteen years of criminal imprisonment with a two-third security period for participation in a terrorist organisation.
    Sentence pronounced: Ten years of imprisonment for participation in a common criminal organisation.
14. Miguel Martinez:
    Sentence requested: Fifteen years of criminal imprisonment with a two-third security period for participation in a terrorist organisation.
    Sentence pronounced: Seven years of imprisonment for participation in a common criminal organisation.

TABLE 6A.4 The Bataclan trial: penalties

The trial began on 8 September 2021, and concluded on 29 June 2022, lasting ten months. All defendants were convicted, receiving sentences ranging from life imprisonment with an irreducible security period to two years in prison.

Name and Accusation Accused persons in detention	Sentence Requested	Sentence
Salah Abdelslam • Participation in a terrorist criminal organisation • Murders in an organised group, in connection with a terrorist enterprise (Bataclan, terraces, Stade de France) • Attempts to murder in an organised group, in connection with a terrorist enterprise (Bataclan, terraces, Stade de France) • Complicity in kidnapping, without voluntary release before the seventh day, in an organised group and in connection with a terrorist enterprise (Bataclan) • Complicity in attempted murders of public authorities, in an organised group, in connection with a terrorist enterprise (Bataclan)	**Life imprisonment** Non-reviewable period of security	Life imprisonment Perpetual period of security
Mohamed Abrini • Participation in a terrorist criminal organisation. • Complicity in murders in an organised group, in connection with a terrorist enterprise (Bataclan, terraces, Stade de France)	Criminal imprisonment for life Twenty-two years of period of security	Criminal imprisonment for life twenty-two years of period of security

• Complicity in attempted murders in an organised group, in connection with a terrorist enterprise (Bataclan, terraces, Stade de France) • Complicity in kidnapping, without voluntary release before the seventh day, in an organised group and in connection with a terrorist enterprise (Bataclan) • Complicity in attempted murders of public authorities, in an organised group, in connection with a terrorist enterprise (Bataclan)		
Yassine Atar • Participation in a terrorist criminal organisation	Nine years + two-thirds security period	Life imprisonment eight years – two-thirds security period
Osama Krayem • This defendant is being prosecuted for the same charges as Mohamed Abrini	Life imprisonment thirty-year security period	Thirty years of imprisonment Security period: two-thirds
Sofien Ayari • This defendant is being prosecuted for the same charges as Mohamed Abrini.	Life imprisonment thirty-year security period	Thirty years of imprisonment Security period: two-thirds
Mohamed Bakkali • This defendant is being prosecuted for the same charges as Mohamed Abrini.	Life imprisonment twenty-two-year security period	Thirty years of imprisonment Security period: two-thirds
Farid Kharkach • Participation in a terrorist criminal organisation	Six years	Requalified charges: fraud. two years in prison
Adel Haddadi • Participation in a terrorist criminal organisation	Twenty years two-thirds of the security period	Eighteen years of criminal imprisonment two-thirds security period

TABLE 6A.4 *(cont.)*

Name and Accusation Accused persons in detention	Sentence Requested	Sentence
Mohamed Amri • Participation in a terrorist criminal organisation • Receiving stolen goods in connection with a terrorist organisation	Eight years	Eight years of criminal imprisonment two-thirds security period
Muhammad Usman • Participation in a terrorist criminal organisation	Twenty years two-thirds of the security period	Eighteen years of criminal imprisonment two-thirds security period
Ali El Haddad Asufi • Participation in a terrorist criminal organisation	Sixteen years imprisonment two-thirds of the sentence as a safety period	Ten years of criminal imprisonment two-thirds security period
Name and Accusation Accused persons under judicial control (Free at the hearing)		
Hamza Attou • Receiving stolen goods in connection with a terrorist organisation	Six years imprisonment with a deferred detention order	Four years of imprisonment, including two years suspended
Abdellah Chouaa • Participation in a terrorist criminal organisation	Six years imprisonment with a deferred detention order	Four years of imprisonment, including three years suspended
Ali Oulkadi • Participation in a terrorist criminal organisation	Five years without a detention order	Five years of imprisonment, including three years suspended

Defendants absent, judged in *abstensia*	**Sentences**
Oussama Atar: Leadership of a terrorist organisation	Criminal imprisonment for life
• Murders in an organised group, in connection with a terrorist enterprise (Bataclan, terraces, Stade de France)	Period of perpetual security
• Attempts to murder in an organised group, in connection with a terrorist enterprise (Bataclan, terraces, Stade de France)	
• Complicity in kidnapping, without voluntary release before the seventh day, in an organised group and in connection with a terrorist enterprise (Bataclan)	
• Complicity in attempted murders of public authorities, in an organised group, in connection with a terrorist enterprise (Bataclan)	
Ahmad Dahmani: in prison in Turkey	Thirty years of imprisonment
• Same accusations as Oussama Atar except for the leadership	Security period: two-thirds
Fabien and Jean-Michel Clain, Oumar Darif, Obeida Aref Dibo	Criminal imprisonment for life
• Same accusations as Oussama Atar except for the leadership	Period of perpetual security

TABLE 6A.5 Statistics regarding the severity of punishment in terrorism AMT cases before the lower courts – 16th Chamber (up to ten years imprisonment)
Appeals were lodged by either the State or the convict or both, and they include appeals on non-convictions.[15]

2018: Number of defendants 67
- Thirty-six aggravations of sentence
- Nine reductions of sentence
- Eleven confirmations of sentence
- Two withdrawals of appeal
- Two deliberations in 2019

2019: Number of terrorism appeal cases (lower court) – sixty-three; Number of defendants – ninety-seven
- Twenty-two aggravations of sentence
- Twenty-two reductions of sentence
- Twenty-four confirmations of sentence
- Twelve withdrawals of appeal
- Seventeen cases postponed to 2020
- One case awaiting deliberation

2020: Number of terrorism appeal cases (lower court) – fifty-one; Number of defendants – sixty-three
- Eleven aggravations of sentence
- Nine reductions of sentence
- Fifteen confirmations of sentence
- Thirteen appeals withdrawn
- Six cases postponed to 2021
- Twelve cases awaiting deliberation in 2021

2021: Number of terrorism appeal cases (lower court) – thirteen; Number of defendants – forty-six
- Fourteen aggravations of sentence
- Nine reductions of sentence
- Ten confirmations of sentence
- Four appeals withdrawn
- Six cases postponed to 2022
- Two cases awaiting deliberation in 2022
- One case resumed

Additional resources for this publication at www.cambridge.org/9781009333221

[15] Official data from the Prosecution office obtained by the author (in the data is unpublished, in file with the author).

TABLE 6A.6 Convictions and sentences for terrorism AMT cases in the Assize Court since 1994

TABLE 6A.6.1 Convictions for AMT

Type of Conviction	1994	1995	1996	1997	1998	1999	2000	2001	2002	2003	2004	2005	2006	2007	2008	2009	2010	2011	2012	2013	2014	2015	2016
Conviction for AMT with other incriminations	10	1	—	23	50	119	138	68	36	60	46	67	89	70	96	87	56	56	56	84	54	81	63
Conviction for AMT as the main incriminations	8	1	—	22	50	116	135	68	35	43	42	54	69	44	62	58	33	40	44	67	44	65	59

Source: Ministry of Justice – National Criminal Records Statistical File.

TABLE 6A.6.2 Total prison sentences pronounced for convictions for AMT (main incrimination)

Total Period of Imprisonment	1994	1995	1996	1997	1998	1999	2000	2001	2002	2003	2004	2005	2006	2007	2008	2009	2010	2011	2012	2013	2014	2015	2016
Less than 5 years	4	1	-	19	30	63	106	48	17	21	18	17	27	23	27	39	13	21	26	38	17	46	16
5 to 10 years	4	-	-	3	19	53	29	20	18	22	24	37	42	21	34	19	20	19	18	29	27	19	42
10 to 15 years	-	-	-	-	-	-	-	-	-	-	-	-	-	-	1	-	-	-	-	-	-	-	1

Source: Ministry of Justice – National Criminal Records Statistical File.

TABLE 6A.6.3 Convictions for AMT (main incrimination) by jurisdiction

Jurisdiction	1994	1995	1996	1997	1998	1999	2000	2001	2002	2003	2004	2005	2006	2007	2008	2009	2010	2011	2012	2013	2014	2015	2016
Specially Composed Assize Court	-	-	-	-	-	-	-	-	-	1	2	5	2	3	3	-	1	3	2	3	-	1	-
Appeals Court	3	-	-	2	-	14	47	25	17	7	11	12	8	13	6	15	10	6	16	23	4	18	13
Lower Criminal Court	5	1	-	20	50	101	87	43	18	34	29	37	59	28	53	43	22	31	26	41	40	45	43
Tribunal for Minor	-	-		-	-	1	1	-	-	1	-	-	-	-	-	-	-	-	-	-	-	1	3

Source: Ministry of Justice – National Criminal Records Statistical File.

TABLE 6A.6.4 Convictions for AMT (main incrimination) by nationality

Nationality	1994	1995	1996	1997	1998	1999	2000	2001	2002	2003	2004	2005	2006	2007	2008	2009	2010	2011	2012	2013	2014	2015	2016
French	5	-	-	16	20	31	45	21	23	13	14	25	19	15	27	20	10	7	15	13	30	28	45
Spanish	3	1	-	2	15	21	22	11	6	20	16	19	35	17	24	5	16	16	17	24	8	4	2
Turkish	-	-	-	-	10	9	30	-	1	-	-	-	-	-	-	10	-	7	1	27	1	25	6
Algerian, Moroccan, Tunisian	-	-	-	3	4	51	31	34	4	10	11	6	13	11	8	9	4	4	1	1	4	3	5
Other	-	-	-	1	-	2	3	1	1	-	-	2	1	1	2	11	1	2	3	2	1	5	1
Unknown/stateless	-	-	-	-	1	2	4	1	-	-	1	2	1	-	1	3	2	4	7	-	-	-	-

Source: Ministry of Justice – National Criminal Records Statistical File.

TABLE 6A.6.5 Length of time between the end date of the facts and the date of conviction for AMT (main incrimination)

	1994	1995	1996	1997	1998	1999	2000	2001	2002	2003	2004	2005	2006	2007	2008	2009	2010	2011	2012	2013	2014	2015	2016
Length of time (years)	nd	nd	nd	6.8	3.8	3.6	4.2	4.6	5.1	3.4	5.1	4,7	4.8	6.3	5.1	4.2	5.6	5.3	6.7	6.7	4.7	5.5	3.7

Source: Ministry of Justice – National Criminal Records Statistical File.

BIBLIOGRAPHY

Aaronson, E. and Shaffer, G. (eds.) (2020). *Transnational Legal Ordering of Criminal Justice Cambridge*. Cambridge University Press.

Abboud, L. (2021). 'A "Truth Commission": Paris Terror Trial Grips France'. in: *Financial Times*, 12 November.

Abel, R. (2019). *Law's Wars: The Fate of the Rule of Law in the US 'War on Terror'*. Cambridge University Press.

Agamben, G. (2003). *Etat d'exception: Homo sacer*. Paris, Editions du Seuil.

Ali-Adraoui, M. and Roy, O. (2018). *The Foreign Policy of Islamist Political Parties: Ideology in Practice*. Edinburgh University Press.

Alix, J. (2010). *Terrorisme et droit pénal. Étude critique des incriminations terroristes*. Paris: Dalloz, coll. 'Nouvelle bibliothèque de thèses', 91, p. 380.

(2014). 'Réprimer la participation au terrorisme'. in: *Revue de Science Criminelle et de Droit Pénal Comparé*, 4, 849–865.

(2020a). 'La Cour de cassation redessine les contours de la constitution de partie civile des victimes d'attentat terroriste', in: *AJ pénal* 143.

(2020b). 'Radicalisation et droit pénal'. in: *Revue de Science Criminelle et de Droit Pénal Comparé*, 3, 769–786.

(2023). 'La Justice Antiterroriste aux Prises avec l'Imputation des Crimes de Masse', in: *Revue de Science Criminelle et de Droit Pénal Comparé*, 2(2), 443.

Alix, J. and Cahn, O. (2023). 'Les procès, révélateurs des mutations de la lutte contre le terrorisme', in: *AJ Pénal*, 33.

Allo, A. (2015). *The Courtroom as a Space of Resistance: Reflections on the Legacy of the Rivonia Trial*. London, Routledge.

Alonso, P. (2016). 'Notes blanches: Les corbeaux de la place Beauvau'. in: *Libération*, 15 February. www.liberation.fr/france/2016/02/15/notes-blanches-les-corbeaux-de-la-place-beauvau_1433587/.

Alter, K. J. (2009). *The European Court's Political Power: Selected Essays*. Oxford, Oxford University Press.

(2014). *The New Terrain of International Law: Courts, Politics, Rights*. Princeton, NJ, Princeton University Press.

Ambos, K. (2003). 'International Criminal Procedure: 'Adversarial,' 'Inquisitorial' or Mixed?', in: *International Criminal Law Review*, 3(1), 1–37.

Ambos, K. and Peters, S. (eds.) (2022). *Transitional Justice in Colombia: The Special Jurisdiction for Peace*. Nomos Verlagsgesellschaft.

Amimour, A. and Salines, G. (2022). *Il nous reste les mots*. Robert Lafont.

Antichan, S. et al. (2021). 'La "grande famille" des victimes des attentats du 13 novembre 2015', in: AOC, 8 December. https://aoc.media/analyse/2021/12/07/la-grande-famille-des-victimes-des-attentats-du-13-novembre-2015/.

Antichan, S., Gensburger, S. and Jarroux P. (eds.) (2023). '*Victimes et associations de victimes dans les procès des attentats de janvier 2015, de novembre 2015 et de Nice le 14 juillet 2016*'. Report for *IERDJ*, available at ierdj.fra1.digitaloceanspaces.com/media_library/2023/10/.19.29_VICTIMES_ATTENTATS_rapport-.pdf.

Anwar, T. and de Goede, M. (2021). 'From Contestation to Conviction: Terrorism Expertise Before the Courts', in: *Journal of Law and Society*, 48(2), 137–157.

Arendt, H. (1963). *Eichmann in Jerusalem: A Report on the Banality of Evil*. London, Faber & Faber.

Ashworth, A. J. and Zedner, L. (2014). *Preventive Justice*. Oxford, Oxford University Press.

Atlani-Duault, L. and Dufoix, S. (2014). 'Les Sciences Sociales Saisies par la Justice', in: *Socio*. 3, 9–47.

Baczko, A. (2021). *La guerre par le droit. Les tribunaux Taliban en Afghanistan*. Paris, CNRS.

Baranger, T., Bonelli, L. and Pichaud, F. (2017). 'La justice des mineurs et les affaires de terrorisme', in: 'A l'épreuve du terrorisme'. *Les cahiers de la justice*, 2, 253–264.

Barbot, J. and Dodier, N. (2023). *Des victimes en procès: Essai sur la réparation*. Presses de l'Ecole des Mines.

Barrelle, K. (2014). 'Pro-integration: Disengagement From and Life After Extremism', in: *Behavioral Sciences of Terrorism and Political Aggression*, 7(2), 129–142.

et al. (2017). 'Does the Pursuit of Meaning Explain the Initiation, Escalation, and Disengagement of Violent Extremists?', in: *Aggression and Violent Behavior*, 34, 185–192

Beaud, S. (1996). 'L'usage de l'entretien en sciences sociales. Plaidoyer pour l'entretien ethnographique', in: *Politix*, 9(35), 226–257.

Beck, C. J. (2015). *Radicals, Revolutionaries and Terrorists*. Polity Press.

Bellanger, H., et al. (2023). 'Filmer les procès pour l'histoire, de Klaus Barbie au procès V13. Évolution des injonctions et des pratiques (1987–2022)' ['Filming trials for history, from Klaus Barbie to the V13 trial. Changes in injunctions and practices (1987–2022], in: *Politika* [online], 9 January, www.politika.io/fr/article/filmer-proces-lhistoire-klaus-barbie-au-proces-v13-evolution-injonctions-pratiques-19872022.

Bens, J. (2022). *The Sentimental Court: The Affective Life of International Criminal Justice*. Cambridge, Cambridge University Press.

Benvenisti, E. (1993). 'Judicial Misgivings Regarding the Application of International Law: An Analysis of Attitudes of National Courts', in: *European Journal of International Law*, 4(2), 159–183

Bergman Blix, S. and Wettergren, Å. (2018). *Professional Emotions in Court: A Sociological Perspective*. Routledge.

Bergman Blix, S., et al. (eds.) (2019). 'Introducing an Interdisciplinary Frontier to Judging, Emotion and Emotion Work', in: *Oñati Socio-Legal Series*, 9(5), 548–556.

Besnier, C. (2007a). 'La cour d'assises. Approche ethnologique du judiciaire' in: *Droit et Cultures*, revue semestrielle d'anthropologie et d'histoire, 54(2), 179–202, L'Harmattan.

(2007b). 'La notion spatio-temporelle dans le processus judiciaire: l'exemple du procès criminel' in: *Le procès: enjeu de droit, enjeu de vérité*, sous la direction de Edwige Rude-Antoine, Paris CURAPP (CNRS), PUF, pp. 41–55.

(2017). *La vérité côté cour. Une ethnologue aux assises*. Paris, La Découverte.

(2023). 'Entretien avec Safya Akorri, avocate au barreau de Paris'. in: *Les Cahiers de la Justice*, 1, 101–102.

Besnier, C. and Weill, S. et al. (2019). 'Les filières djihadistes en procès. Approche ethnographique des audiences criminelles et correctionnelles (2017–2019)', in: *Mission de Recherche Droit & Justice*, 177

Bienvault, P. (2020). 'Procès Charlie Hebdo – Hyper Cacher: 'Ne pas faire peser sur les accusés le poids des attentes de la société'. in: *La Croix* [online], 2 September, www.la-croix.com/France/Proces-Charlie-Hebdo-Hyper-Cacher-Ne-pas-faire-peser-accuses-poids-attentes-societe-2020-09-02-1201111869.

Bigo, D. (2007). *The Field of the EU Internal Security Agencies*. Paris, L'Harmattan.

(2016). *Terrorisme, Guerre, Sécurité intérieure, Sécurité extérieure*. Edition Universitaire Européenne.

Bigo, D. and Bonelli, L. (eds.) (2018). 'Introduction: Ni État de droit, ni État d'exception. L'état d'urgence comme dispositif spécifique?', in: *Cultures & Conflits*, 112(4), 7–14.

Bigo, D., Mc Cluskey, E. and Tréguer F. (eds.) (2023). *Intelligence Oversight in Times of Transnational Impunity*. New Intelligence Studies, New York, Routledge.

Bigo, D. and Tsoukala, A. (2008). *Terror, Insecurity and Liberty: Illiberal Practices of Liberal Regimes After 9/11*. London. New York, Routledge.

Biland, E. and Steinmetz, H. (2017). 'Are Judges Street-Level Bureaucrats? Evidence from French and Canadian Family Courts', in: *Law & Social Inquiry*, 42(2), 298–324.

Bilsky, L. Y. (1996). 'When Actor and Spectator Meet in the Courtroom: Reflections on Hannah Arendt's Concept of Judgment', in: *History and Memory*, 8(2), 137–173.

Blom, A. (2011). 'Les 'martyrs' jihadistes veulent-ils forcément mourir? Une approche émique de la radicalisation autosacrificielle au Pakistan', in *Revue française de science politique*, 5(61), 867–891.

Bögelein, N., Eppert, K., Roth, V. and Schmidt-Kleinert, A. (2022). 'Courtroom Ethnography in the Context of Terrorism: A Multi-Level Approach'. in: *International Journal of Qualitative Methods*, 21, 1–11.

Bonelli, L. and Carrié, F. (2018). *La fabrique de la radicalité. Une sociologie des jeunes djihadistes français*. Paris, Le Seuil.

Bourdieu, P. (1987). 'The Force of Law: Toward a Sociology of the Juridical Field', in: *Hastings Law Journal*, 38(5), 828–829.

(1991). *Language and Symbolic Power*. Translated by Raymond, G. and Adamson, M. Cambridge, Polity Press.

Bourles, Jean-Michel (2021). 'Entretien avec le Procureur national antiterroriste, Jean-François Ricard et le Procureur adjoint, Jean-Michel Bourles', in: *Les Cahiers de la Justice*, 2, 212.

Boussaguet, L. and Faucher, F. (2018). 'La construction des discours présidentiels post-attentats à l'épreuve du temps', in: Mots. *Les langages du politique*, 118, 95–115.

Bouvier, E. and Martelet, C. (2018). *Un parfum de Djihad*. Paris, Plon.

Braconnier Moreno, L. (2024). *Vers une justice interculturelle pour la paix ? Harmonisation de la justice transitionnelle et du droit propre des peuples autochtones en Colombie (2018–2023)*. Joint thesis under the supervision of Véronique Champeil-Desplats (Université Paris Nanterre) and Camilo Borrero García (Universidad Nacional de Colombia).

Braithwaite, J. (2004). 'Restorative Justice and De-Professionalization', in: *The Good Society*, 13(1), 28.

Branco, P. (2023). 'Analysing Courthouses' Spaces, Places and Architecture: Some Methodological Outlines', in: *Oñati Socio-Legal Series*, 13(S1), S278–S298.

Brisard, J. C. et al. (2018). *'La justice pénale face au djihadisme: Le traitement judiciaire des filières syro-irakiennes (2014–2017)'*. May. Centre d'Analyse du Terrorisme (CAT).

Broekman, J. M. (1993). *Droit et anthropologie*. Paris, Librairie générale de droit et de jurisprudence (L.G.D.J.).

Burns, R. P. (1999). *A Theory of the Trial*. Princeton, NJ, Princeton University Press.

Cahn O. (2009). 'The Fight against Terrorism and Human Rights: The French Perspective'. in: Wade, M. and Maljevic, A. (eds.) *A War on Terror? The European Stance on a New Threat, Changing Laws and Human Rights*. New York, Springer, pp. 467–503.

(2016). 'Le dispositif antiterroriste français, une manifestation du droit pénal de l'ennemi', in: *Archives de Politique Criminelle*, 1, 91–99.

Caldwell, R. A. (2012). *Fallgirls: Gender and the Framing of Torture at Abu Ghraib*. Routledge.

Canivez, P. (1995). *Éduquer le Citoyen?* Paris, Hatier.

Capdeville, C. and Popelin, P. (2016). 'Rapport fait au nom de la commission des lois constitutionnelles, de la législation et de l'administration générale de la république, sur le projet de loi (no 3473) renforçant la lutte contre le crime organisé, le terrorisme et leur financement, et améliorant l'efficacité et les garanties de la procédure pénale', in: *Assemblée Nationale*, Report No. 3515, 18 February.

Cardi, C. and Pruvost, G. (eds.) (2012). *Penser la violence des femmes*, Paris, La Découverte.

Carlson, K. (2018). *Model(ing) Justice: Perfecting the Promise of International Criminal Law*. Cambridge University Press.

(forthcoming). 'Ties That Sever: Losing the Right to Belong in Denmark'. in: *Law & Critique*.

Cassese, A. (1989a). *Terrorism, Politics, and Law: The Achille Lauro Affair*, Cambridge, Cambridgeshire, Polity.

(1989b). 'The International Community's Legal Response to Terrorism', in: *International And Comparative Law Quarterly*, 38, 589–608.

Cassia, P. (2016). *Contre l'état d'urgence*. Paris, Dalloz.

Cefaï, D. (2010). *L'engagement ethnographique*. Aubervilliers: Éditions EHESS, coll. 'En temps et lieux'.

Chesnelong, B. (2022). 'Un Procès pour l'exemple Justifier la Force Plutôt que Fortifier la Justice', in: *Revue Esprit*, 91, 97.

Chinkin, C. and Kaldor, M. (2017). *International Law and New Wars*. Cambridge University Press.

Choblet, J. (2022). 'Courtroom or Stage? Performance Versus a Fair Trial in the Paris Attacks Case', in: *ICCT*, 25 Mar 2022, available at www.icct.nl/publication/courtroom-or-stage-performance-versus-fair-trial-paris-attacks-case.

Christensen, M.J. (2017). 'Crafting and Promoting International Crimes: A Controversy Between Legal Professionals of Core Crimes and Anti-Corruption', in: *Leiden Journal of International Law*, 30(2), 501–521.

Christie, N. (1977). 'Conflicts as Property', in: *British Journal of Criminology* 1, 17.

Claverie, E. (2012). 'Mettre en cause la légitimité de la violence d'État La justice pénale internationale comme institution, comme dispositif et comme scène', in: *Quaderni*, 2, 78.

(2018a). 'Juger, dire le vrai, réconcilier', in: Cabanes, B. (eds.) *Une Histoire de la Guerre, XIXème-XXème siècles*. Paris, Le Seuil, pp. 733–741.

(2018b) 'Les Combattants, les fétiches et le prétoire, le procès de Germain Katanga devant la Cour pénale internationale'. in: *'Face à la sorcellerie'. Cahiers d'Etudes africaines*, LVIII, 231–232.

Codaccioni, V. (2015). *Justice d'exception: L'État Face Aux Crimes Politiques et Terroristes*. Paris, CNRS.

Collectif Onze. (2013). *Au tribunal des couples. Enquête sur des affaires familiales*, Paris, Odile Jacob.

Collective of defence lawyers (2022). 'Le procès des attentats du 13-Novembre n'a pas été exemplaire et les droits de la défense ont été malmenés' ('The trial of the November 13 attacks was not exemplary, and the rights of the defence were mishandled'), in: *Le Monde*, 18 July. www.lemonde.fr/idees/article/2022/07/18/le-proces-des-attentats-du-13-novembre-n-a-pas-ete-exemplaire-et-les-droits-de-la-defense-ont-ete-malmenes_6135154_3232.html.

Colemans, J. (2015). 'Ce que les émotions font faire aux professionnels du droit: Jalons pour une approche praxéologique des expressions émotionnelles dans la sphère judiciaire', in: *Social Science Information*, 54, 525–542.

Colemans, J. and Dupret, B. (2018). *Ethnographies du raisonnement juridique*. Paris, Librairie générale de droit et de jurisprudence (L.G.D.J.).

Conti, B. (2019). 'Between Deradicalisation and Disengagement: The Re-engagement of the Radical Actor?', in Jayakumar, S. (ed.) *Terrorism, Radicalisation & Countering Violent Extremism: Practical Considerations & Concerns*. Palgrave Pivot, pp. 43–56.

(2020). 'The impact of policies of counter-radicalisation in prison: a cumulative production?', in: *DARE Report*. https://documents.manchester.ac.uk/display.aspx?DocID=58622.

(2021). 'The Rise and Fall of a Jihadist Neo-Family: The Cannes-Torcy Cell', in: Ferret J. and Khosrokhavar, F. (eds.) *Family and Jihadism A Socio-Anthropological Approach to the French Experience*. London, Routledge, pp. 111–150.

(2023). 'Trajectories of (Non)Radicalisation in a French Prison', in: Pilkington, H. (ed.) *Resisting Radicalisation? Understanding Young People's Journeys through Radicalising Milieus*. New York, Berghahn Books, pp. 262–292.

(2024). *Presque rien. Une ethnographie carcérale des inégalités, des injustices et de la radicalisation. Paris*, Edition Le Croquant.

Contrôleur général des lieux de privation de liberté (2015). *La prise en charge de la radicalisation islamiste en milieu carcéral*. Online report: www.cglpl.fr/2015/avis-relatif-a-la-prise-en-charge-de-la-radicalisation-islamiste-en-milieu-carceral/.

Court of Cassation, 1st Civil Chamber, 17 October 1995, Decision No. 93-14.837. www.legifrance.gouv.fr/juri/id/JURITEXT000007035042/.

Criminal Chamber, 8 July 2015, Decision No. 14-88.329. www.legifrance.gouv.fr/juri/id/JURITEXT000030869110/.

Court of Cassation, Criminal Chamber, 10 January 2017, Decision No. 16-84.596. www.courdecassation.fr/decision/5fd911e5e32854ac37e6165b?search_api_fulltext=16-84.596&op=Rechercher&expression_exacte=1&date_du=&date_au=&judilibre_juridiction=all&previousdecisionpage=&previousdecisionindex=&nextdecisionpage=&nextdecisionindex.

Cotterrell, R. (1984). *The Sociology of Law*. Oxford, Oxford University Press.

(1995). *Law's Community: Legal Thought in Sociological Perspective*. Oxford, United Kingdom, Clarendon Press.

(2012). 'What Is Transnational Law?' in: *Law and Social Inquiry*, 37(2), 500–524.

Council of State, (2003) *Ministre de l'Intérieur c. Diouri*, Case No. 128128, 11 October 1991; Council of State, *Ministre de l'Intérieur c. Rakhimov*, Case No. 238662, 3 March 2003

Crctticz, X. Seze, R. (2022). 'Sociology of French Jihadism, Prosopographic Analysis of Over 350 Incarcerated Jihadist Terrorists'. Research Report, French Ministry of Justice.

Creux-Thomas, F. (2022). 'Avocats de parties civiles au procès des attentats du 13 novembre 2015: Coulisses d'une coordination inédite', in: *La Semaine Juridique – Édition Générale*, 22, 1064–1068.

Dahlberg, L. (2009). 'Emotional Tropes in the Courtroom: On Representation of Affect and Emotion in Legal Court Proceedings', in: *Law and Humanities*, 3, 175.

Daho, G. Guittet, E.-P.. and Pomarède, J. (2020). 'Les territoires du secret: confidentialité et enquête dans les mondes pluriels de la sécurité', in: *Cultures & Conflits*, 118, 71–77.

Danet, J. (2001). *For a Critical Criminal Defense*, Dalloz.

De Galembert, C. (2016) 'Le 'radical', une nouvelle figure de dangerosité carcérale aux contours flous', *Critique internationale*, 72, 53–74.

De Goede, M. (2008). 'Money, Media and the Anti-Politics of Terrorist Finance', in: *European Journal of Cultural Studies*, 11(3), 289–310.

(2012). *Speculative Security: The Politics of Pursuing Terrorist Monies*. University Of Minnesota Press.

(2020). 'Engagement all the Way Down', in: *Critical Studies on Security*, 8(2), 101–115.

De Graaf, B. (2019). 'Foreign Fighters on Trial: Sentencing Risk, 2013–2017', in: Fadil, N., de Koning, M. and Ragazzi, F. *(eds.) Radicalization in Belgium and the Netherlands: Critical Perspectives on Violence and Security*. Bloomsbury, pp. 97–130.

De Graaf, B. and Schmid, A. P. (eds.) (2016). *Terrorists on Trial: A Performative Perspective*. Leiden University Press.

De Guttry, A., et al., (2016). *Foreign Fighters Under International Law and Beyond*. Asser Press Springer.

Delmas-Marty, M. (2007). 'The Paradigm of the War on Crime', in: *Journal of International Criminal Justice*, 5, 584–598.

(2010). *Libertés et sûreté dans un monde dangereux*. Paris, Seuil.

De Londras, F. (2019). 'Transnational Counter-Terrorism: A Problématique', in: *Current Legal Problems*, 72, 203–251.

(2022). *The Practice and Problems of Transnational Counter-Terrorism*. Cambridge University Press.

Derrida, J. (1992). 'Force of Law: The "Mystical Foundation of Authority", in: Cornell, D., Rosenfield, M. and Carlson, D. G. (eds.) *Deconstruction and the Possibility of Justice*. Routledge, pp. 3–67.

Dezalay, S. (2020). 'Introduction: Wars on Law, Wars through Law? Law and Lawyers in Times of Crisis', in: *Journal of Law and Society*, 47(S1), S1–S13.

Dezalay, Y. and Garth, B. G. (2002). *Global Prescriptions: The Production, Exportation, and Importation of a New Legal Orthodoxy*. University of Michigan Press.

DNA (2023). 'Attaque à Paris: quelle surveillance existe-t-il pour les ex-détenus radicalisés?' in: *DNA*, 5 December. www.dna.fr/faits-divers-justice/2023/12/05/quelle-surveillance-existe-t-il-pour-les-ex-detenus-radicalises.

Dubois, Chloé (2024), 'Yazidi genocide trial to take place in France', *justiceinfo.net*, 26 November 2024. www.justiceinfo.net/en/138787-yazidi-genocide-trial-france.html

Dupret, B. (2010). 'Droit et sciences sociales. Pour une respécification praxéologique', in: *Droit et société*, 75(2), 315–335.

(2021). *In Positive Law from the Muslim World: Jurisprudence, History, Practices*. Cambridge University Press.

et al. (eds.) (2015). *Law at Work: Studies in Legal Ethnomethods*. Oxford University Press.

Durand-Souffland, S. (2017). 'Quand le Renseignement voulait recruter Mohamed Merah'. in: *Le Figaro*, 16 October. www.lefigaro.fr/actualite-france/2017/10/16/01016-20171016ARTFIG00310-quand-le-renseignement-voulait-recruter-merah.php.

Durkheim, E. (1893). *De la division du travail social*, PUF, 1996.

Edelman, M. (1971). *Politics as Symbolic Action: Mass Arousal and Quiescence*. Chicago: Markham Publishing Co.

European Court of Human Rights. (2022). *H.F. and Others v. France* (Applications Nos. 24384/19 and 44234/20). Grand Chamber Judgment, 14 September 2022.

(2001). *Krombach v. France*, Judgement, 13 February 2001, Application No. 29731/96.

Fassin, D. (2005). 'Compassion and Repression: The Moral Economy of Immigration Policies in France', in: *Cultural Anthropology*, 20(3), 362–387.

(2009). 'Les économies morales revisitées'. in: *Annales. Histoire, Sciences Sociales*, 64, 1257.

(2013). *Enforcing Order: An Ethnography of Urban Policing*. Cambridge, Polity Press.

(2017). *Punir: une passion contemporaine*. Seuil.

Fassin, D. and Kobelinsky, C. (2012). 'Comment on juge l'asile: l'institution comme agent moral'. in: *Revue française de sociologie*, 53(4), 657–688.

Faucher-King, F. and Truc, G. (eds.) (2022). *Facing Terrorism in France: Lessons From the 2015 Paris Attacks*. New-York, Palgrave MacMillan.

Fédération internationale des droits de l'homme (FIDH) (1999) . 'France: Paving the Way for Arbitrary Justice', in: *Fédération internationale des droits de l'homme*. No. 271–2, March.

Feeley, M. (1982). 'Plea Bargaining and the Structure of the Criminal Process'. in: *Justice System Journal*, 7, 338–354.

Feeley, M. M. (1979). *The Process is the Punishment: Handling Cases in a Lower Criminal Court*. New York, Russell Sage Foundation.

Feeley, M. M. and Simon, J. (1992). 'The New Penology: Notes on the Emerging Strategy of Corrections and Its Implications', in: *Criminology*, 30, 449.

Ferret, J. and Khosrokhavar, F. (2021). *Family and Jihadism A Socio-Anthropological Approach to the French Experience*'. Routledge.

Fillieule, O. (2012). 'Le désengagement d'organisations radicales. Approche par les processus et les configurations', in: *Lien social et Politiques*, 68, 37–59.

Foley, F., (2013). *Countering Terrorism in Britain and France: Institutions, Norms and the Shadow of the Past*. Cambridge, Cambridge University Press.

Foucault, M. (1975). *Surveiller et punir: naissance de la prison*. Paris, Gallimard. Texte no. 194, 4.

(1977). 'Michel Foucault et les juges', in: *Antenne 2*. INA archive, Online video clip. www.ina.fr/ina-eclaire-actu/video/i06277672/michel-foucault-et-les-juges.

(1994). *Dits et Ecrits (1954–1988), Tome III: 1976–1979*. Gallimard.

Freedman, J. (2012) 'La violence des femmes pendant les conflits armés et la (non)-réaction des organisations internationales', in: Cardi, C. and Pruvost, G. (eds.) *Penser la violence des femmes*. Paris, La Découverte, pp. 330–340.

French Ministry of Justice (2016). 'La lettre du porte-parole du Ministère de la Justice: la législation anti-terroriste'. in: *Ministère de la Justice*, 23 November. www.gip-recherche-justice.fr/conference-consensus/presse.justice_subdomain/info-justice-11598/la-lettre-du-porte-parole-23-novembre-2016-29479/.

French National Assembly (2015). 'Bilan statistique de l'état d'urgence'. in: *Assemblée Nationale*, 14 November. www2.assemblee-nationale.fr/static/15/lois/bilan_contentieux.pdf.

Galanter, M. (1974). 'Why the "Haves" Come Out Ahead: Speculations on the Limits of Legal Change'. in: *Law and Society Review*, 9(1), 165–230.

Garapon, A. (1985). *L'âne portant des reliques. Essai sur le rituel judiciaire*, Paris, Le Centurion.

(1997). *Bien juger: essai sur le rituel judiciaire*, Paris, Odile Jacob.

Garapon, A. and Papadopoulos, I. (2003). *Juger en Amérique et en France*. Paris, Odile Jacob.

Garapon, A. and Rosenfeld, M. (2016). *Démocraties sous stress: Les défis du terrorisme global*. Paris, Presses Universitaires de France.

Garapon, A. and Salas, D. (1997). *La justice et le mal*. Paris, Éditions Odile Jacob.

Garfinkel, H. (1967). 'What is Ethnomethodology?' in: Garfinkel, H. (ed.) *Studies in Ethnomethodology*. Englewood Cliffs, Prentice-Hall, pp. 1–35.

Garland, D. (2001). *The Culture of Control – Crime and Social Order in Contemporary Society*. Oxford University Press.

Gensburger, S. and Lefranc, S. (2020). *Beyond Memory. Can We Really Learn From the Past?* Palgrave Pivot Cham.

Gensburger, S. and Truc, G. (2020). *Les mémoriaux du 13 novembre*. Aubervilliers: Éditions EHESS, coll. 'Représentations'.

Gill, N. and Good, A. (eds.) (2019). *Asylum Determination in Europe: Ethnographic Perspectives*. 1st ed. Basingstoke: Springer Nature.

Ginsburg, T. and Moustafa, T. (eds.) (2008). *Rule by Law: The Politics of Courts in Authoritarian Regimes*. Cambridge, Cambridge University Press.

Goffman, E. (1974). *Frame Analysis: An Essay on the Organization of Experience*. Cambridge, Harvard University

Gorce, R. (2023). "What the Film Does to the Trial," in "Victims in the Trials of the January and November 2015 Attacks," *IERDJ*, September 2023 (online) (in French), https://ierdj.fra1.digitaloceanspaces.com/media_library/2023/10/19.29_VICTIMES_ATTENTATS_rapport-.pdf.

Gready, P. and Robins, S. (2014). 'From Transitional to Transformative Justice: A New Agenda for Practice', in: *International Journal of Transitional Justice*, 8(3), 339.

Guittet, E.-P. (2018). 'Les maux de l'urgence et de l'exception', in: *Cultures et Conflits*, 112.

Guittet, E., Mégie, A. and Weill, S. (2021). 'Ce que la 'guerre au terrorisme' fait à la justice'. in: *Cultures & Conflits*, 123/124, 95–103.

Hacking, I. (1991). 'The Making and Molding of Child Abuse', in: *Critical Inquiry*, 17(2), 253.

Haenel, Y. and Bouck, F. (2020). *Janvier 2015: le procès*. Paris, Les échappés Charlie Hebdo.

Hagedorn, J. M. (2022). *Gangs on Trial: Challenging Stereotypes and Demonization in the Courts*. Temple University Press.

Halliday, T. C. and Shaffer, G. (2015). *Transnational Legal Orders*. Cambridge University Press.

Hambly, J. (2023). 'Framing the View', in Flower, L. and Klosterkamp, S. (eds.) *Courtroom Ethnography Exploring Contemporary Approaches, Fieldwork and Challenges*. Basingstoke, Palgrave Macmillan, p. 20.

Hayaert, V. (2023). 'Friday the 13th: The Symbolic Power of Trials on Countering Terrorism With Democracy', in: *Law, Technology and Humans*, 5(1), 125.

Hayner, P. (2002). *Unspeakable Truths. Confronting State Terror and Atrocity*. Routledge.

Hecker, M. (2018 City). '137 nuances de terrorisme. Les djihadistes de France face à la justice', in: *Focus stratégique, études de l'IFRI*. 79, 56 p.

Hecker, M. and Koller, S. (2024). 'Les femmes sont-elles des djihadistes comme les autres?', in: *Esprit magazine*, 3, 133–144.

Heller, K. and Simpson, G. (eds.) (2013). *The Hidden Histories of War Crimes Trials*. Oxford University Press.

Hennette-Vauchez, S. (2019). 'La fabrique législative de l'état d'urgence : lorsque le pouvoir n'arrête pas le pouvoir' ['The Legislative Fabric of the State of Emergency: When Power Doesn't Stop Power']. in: *Cultures & Conflits*, 112, 17–41.

(2021). 'The State of Emergency in France: Days Without End?', in: *European Constitutional Law Review*, 14(4), 700.

(2022a). *La démocratie en état d'urgence. Quand l'exception devient permanente*. Paris, Seuil.

(2022b). 'Taming the Exception? Lessons From the Routinisation of States of Emergency in France', in: *International Journal of Constitutional Law*, 20(5), 1793–1819.

Hennette-Vauchez, S. and Slama, S. (2017). 'Harry Potter au Palais Royal? La lutte contre le terrorisme comme cape d'invisibilité de l'état d'urgence et la transformation de l'office du juge administrative', in: *Les Cahiers de la Justice*, 2(2), 287.

et al. (2018). 'Ce que le contentieux administratif révèle de l'état d'urgence'. in: *Cultures & Conflits*, 112, 35–74.

Henrion-Stoffel, H. and Lazerges, C. (2016). 'The Decline of Criminal Law and the Rise of the Concept of Enemy Criminal Law', in: *Revue de sciences criminelles*, 649–662.

Hirschl, R. (2004). *Towards Juristocracy: The Origins and Consequences of the New Constitutionalism*. Harvard University Press.

Hodgson, J. (2005). *French Criminal Justice: A Comparative Account of the Investigation and Prosecution of Crime in France*. Oxford and Portland, Hart Publishing.

(2010a). 'The French Prosecutor in Question'. in: *Washington & Lee Law Review*, 67, 1361.

(2010b). 'Guilty Pleas and the Changing Role of the Prosecutor in French Criminal Justice'. in: *University of Warwick*, No. 15, July 29.

(2020). *Metamorphosis of Criminal Justice: A Comparative Account*. Oxford University Press.

Hodgson, J. and Roberts, A. (2010). 'Criminal Process and Prosecution'. In Cane, P. and Kritzer, B. (eds.) *Oxford Handbook of Empirical Legal Research*. Oxford, Oxford University Press, pp. 64–95.

Hodgson, J. and Soubise, L. (2016). *Prosecution in France*. New York, Oxford University Press.

Holden, L. (2019). 'Cultural Expertise and Socio-Legal Studies. Introduction', in: Sarat A. (eds.) *Cultural Expertise and Socio-Legal Studies*, p. 1.

Holmes, L. (2016). *Advanced Introduction to Organised Crime*. Edward Elgar Publishing.

Hor, M. Y. M., Ramraj, V. V., Roach, K. and Williams, G. (2012). *Global Anti-Terrorism Law and Policy*. (2nd ed.). Cambridge University Press.

Hubrecht, J. (2019). Le terrorisme. Un défi pour la justice transitionnelle. in: *Les Cahiers de la Justice*, 3(3), 393–402.

Human Rights Watch (2007). 'France. In the Name of Prevention: Insufficient Safeguards in National Security Removals', in: *Human Rights Watch*, 19(3).

(2008). 'Pre-empting Justice: Counterterrorism Laws and Procedures in France'. in: *Human Rights Watch*, 1 July. www.hrw.org/report/2008/07/01/preempting-justice/counterterrorism-laws-and-procedures-france.

Humbert, S., Ludwiczak, F. and Salas, D. (2015). *Juste victime dans le procès pénal*. Paris, L'Harmattan.

Huneeus, A. V. and Rueda-Saiz, P. (2021). 'Territory as a Victim of Armed Conflict'. in: *International Journal of Transitional Justice*, 15, 210.

Huysmans, J. (2008). 'The Jargon of Exception – on Schmitt, Agamben and the Absence of Political Society'. in: *International Political Sociology*, 2(2), 165–183.

IERDJ (2023). *Victims in the Trials of the January and November 2015 Attacks*. September (online).

Immler, N. L. and Wentholt, N. (2023). 'How Tort Can Address Historical Injustice'. in: *Netherlands Journal of Legal Philosophy*, 2, 189–210.

Institut d'études politiques de Paris. (2022). *Bibliographie: Terrorisme en France: procès historiques*. Bibliothèque de Sciences Po.

International Commission of Jurists (2010). 'France: ICJ submission to the committee against torture on the 6h periodic report of France'. *International Commission of Jurists*, April. www.icj.org/wp-content/uploads/2012/06/France-torture-thematic-report-2010.pdf.

Israël, L. and Malatesta, M. (2012). 'Défendre l'ennemi public', in: *Le Mouvement social*, 240(3), 2.

Jackson, J. (2023). *France on Trial: The Case of Marshal Pétain*. London, Allen Lane, Penguin Books.

Jacquin, J. B. (2020). 'Procès de terroristes : 'Il y a une tension entre le contexte sécuritaire et l'audience où l'on revient à une justice plus ordinaire'. in: *Le Monde* [online], 10 March, www.lemonde.fr/idees/article/2020/03/10/proces-de-terroristes-il-y-a-une-tension-entre-le-contexte-securitaire-et-l-audience-ou-l-on-revient-a-une-justice-plus-ordinaire_6032428_3232.html.

Jacquin, J.-B., Seelow S., and Vincent, E. (2018) 'Justice antiterroriste: "Nous constatons un durcissement de la repression"', *in: Le Monde*, 29 March. www.lemonde.fr/police-justice/article/2018/03/29/justice-antiterroriste-nous-constatons-un-durcissement-de-la-repression_5277824_1653578.html.

Jakobs, G. (1985). 'Kriminalisierung im Vorfeld einer Rechtsgutsverletzung'. in: *Zeitschrift für die gesamte Strafrechtswissenschaft*, 97(4), 751–785.

Jarroux, P., Mégie, A., Ortin, J. and Salas, D. (2021). 'Entretien avec le président Régis de Jorna', in: *Les Cahiers de la Justice*, 2(2), 228.

Jayakumar, S. (ed.) (2019). *Terrorism, Radicalisation & Countering Violent Extremism: Practical Considerations & Concerns*, Palgrave Pivot.

Kampf, R. (2024). *Justice antiterroriste, vengeance d'État*. Séminaire au Collège de France, 7 May.

Karpik, L. and Halliday, T. (2011). 'The Legal Complex', in: *Annual Review of Law and Social Science*, 7(1), 217–236.

Kennedy, D. (1997). *A Critique of Adjudication (Fin de Siècle)*. Cambridge, MA, Harvard University Press.

Khosrokhavar, F. (2017). *Radicalization Why Some People Choose the Path of Violence*. The New Press.

(2018). *Le nouveau jihad en Occident*. Paris, Robert Laffont.

(2021) *Jihadism in Europe: European Youth and the New Caliphate*, Oxford, Oxford University Press.

Kim, M. (2021). 'Transformative Justice and Restorative Justice: Gender-Based Violence and Alternative Visions of Justice in the United States'. *in: International Review of Victimology*, 27(2), 162.

Kirchheimer, O. (1961). *Political Justice: The Use of Legal Procedure for Political Ends*. Princeton, Princeton University Press.

Koehler, D. (2016). Understanding Deradicalization. Methods, Tools and Programs for Countering Violent Extremism. Oxon/New York: Routledge, 2016.

Kohler-Hausmann, I. (2018). *Misdemeanorland: Criminal Courts and Social Control in an Age of Broken Windows Policing*. Princeton. NJ: Princeton University Press.

Koller, S. (2023). *Prosecution of Returnees from Syria and Iraq in France: Insights and Recommendations for Policymakers and Security Agencies*. Counter-Extremism Project.

Koskenniemi, M. (2002). 'Between Impunity and Show Trials', in: *Max Planck Yearbook of United Nations Law Online*, 6(1), 1–35.

Krähenmann, S. (2014). *Foreign Fighters Under International Law*. Geneva, Geneva Academy of International Humanitarian Law and Human Rights (Geneva Academy).

Laacher, S. (2022). *Juger la terreur. Le procès des attentats de janvier 2015*. Édition De l'aube.

Lahire, B. (2016). *Pour La Sociologie: Et Pour en Finir avec une Prétendue 'Culture de l'Excuse'*. La Découverte.

Latour, B. (2002). *La fabrique du droit Une ethnographie du Conseil d'État*. Paris, La Découverte.

(2010). *The Making of Law. An Ethnography of the Conseil d'Etat*. Translated by Brilman, M. and Pottage, A. Cambridge, Polity Press.

Laugerud, S. and Langballe, Å. (2017). 'Turning the Witness Stand into a Speaker's Platform: Victim Participation in the Norwegian Legal System as Exemplified by the Trial Against Anders Behring Breivik', in: *Law & Society Review*, 51(2), 227, 241–243.

Le Monde (2016). 'François Molins annonce un 'durcissement considérable' de la politique pénale en matière de terrorisme'. in: *Le Monde*, 2 September. www.lemonde.fr/police-justice/article/2016/09/02/francois-molins-annonce-un-durcissement-considerable-de-la-politique-penale-en-matiere-de-terrorisme_4991487_1653578.html.

Leader, K. (2020). 'The Trial's the Thing: Performance and Legitimacy in International Criminal Trials', in: *Theoretical Criminology*, 24(2), 241–257.

Leebaw B. (2011). *Judging State-Sponsored Violence, Imagining Political Change*. Cambridge University Press.

Lefranc, S. (2021). 'A Tale of Many Jurisdictions: How Universal Jurisdiction is Creating a Transnational Judicial Space', in: *Journal of Law and Society*, 48(4), 573–594.

(2022a). *Comment Sortir de la Violence-? Enjeux et Limites de la Justice Transitionnelle*. CNRS Editions.

(2022b). 'Extraire les victims de violences du marbre de leur trauma: Retour sur le proces des attentas du 13-Novembre', in: AOC, 10 June, available at aoc.media/analyse/2022/06/09/extraire-les-victimes-de-violences-du-marbre-de-leur-trauma-retour-sur-le-proces-des-attentats-du-13-novembre/.

Lefranc, S. and Weill, S. (2023). 'Le procès V13 comme expérimentation judiciaire: entre justices pénale et transformative', in: *Les Cahiers de la Justice*, 1, 41–57.

Lerner, R. L. (2001). 'The Intersection of Two Systems: An American on Trial for an American Murder in the French cour d'assises', in: *University of Illinois Law Review*, 791, 791–856.

Les Cahiers de la Justice (2017). 'Entretien avec David De Pas, juge d'instruction au pôle antiterroriste (TGI de Paris): Entretien réalisé le 16 février 2017 à Paris [Interview with David De Pas, investigating judge at the counter-terrorism unit]'. in: *Les Cahiers de la Justice*, 2, 265–273.

(2021). 'Le procès des attentats des 7, 8 et 9 janvier 2015'. in: *Les Cahiers de la Justice*. www.lgdj.fr/les-cahiers-de-la-justice-2021-n2-9782247208609.html.

(2023). 'Le procès du 13 novembre : témoignages et analyses'. in: *Les Cahiers de la Justice* [online], 2023(1). www.lgdj.fr/les-cahiers-de-la-justice-2023-n1-9782247224937.html.

Levy, H., Apelbaum, D., Pugliese, M., Witt, C. and Tardé, C. (2021). 'Procès des attentats des 7, 8 et 9 janvier 2015: Table ronde avec les avocats de la défense (David Apelbaum Hugo Lévy, Margot Puglièse, Clémence Witt, Camille Tardé)' in: *Les Cahiers de la Justice*, 2, 245.

Lienhard, C. and Szwarc, C. (2021). 'Le parcours des victimes, parties civiles'. in: *Les Cahiers de la Justice*, 2, 261.

Lindeperg, S. (2012). 'From Courtrooms to the Screen, Elements of Reflection on the Filming of Court Proceedings' in: *Etudes*, 416, 507–518.

(2021). *Nuremberg, la bataille des images*. Paris, Éditions Payot & Rivages.

(2023). 'V13, un procès pour l'histoire?', in: *L'histoire*, May, 58.

Linhardt, D. and Moreau de Bellaing, C. (2017). 'The Doctrine of Enemy Criminal Law and the Idea of Counterterrorism: Genesis and Circulation of a Legal Dogmatic Enterprise'. in: *Droit et société*, 97(3), 615–640.

Linhardt, D. and Vitale, T. (2012 [1980]). 'Foreword: Tests of the State', in: *Quaderni*, 78, 5–22.

Lipsky, M. (1980). *Street-Level Bureaucracy*, New York, Russell Sage Foundation.

Malinowski, B. (1926). *Crime and Custom in Savage Society*. Martino Fine Books.

(1927). *Sex and Repression in Savage Society*. London, Harcourt Brace.

Malka, R. (2021). *The Right to Annoy God*. Grasset.

Marchand, E. and Werner, A. (2020). 'Supporting Victims at Trial: Civil Parties' Perspective' in: Weill, S. et al. (eds.) *The President on Trial, Prosecuting Hissene Habre*. Oxford: Oxford University Press, pp. 126–133.

Marlière, P. (2023). 'The 'Islamo-gauchiste threat' as Political Nudge', in: *French Cultural Studies*, 43(3), 234.

Maroney, T. (2019). 'Empirically Investigating Judicial Emotion', in: *Oñati Socio-Legal Series*, 9(5), 799.

Masferrer, A. (2012). *Post 9/11 and the State of Permanent Legal Emergency*. New York, Springer.

Massoud, M. (2021). *Shari'a, Inshallah Finding God in Somali Legal Politics*. Cambridge University Press.

Mayur, S. (2023). *Terror Trials: Life and Law in Delhi's Courts*. Hyderabad: Orient Blackswan.

McColgan, M. and Attanasio, A. (1999). 'International Mission of Inquiry. France: Paving the Way for Arbitrary Justice', in: *International Federation of Human Rights Leagues*, 271(2), 18.

McEvoy, K. et al. (2022). *Lawyers in Conflict and Transition*. Cambridge University Press.

Mégie A. (2010). 'The 'Terrorist Scene: Theoretical Reflections on "Old" and "New" Terrorism', in: *Canadian Journal of Political Science*, 43(4), 983–1003.

(2014). 'The Origin of EU Authority in Criminal Matters: A Sociology of Legal Experts in European Policy-making', in: *Journal of European Public Policy*, 21(2), 230–247.

(2017). 'La réponse judiciaire au terrorisme au regard de la Charte des droits fondamentaux de l'UE'. in: *L'enquête judiciaire et les techniques de renseignement*. European project report. Brussels, February. p. 18.

(2020a). 'C'est ouvert au public ces procès? Les secrets d'une scène d'audience au prisme de la lutte contre le terrorisme', in: *Revue Rue Descartes*, 2, 85.

(2020b). '"So these trials are open to the public?" The Secrets of Trial Proceedings Through the Lens of the Fight against Terrorism'. in: *Journal of the CIPH*, 2 n.98, Collège international de Philosophie, pp. 64–80

(2021). 'Maintenant on va juger les morts?! Ethnographie des procès du terrorisme à l'épreuve des présumés morts', in: *Cultures & Conflits*, 121, 15–34.

(2023). 'Le parquet national antiterroriste La fabrication d'une 'figure experte' de la lutte contre le terrorisme en France', in: *Gouvernement et action publique*. 12(3), 127–149.

Mégie, A. and Pawella, J. (2017). 'Les procès correctionnels des filières djihadistes. Juger dans le contexte de la guerre contre le terrorisme', in: *Les Cahiers de la Justice*, 2, 235–251.

Mégie, A., Piret, C., Sturm, F., Peyrucq, B. and Leclerc, H. (2019). *Chroniques d'un procès du terrorisme: L'Affaire Merah*. Editions de La Martinière.

Mégie, A. and Sansico, V. (2021). 'Terrorism on Trial: A History', in: *Histoire @ Politique, Revue du Centre d'Histoire de Sciences Po*, 45, 3–10.

Mehra T., Renard T. and Herbach M. (eds.) (2024). *Female Jihadis Facing Justice: Comparing Approaches in Europe*. International Center for Counter-Terrorism.

Mercier, M. (2016). 'Proposition de loi relative à la composition de la cour d'assises de l'article 698-6 du code de procédure pénale'. in: *Sénat*, Report No. 252, 21 December. p. 13. www.senat.fr/rap/l16-252/l16-2521.pdf.

Merry, S. E. (1990). *Getting Justice and Getting Even: Legal Consciousness among Working-Class Americans*. Chicago, University of Chicago Press.

(2006). 'New Legal Realism and the Ethnography of Transnational Law', in: *Law and Social Inquiry*, 31(4), 975–995.

Mertz, E. (1994). 'Legal Language: Pragmatics, Poetics and Social Power', in: *Annual Review of Anthropology*, 23, 435–455.

(2007). *The Language of Law School: Learning to 'Think like a Lawyer'*. Oxford, Oxford University Press.

Mertz, E. and Jothie R. (2014). 'Language- and Law Scholarship: An Interdisciplinary Conversation and a Post-9/11 Example', in: *Annual Review of Law and Social Sciences*, 10, 169–183.

Mestren, A. (2023). 'France incarceration numbers hit record high, and set to rise further with riot-related verdicts', in: *Le Monde*, 2 August. www.lemonde.fr/en/france/article/2023/08/02/france-s-prison-record-high-incarceration-numbers-set-to-rise-further-with-riot-related-verdicts_6077261_7.html.

Ministère de la Justice (2016). 'La lettre du porte-parole du Ministère de la Justice: la législation anti-terroriste', in: *Ministère de la Justice*, 23 November.

(2019). 'Zoom sur le nouveau Parquet National antiterroriste', in: *Justice.gouv.fr*, 30 September.

Ministère de l'Intérieur (2022). 'La prise en compte des sortants de prison radicalisés'. in: *Direction Générale de la Sécurité Intérieure*, updated 31 July 2024.

Monod, J. (2016). *Penser l'ennemi, affronter l'exception: Réflexions critiques sur l'actualité de Carl Schmitt*. Paris, La Découverte.

Mucchielli, J. (2017). 'Procès Merah: La défense demande l'acquittement'. in: *Dalloz Actualité*, 2 November. www.dalloz-actualite.fr/flash/condamnation-d-abdelkader-merah-motivation-de-cour-d-assises.

Mulcahy, L. (2007). 'Architects of Justice: The Politics of Courtroom Design', in: *Social and Legal Studies*, 16(3), 383–403.

(2011). *Legal Architecture. Justice, Due Process and the Place of Law*. London, Routledge.

Mulcahy, L. and Rowden, E. (2019). *The Democratic Courthouse: A Modern History of Design, Due Process and Dignity*. London, Routledge.

Murphy, C. (2015). *EU Counter-Terrorism Law: Pre-emption and the Rule of Law*. Hart Publishing.

(2019). 'Terrorism and Transnational Law: Rules of Law Under Conditions of Globalisation'. in: Zumbansen, P. (ed.). *The Oxford Handbook of Transnational Law*, University of Bristol Law Research Paper Series, pp. 845–866.

Mustafina, R. (2022). 'Turning on the Lights? Publicity and Defensive Legal Mobilization in protest-Related Trials in Russia', in: *Law & Society Review*, 56(4), 601–622.

Naftali, P. (2016). 'Crafting a 'Right to Truth' in International Law: Converging Mobilizations, Diverging Agendas?', in: *Champ pénal/Penal field*, 13.

Nelken, D. (eds.) (1997). *Comparing Legal Cultures*. Aldershot: Ashgate.

Ní Aoláin, F. (2018). 'L'exercice contemporain des pouvoirs d'urgence : réflexions sur la permanence, la non-permanence et les ordres juridiques administratifs', in: *Cultures & Conflits*, 112(4), 15–34.

(2020). 'The Contemporary Exercise of Emergency Powers: Reflections on Permanence, Impermanence and Challenging Times'. in: *Political Anthropological Research on International Social Sciences (PARIS)*, 1, 197.

(2021). "Soft Law', Informal Lawmaking and 'New Institutions' in the Global Counter-Terrorism Architecture', in: *European Journal of International Law*, 32, 919.

Ní Aoláin, F. and Gross, O. (2013). *Guantánamo and Beyond Exceptional Courts and Military Commissions in Comparative Perspective*. Cambridge University Press.

Noack, R. (2021). 'In a custom-built courtroom, the trial begins for the November 2015 Paris attacks', in: *The Washington Post*, 8 September.

Nossiter, A. (2018). 'Paris Trial Shows Faltering Evolution of a Jihadist Cell'. in: *The New York Times*, 13 April.

Odinet, G. (2017). 'Le rôle du juge administratif dans le contrôle de l'état d'urgence'. in: *Les Cahiers de la Justice*, 2(2), 278.

Ojanen, T. (2013). 'Administrative Counter-Terrorism Measure – A Strategy to Circumvent Human Rights in the Fight Against Terrorism?', in: Cole, D., Fabbrini, F., and Vedaschi A. (eds.) *Secrecy, National Security and the Vindication of Constitutional Law*. Cheltenham, Edward Elgar Publishing, pp. 249–266.

Olalde, A. J. (2014). 'Restorative Encounters in Terrorist Victimization in Spain: Theoretical Reflections and Practical Insights from Social Work', in: *Oñati Socio-legal Series*, 4(3), 404.

Olson, S. M. and Dzur, A. W. (2004). 'Revisiting Informal Justice: Restorative Justice and Democratic Professionalism', in: *Law and Society Review*, 38(1), 139.

Osiel, M. J. (2008). 'In Defense of Liberal Show Trials – Nuremberg and Beyond', in: Mettraux, G. (eds.) *Perspectives on the Nuremberg Trial*. Oxford University Press, pp. 704–725

Parmentier, S. (2018). 'Dans le prétoire. Quelle défense aujourd'hui pour les terroristes dans les tribunaux?', in: *France Inter*. 28 September. www.radiofrance.fr/franceinter/podcasts/dans-le-pretoire/quelle-defense-aujourd-hui-pour-les-terroristes-dans-les-tribunaux-8769649.

Parsons, T. (1962). 'The Law and Social Control', in *Law and Sociology: Exploratory Essays*, W. M. Evan (ed.), Free Press.

Pawella, J. (2019). Chiffres 2018–2019. *Radicalisations*. https://doi.org/10.58079/t5qw.

Pereira Rui, M. (2017). 'Judging Terrorism with or without a Jury? A Study of the Role of the Popular Jury in Terrorism Trials in France, the United Kingdom, and the United States', in: *Revue de Science Criminelle et de Droit Pénal Comparé*, 2, 215–230.

Piquet, C. and Licourt, J. (2017). 'La réclusion criminelle à perpétuité requise à l'encontre d'Abdelkader Merah. Le second accusé, un homme "sans loi, sans foi, sans morale"', in: *Le Figaro*, 30 October. (Loose translation.) www.lefigaro.fr/actualite-france/2017/10/30/01016-20171030LIVWWW00021-proces-merah-abdelkader-mohamed-fettah-malki-terrorisme-derniere-semaine-en-direct.php.

Politika (2022). 'Jeux de rôles au palais de justice. Réflexion sur la place des chercheurs au tribunal du terrorisme' ('Role-playing at the courthouse. Reflections on the place of researchers at the terrorism court'. Research collective ProMeTe, in: *Politika magazine*.

Pottage, A. (2012). 'The Materiality of What?', in: *Journal of Law and Society*, 39 (1), 167–183.

Promete (2021). 'Les procès 'historiques' du terrorisme'. in: *Politika* [online]. www.politika.io/fr/atelier/proces-historiques-du-terrorisme.

Ragazzi, F. (2016). 'La lutte contre la radicalisation ou deux formes de la pensée magique', in: *Mouvements*, 88(4), 151–158.

Ramati, N. (2020). 'The Rulings of the Israeli Military Courts and International Law', in: *Journal of Conflict and Security Law*, 25(1), Spring, 149–169.

Ricard, Jean-François (2021) in 'Entretien avec le Procureur national antiterroriste, Jean-François Ricard et le Procureur adjoint, Jean-Michel Bourles', in: *Les Cahiers de la Justice*, 2, 213.

Riss (2020), *Charlie Hebdo*, December 23, 2020.

Roach, K. (2015). *Comparative Counter-Terrorism Law*. Cambridge University Press.

Roach Anleu, S. and Mack, K. (2021). *Judging and Emotion: A Socio-Legal Analysis*. London, Routledge.

Robinson, E. (2021). 'L'office du juge d'instruction antiterroriste', in: *Les Cahiers de la Justice*, 2, 365.

Robertson, G. (2007). 'Fair Trials for Terrorists?', in R. A. Wilson (ed.), *Human Rights in the 'War on Terror'*, p. 169.

Rosanvallon, P. (2006). *La contre-démocratie, la politique à l'âge de la défiance*. Seuil.

Rouland, N. (1988). *Anthropologie juridique*. Paris, Les Presses Universitaires de France.

Rousso, H. (2016). *Juger le passé: Le procès Eichmann*. Mémorial de la Shoah.

Roy, O. (2010). *Généalogie de l'islamisme*. Paris, Hachette.

Sadat Wexler, L. (1994). 'The Interpretation of the Nuremberg Principles by the French Court of Cassation: From Touvier to Barbie and Back Again'. in: *Columbia Journal of Transnational Law*, 32, 289–380.

Salas, D. (2002). 'The Role of the Judge'. in: Delmas-Marty, M., and Spencer, J. R. (eds.) *European Criminal Procedures*. Cambridge, Cambridge University Press, pp. 488–540.

(2011). *Du procès pénal*, Paris, originally edited in PUF, 1992, edition Quadrige.

(2018). *La foule innocente*. Paris, Desclée De Brouwer.

(2019). 'Le djihad du silence. Le procès du Musée juif (Bruxelles, 10 janvier - 18 mars 2019)'. in: *Archives de Politique Criminelle*, 41(1), 223–233.

Salas, D. and Besnier, C. (2023). 'Entretien avec Claire Josserand-Schmidt', in: *Les Cahiers de la Justice*, 1, 113.

Salas, D. and Weill, S. (2021). 'France et États-Unis. Deux Réponses au Terrorisme', in: *Revue Études*, 4288.

Sassoli, M. (2006). 'Terrorism and War'. in: *Journal of International Criminal Justice*, 4, 959–981.

Saul, B. (2014). *Research Handbook on International Law and Terrorism*. Edward Elgar.

(eds.) (2020). *Research Handbook on International Law and Terrorism*. 2nd ed., Edward Elgar.

Scheffer, T., Hannken-Illjes, K. and Kozin, A. (2010). *Criminal Defence and Procedure. Comparative Ethnographies in the United Kingdom, Germany, and the United States*. New York, Palgrave Macmillan.

Scheinin, M. (eds.) (2013). *Terrorism And Human Rights*. Edward Elgar Publishing.

(2014). 'Epilogue: Human Rights and Counter-Terrorism – Lessons from a Long Decade'. in: Jenkins, D., Jacobssen A. and Henriksen A. (eds.) *The Long Decade: How 9/11 Changed the Law*. Oxford University Press. pp. 289–303.

Schmid, A. P. (2013). *The Routledge Handbook of Terrorism Research*. Routledge.

Schwartz, O. (2012). *Le monde privé des ouvriers: Hommes et femmes du Nord*. Paris, Presses Universitaires de France, coll. 'Quadrige'.

Seelow, 2022. 'Au procès des attentats du 13-Novembre, Salah Abdeslam irrite, le public applaudit, l'audience est suspendue'. ('At the November 13 Attacks Trial, Salah Abdeslam Provokes, the Public Applauds, and the Hearing is Suspended'). in: *Le Monde*, 16 March. www.lemonde.fr/societe/article/2022/03/16/au-proces-du-13-novembre-salah-abdeslam-irrite-le-public-applaudit-l-audience-est-suspendue_6117682_3224.html?random=755121807.

Seelow, S., Jackson, K. and Otero, N. (2021). *La Cellule: Enquête sur les attentats du 13 novembre 2015*. Paris, Les Arènes.

Seroussi, J. (2018). 'How do International Lawyers Handle Facts? The Role of folk Sociological Theories at the International Criminal Court', in: *British Journal of Sociology*, 69(4), 962.

Settoul, E. (2022). *Radicalization in Theory and Practice: Understanding Religious Violence in Western Europe*. University of Michigan Press.

Sèze, R. (2024). *Se sacrifier pour la cause. Trajectoires des femmes jihadiste*. Seuil.

(2019). *Prévenir la violence djihadiste: les paradoxes d'un modèle sécuritaire*. Paris, Éditions du Seuil.

Sèze, R. and Clément, P. (2021). 'Still routes over roots? Les introuvables racines du djihadisme français', in: *Critique internationale*, 92(3), 173–191.

Shaffer, G. and Ginsburg, T. (2012). 'The Empirical Turn in International Legal Scholarship', in: *American Journal of International Law*, 106(1), 1–46.

Shamir, R. (1990). "Landmark Cases' and the Reproduction of Legitimacy'. in: *Law & Society Review*, 24(3), 781–805.

Shapiro, M. (1986). *Courts: A Comparative and Political Analysis*. University of Chicago Press.

Shapiro, M. and Stone Sweet, A. (2002). *On Law, Politics, and Judicialization*. Oxford University Press.

Shapiro, J. and Suzan, B. (2003). 'The French Experience of Counter-Terrorism', in: *Survival*, 45(1), 67–98.

Sherpa and the European Center for Constitutional and Human Rights (2017). 'Important step in the "Lafarge in Syria" case: Nomination of three investigative judges'. in: *Sherpa*, 13 June.

Sherpa and the European Center for Constitutional and Human Rights (2017). 'Landmark decision: company Lafarge indicted – complicity in crimes against humanity included', in: *Sherpa*, 28 June.

Simon, J. (2007). *Governing through Crime*. New York, Oxford University Press.

Simonson, J. (2014). 'The Criminal Court Audience in a Post-Trial World'. in: *Harvard Law Review*, 127, June 1, pp. 2173–2232.

(2017). 'Democratizing Criminal Justice through Resistance and Contestation'. in: *Northwestern University Law Review*, 111, 1609.

Slaughter, A.-M. (2004). *A New World Order*. Princeton University Press.

Sommier, I. (2000). *Le terrorisme*. Flammarion.

(2012). 'Engagement radical, désengagement et déradicalisation. Continuum et lignes de fracture', in: *Lien social et Politiques*, 68, 30.

Sperfeldt, C. (2022). *Practices of Reparations in International Criminal Justice*. Cambridge, Cambridge University Press.

Starr, J. and Goodale, M. (2002). 'Introduction: Legal Ethnography: New Dialogues, Enduring Methods', in: Starr, J. and Goodale, M. (eds.) *Practicing Ethnography in Law*. New York, Palgrave Macmillan, pp. 1–10.

Stirn, B. (2016). 'President of the State Council's litigation section, Report No. 3784'. in: *Assemblée Nationale*, 25 May, www2.assemblee-nationale.fr/documents/notice/14/rapports/r3784/%28index%29/depots.

Sullivan, G. (2014). 'Transnational Legal Assemblages and Global Security Law: Topologies and Temporalities of the List', in: *Transnational Legal Theory*, 5(1), 81–127.

(2020). *The Law of the List UN Counterterrorism Sanctions and the Politics of Global Security Law*. Cambridge University Press.

Talesh, S. et al. (eds.) (2021). *Research Handbook on Modern Legal Realism*. Cheltenham, Edward Elgar.

Tamanaha, B. Z. (2004). *On the Rule of Law: History, Politics, Theory*. Cambridge, Cambridge University Press.

Tardy-Joubert, S. (2022). 'La Cellule, une bande dessinée pour mieux comprendre le procès du 13 novembre', in: *Actu-Juridique.fr*, 3 June.

Tellier, M. and Sturm, F. (2020). "Association de malfaiteurs terroriste' : une infraction qui pose question'. in: Radio France [online], 16 December. www.radiofrance.fr/franceculture/association-de-malfaiteurs-terroriste-une-infraction-qui-pose-question-9349108.

Thomson, D. (2014). Les français djihadistes. Les arènes.

(2016). *Les Revenants. Ils étaient partis faire le jihad, ils sont de retour en France*. Paris, Seuil.

Tornqvist, N. (2022). 'Drizzling Sympathy: Ideal Victims and Flows of Sympathy in Swedish Courts', in: *International Review of Victimology*, 28(3), 263–285.

Trévidic, M. (2011). *Au cœur de l'antiterrorisme*. Paris, J.C. Lattès.

(2013). *Les Sept piliers de la déraison*. Paris, J.C. Lattès.

(2014). *Qui a peur du petit méchant juge?* Paris, J.C. Lattès.

(2020). *Le roman du terrorisme: discours de la méthode terroriste*. Paris, Flammarion.

(2024). 'Marc Trévidic, magistrat: 'Il ne faut pas attendre quoi que ce soit d'un ministère de la Justice'. Interviewed by Vanhoenacker, C. in: *France Inter*, 2 June. www.radiofrance.fr/franceinter/podcasts/bistroscopie/bistroscopie-du-samedi-16-mars-2024-2950163.

Triet, J. (Director). (2023). *Anatomy of a Fall*. Les Films Pelléas.

Truc, G. (2016) *Sidérations. Une sociologie des attentats*. Presses universitaires de France, Paris.

(2018). *Shell Shocked: The Social Response to Terrorist Attacks*. Cambridge, Polity.

(2022). *Facing Terrorism in France: Lessons from the 2015 Paris Attacks*, Cham, Palgrave MacMillan.

Trujillo, J. V. (2022). 'The Collectivization of Victim Participation: The Case of Colombia's Special Jurisdiction for Peace', in: Ambos, K. and Peters, S. (eds.) *Transitional Justice in Colombia*. Baden-Baden, Nomos, pp. 161–186.

Truong, F. (2017). *Loyautés Radicales: L'Islam et Les "Mauvais Garçons" de la Nation*. La Découverte.

UN Office of the High Commissioner for Human Rights (2019). 'France: UN Experts Denounce Severe Rights Restrictions on 'Gilets Jaunes' Protesters'. in: *United Nations Press Releases*, 14 February.

United Nations Committee on the Rights of the Child. (2022). *F.B. et al. v. France* (Communication No. 79/2019)

Vanhamme, F. and Beyens, K. (2007). 'La recherche en sentencing: un survol contextualisé', in: *Déviance et Société*, 31, 199–228.

Vedaschi, A. and Scheppele, K. (eds.) (2021). *The Rise of Global Anti-Terrorism Law: How the UN Security Council Rules the World (Global Law Series)*. Cambridge University Press.

Verges, J. (1968). *De la stratégie judiciaire*. Paris, Editions de Minuit.

Viennot, C. (2015). 'The Muhammad Caricatures as Seen by the French Courts'. in: *Les Cahiers de la Justice*, 2, 265–282.

Wacquant, L. (2008). 'Ordering Insecurity: Social Polarization and the Punitive Upsurge', in: *Radical Philosophy Review*, 11(1), 1–19.

(2021). *Body & Soul Notebooks of an Apprentice Boxer*. Oxford University Press.

Wacquant, L. (2023). 'La sociologie est un art martial qui permet de se défendre contre le monde social'. Interviewed by Cerf, J. in: *Télérama*, 18 June. www.telerama.fr/debats-reportages/loic-wacquant-la-sociologie-est-un-art-martial-qui-permet-de-se-defendre-contre-le-monde-social-7016061.php.

Waever, O. (1989). 'Security, the Speech Act', in: *Analysing the Politics of a Word*. Research Training Seminar. Copenhagen, pp. 371–383.

Waldron, J. (2003). 'Security and Liberty: The Image of Balance'. in: *Journal of Political Philosophy*, 11(2), 191–210.

(2016). Political Political Theory: Essays on Institutions. Harvard University Press.

(2021). 'The Rule of Law as an Essentially Contested Concept' in: NYU School of Law, Public Law Research Paper No. 21-15, March 19.

Weiler, J. H. H. (1991). 'The Transformation of Europe'. in: *Yale Law Journal*, 100(8), 2403–2483.

Weill, S. (2014). *The Role of National Courts in Applying International Humanitarian Law*. Oxford, Oxford University Press.

(2018). 'French Foreign Fighters: The Engagement of Administrative and Criminal Justice in France', in: *International Review of the Red Cross*, No. 907–909, 211–238.

(2020). 'Transnational Jihadism and the Role of Criminal Judges: An Ethnography of French Courts', in: *Journal of Law and Society*, 47(S1), 30–53.

(2022). 'La société face au terrorisme: quel rôle pour les procès?' Interviewed by Etienne, V. in: *Sciences Po, Centre d'Études Européennes et de Politique Comparée*, 9 November.

(2023). 'Engaging with Court Research: The Case of French Terror Trials'. in: *Oñati Socio-Legal Series*, 13(S1), S225–S251.

Weill, S. and Lefranc, S. (2025). 'The French Bataclan Trial as a judicial experiment: What lessons for the prosecution of mass crimes?', In: *Leiden Journal of International Law*, 38(2), 343–360.

Weill, S. and Robinson, M. (2020). "Chapter 18: Military Courts and Terrorism: The 911 Trial Before the Guantanamo Bay Military Jurisdiction". in: *Research Handbook on International Law and Terrorism*. Cheltenham, UK, Edward Elgar Publishing.

Weill, S., Seelinger, K.T. and Carlson, K.B. (eds.) (2020). *The President on Trial, Prosecuting Hissene Habre*. Oxford University Press.

(2022). 'Theorizing Empirical Court Research: The Test Case of the Trial of Hissène Habré'. in: *International Review of the Red Cross*, 103 (918), 1073–1081.

Weill, S., and Sulzer, J. (2021). 'Droits des accusés et des parties civiles: deux exigences incompatibles? [Rights of the accused and rights of the civil parties: incompatible requirements?]' in: *Les Cahiers de la Justice*, 2(2), 351–360.

Wiebelhaus-Brahm, E. (2010.) *Truth Commissions and Transitional Societies. The Impact on Human Rights and Democracy*. Routledge.

Wilhelm-Olympiou, C. and Köse, H. (2023). 'Jugement des revenantes de Daesh en France : une période charnière'. in: *Centre d'analyse, de vigilance et d'étude de la justice anti-terroriste* (CAVEAT). www.le-caveat.org/publications/jugement-des-revenantes-de-daesh-en-france-une-priode-charnire.

Wilhelm-Olympiou, C. (2024). La prise en charge des retours de zone [panel presentation]. Ecole Nationale de la Magistrature Training: Democratie et Terrorisme, Paris, France, 11 December 2024.

Zagury, D. (2018). *La barbarie des hommes ordinaires*. Paris, Editions de l'Observatoire.

INDEX

CAMBRIDGE STUDIES IN LAW AND SOCIETY

Books in the Series

Diseases of the Will: Alcohol and the Dilemmas of Freedom
Mariana Valverde

The Politics of Truth and Reconciliation in South Africa: Legitimizing the Post-Apartheid State
Richard A. Wilson

Modernism and the Grounds of Law
Peter Fitzpatrick

Unemployment and Government: Genealogies of the Social
William Walters

Autonomy and Ethnicity: Negotiating Competing Claims in Multi-Ethnic States
Yash Ghai

Constituting Democracy: Law, Globalism and South Africa's Political Reconstruction
Heinz Klug

The Ritual of Rights in Japan: Law, Society, and Health Policy
Eric A. Feldman

Governing Morals: A Social History of Moral Regulation
Alan Hunt

The Colonies of Law: Colonialism, Zionism and Law in Early Mandate Palestine
Ronen Shamir

Law and Nature
David Delaney

Social Citizenship and Workfare in the United States and Western Europe: The Paradox of Inclusion
Joel F. Handler

Law, Anthropology, and the Constitution of the Social: Making Persons and Things
Edited by Alain Pottage and Martha Mundy

Judicial Review and Bureaucratic Impact: International and Interdisciplinary Perspectives
Edited by Marc Hertogh and Simon Halliday

Immigrants at the Margins: Law, Race, and Exclusion in Southern Europe
Kitty Calavita

Lawyers and Regulation: The Politics of the Administrative Process
Patrick Schmidt

Law and Globalization from Below: Towards a Cosmopolitan Legality
Edited by Boaventura de Sousa Santos and César A. Rodríguez-Garavito

Public Accountability: Designs, Dilemmas and Experiences
Edited by Michael W. Dowdle

Law, Violence and Sovereignty among West Bank Palestinians
Tobias Kelly

Legal Reform and Administrative Detention Powers in China
Sarah Biddulph

The Practice of Human Rights: Tracking Law between the Global and the Local
Edited by Mark Goodale and Sally Engle Merry

Judges beyond Politics in Democracy and Dictatorship: Lessons from Chile
Lisa Hilbink

Paths to International Justice: Social and Legal Perspectives
Edited by Marie-Bénédicte Dembour and Tobias Kelly

Law and Society in Vietnam: The Transition from Socialism in Comparative Perspective
Mark Sidel

Constitutionalizing Economic Globalization: Investment Rules and Democracy's Promise
David Schneiderman

The New World Trade Organization Knowledge Agreements: Second Edition
Christopher Arup

Justice and Reconciliation in Post-Apartheid South Africa
Edited by François du Bois and Antje du Bois-Pedain

Militarization and Violence against Women in Conflict Zones in the Middle East: A Palestinian Case-Study
Nadera Shalhoub-Kevorkian

Child Pornography and Sexual Grooming: Legal and Societal Responses
Suzanne Ost

Darfur and the Crime of Genocide
John Hagan and Wenona Rymond-Richmond

Fictions of Justice: The International Criminal Court and the Challenge of Legal Pluralism in Sub-Saharan Africa
Kamari Maxine Clarke

Conducting Law and Society Research: Reflections on Methods and Practices
Simon Halliday and Patrick Schmidt

Planted Flags: Trees, Land, and Law in Israel/Palestine
Irus Braverman

Culture under Cross-Examination: International Justice and the Special Court for Sierra Leone
Tim Kelsall

Cultures of Legality: Judicialization and Political Activism in Latin America
Javier Couso, Alexandra Huneeus, and Rachel Sieder

Courting Democracy in Bosnia and Herzegovina: The Hague Tribunal's Impact in a Postwar State
Lara J. Nettelfield

The Gacaca Courts, Post-Genocide Justice and Reconciliation in Rwanda: Justice without Lawyers
Phil Clark

Law, Society, and History: Themes in the Legal Sociology and Legal History of Lawrence M. Friedman
Edited by Robert W. Gordon and Morton J. Horwitz

After Abu Ghraib: Exploring Human Rights in America and the Middle East
Shadi Mokhtari

Adjudication in Religious Family Laws: Cultural Accommodation, Legal Pluralism, and Gender Equality in India
Gopika Solanki

Water on Tap: Rights and Regulation in the Transnational Governance of Urban Water Services
Bronwen Morgan

Elements of Moral Cognition: Rawls' Linguistic Analogy and the Cognitive Science of Moral and Legal Judgment
John Mikhail

Mitigation and Aggravation at Sentencing
Edited by Julian V. Roberts

Institutional Inequality and the Mobilization of the Family and Medical Leave Act: Rights on Leave
Catherine R. Albiston

Authoritarian Rule of Law: Legislation, Discourse and Legitimacy in Singapore
Jothie Rajah

Law and Development and the Global Discourses of Legal Transfers
Edited by John Gillespie and Pip Nicholson

Law against the State: Ethnographic Forays into Law's Transformations
Edited by Julia Eckert, Brian Donahoe, Christian Strümpell, and Zerrin Özlem Biner

Transnational Legal Ordering and State Change
Edited by Gregory C. Shaffer

Legal Mobilization under Authoritarianism: The Case of Post-Colonial Hong Kong
Waikeung Tam

Complementarity in the Line of Fire: The Catalysing Effect of the International Criminal Court in Uganda and Sudan
Sarah M. H. Nouwen

Political and Legal Transformations of an Indonesian Polity: The Nagari from Colonisation to Decentralisation
Franz von Benda-Beckmann and Keebet von Benda-Beckmann

Pakistan's Experience with Formal Law: An Alien Justice
Osama Siddique

Human Rights under State-Enforced Religious Family Laws in Israel, Egypt, and India
Yüksel Sezgin

Why Prison?
Edited by David Scott

Law's Fragile State: Colonial, Authoritarian, and Humanitarian Legacies in Sudan
Mark Fathi Massoud

Rights for Others: The Slow Home-Coming of Human Rights in the Netherlands
Barbara Oomen

European States and Their Muslim Citizens: The Impact of Institutions on Perceptions and Boundaries
Edited by John R. Bowen, Christophe Bertossi, Jan Willem Duyvendak, and Mona Lena Krook

Environmental Litigation in China: A Study in Political Ambivalence
Rachel E. Stern

Indigeneity and Legal Pluralism in India: Claims, Histories, Meanings
Pooja Parmar

Paper Tiger: Law, Bureaucracy and the Developmental State in Himalayan India
Nayanika Mathur

Religion, Law and Society
Russell Sandberg

The Experiences of Face Veil Wearers in Europe and the Law
Edited by Eva Brems

The Contentious History of the International Bill of Human Rights
Christopher N. J. Roberts

Transnational Legal Orders
Edited by Terence C. Halliday and Gregory Shaffer

Lost in China? Law, Culture and Society in Post-1997 Hong Kong
Carol A. G. Jones

Security Theology, Surveillance and the Politics of Fear
Nadera Shalhoub-Kevorkian

Opposing the Rule of Law: How Myanmar's Courts Make Law and Order
Nick Cheesman

Ironies of Colonial Governance: Law, Custom and Justice in Colonial India
James Jaffe

The Clinic and the Court: Law, Medicine and Anthropology
Edited by Ian Harper, Tobias Kelly, and Akshay Khanna

The World of Indicators: The Making of Government Knowledge through Quantification
Edited by Richard Rottenburg, Sally E. Merry, Sung-Joon Park, and Johanna Mugler

Contesting Immigration Policy in Court: Legal Activism and Its Radiating Effects in the United States and France
Leila Kawar

The Quiet Power of Indicators: Measuring Governance, Corruption, and Rule of Law
Edited by Sally Engle Merry, Kevin E. Davis, and Benedict Kingsbury

Investing in Authoritarian Rule: Punishment and Patronage in Rwanda's Gacaca Courts for Genocide Crimes
Anuradha Chakravarty

Contractual Knowledge: One Hundred Years of Legal Experimentation in Global Markets
Edited by Grégoire Mallard , and, Jérôme Sgard

Iraq and the Crimes of Aggressive War: The Legal Cynicism of Criminal Militarism
John Hagan, Joshua Kaiser, and Anna Hanson

Culture in the Domains of Law
Edited by René Provost

China and Islam: The Prophet, the Party, and Law
Matthew S. Erie

Diversity in Practice: Race, Gender, and Class in Legal and Professional Careers
Edited by Spencer Headworth, Robert L. Nelson, Ronit Dinovitzer, and David B. Wilkins

A Sociology of Constitutions: Constitutions and State Legitimacy in Historical-Sociological Perspective
Chris Thornhill

A Sociology of Transnational Constitutions: Social Foundations of the Post-National Legal Structure
Chris Thornhill

Genocide Never Sleeps: Living Law at the International Criminal Tribunal for Rwanda
Nigel Eltringham

Shifting Legal Visions: Judicial Change and Human Rights Trials in Latin America
Ezequiel A. González-Ocantos

The Demographic Transformations of Citizenship
Heli Askola

Criminal Defense in China: The Politics of Lawyers at Work
Sida Liu and Terence C. Halliday

Contesting Economic and Social Rights in Ireland: Constitution, State and Society, 1848–2016
Thomas Murray

Buried in the Heart: Women, Complex Victimhood and the War in Northern Uganda
Erin Baines

Palaces of Hope: The Anthropology of Global Organizations
Edited by Ronald Niezen and Maria Sapignoli

The Politics of Bureaucratic Corruption in Post-Transitional Eastern Europe
Marina Zaloznaya

Revisiting the Law and Governance of Trafficking, Forced Labor and Modern Slavery
Edited by Prabha Kotiswaran

Incitement on Trial: Prosecuting International Speech Crimes
Richard Ashby Wilson

Criminalizing Children: Welfare and the State in Australia
David McCallum

Global Lawmakers: International Organizations in the Crafting of World Markets
Susan Block-Lieb and Terence C. Halliday

Duties to Care: Dementia, Relationality and Law
Rosie Harding

Insiders, Outsiders, Injuries, and Law: Revisiting "The Oven Bird's Song"
Edited by Mary Nell Trautner

Hunting Justice: Displacement, Law, and Activism in the Kalahari
Maria Sapignoli

Injury and Injustice: The Cultural Politics of Harm and Redress
Edited by Anne Bloom, David M. Engel, and Michael McCann

Ruling Before the Law: The Politics of Legal Regimes in China and Indonesia
William Hurst

The Powers of Law: A Comparative Analysis of Sociopolitical Legal Studies
Mauricio García-Villegas

A Sociology of Justice in Russia
Edited by Marina Kurkchiyan and Agnieszka Kubal

Constituting Religion: Islam, Liberal Rights, and the Malaysian State
Tamir Moustafa

The Invention of the Passport: Surveillance, Citizenship and the State, Second Edition
John C. Torpey

Law's Trials: The Performance of Legal Institutions in the US "War on Terror"
Richard L. Abel

Law's Wars: The Fate of the Rule of Law in the US "War on Terror"
Richard L. Abel

Transforming Gender Citizenship: The Irresistible Rise of Gender Quotas in Europe
Edited by Eléonore Lépinard and Ruth Rubio-Marín

Muslim Women's Quest for Justice: Gender, Law and Activism in India
Mengia Hong Tschalaer

Children as 'Risk': Sexual Exploitation and Abuse by Children and Young People
Anne-Marie McAlinden

The Legal Process and the Promise of Justice: Studies Inspired by the Work of Malcolm Feeley
Jonathan Simon, Rosann Greenspan, Hadar Aviram

Gift Exchanges: The Transnational History of a Political Idea
Grégoire Mallard

Measuring Justice: Quantitative Accountability and the National Prosecuting Authority in South Africa
Johanna Mugler

Negotiating the Power of NGOs: Women's Legal Rights in South Africa
Reem Wael

Indigenous Water Rights in Law and Regulation: Lessons from Comparative Experience
Elizabeth Jane Macpherson

The Edge of Law: Legal Geographies of a War Crimes Court
Alex Jeffrey

Everyday Justice: Law, Ethnography, and Injustice
Sandra Brunnegger

The Uncounted: Politics of Data in Global Health
Sara L. M. Davis

Transnational Legal Ordering of Criminal Justice
Gregory Shaffer and Ely Aaronson

Five Republics and One Tradition
Pablo Ruiz-Tagle

The Law Multiple: Judgment and Knowledge in Practice
Irene van Oorschot

Health as a Human Right: The Politics and Judicialisation of Health in Brazil
Octávio Luiz Motta Ferraz

Shari'a, Inshallah: Finding God in Somali Legal Politics
Mark Fathi Massoud

Policing for Peace: Institutions, Expectations, and Security in Divided Societies
Matthew Nanes

Rule of Law Intermediaries: Brokering Influence in Myanmar
Kristina Simion

Lactation at Work: Expressed Milk, Expressing Beliefs, and the Expressive Value of Law
Elizabeth A. Hoffmann

The Archival Politics of International Courts
Henry Redwood

Global Pro Bono: Causes, Context, and Contestation
Edited by Scott L. Cummings, Fabio de Sa e Silva, and Louise G. Trubek

The Practice and Problems of Transnational Counter-Terrorism
Fiona de Londras

Decoupling: Gender Injustice in China's Divorce Courts
Ethan Michelson

Anti-Constitutional Populism
Martin Krygier, Adam Czarnota, and Wojciech Sadurski

Lawyers in Conflict and Transition
Kieran McEvoy, Louse Mallinder, and Anna Bryson

The Ghostwriters: Lawyers and the Politics behind the Judicial Construction of Europe
Tommaso Pavone

The Sentimental Court: The Affective Life of International Criminal Justice
Jonas Bens

Practices of Reparations in International Criminal Justice
Christoph Sperfeldt

Seeking Supremacy: The Pursuit of Judicial Power in Pakistan
Yasser Kureshi

The Power of the Jury: Transforming Citizens into Jurors
Nancy S. Marder

Undue Process: Persecution and Punishment in Autocratic Courts
Fiona Feiang Shen-Bayh

Discounting Life: Necropolitical Law, Culture, and the Long War on Terror
Jothie Rajah

Clean Air at What Cost? The Rise of Blunt Force Regulation in China
Denise Sienli van der Kamp

Law and Precarity: Legal Consciousness and Daily Survival in Vietnam
Tu Phuong Nguyen

Prosecutors, Voters and The Criminalization of Corruption in Latin America: The Case of Lava Jato
Ezequiel A. Gonzalez-Ocantos and Paula Muñoz Chirinos

Entangled Domains: Empire, Law and Religion in Northern Nigeria
Rabiat Akande

The Social Constitution: Embedding Social Rights Through Legal Mobilization
Whitney K. Taylor

Out of Place: Fieldwork and Positionality in Law and Society
Edited by Lynette J. Chua and Mark Fathi Massoud

Negotiating Legality: Chinese Companies in the U.S. Legal System
Ji Li

Law and Jewish Difference: Ambivalent Encounters
Mareike Riedel

A Sociology of Post-Imperial Constitutions: Suppressed Civil War and Colonized Citizens
Chris Thornhill

The Regulation of Prostitution in China: Law in the Everyday Lives of Sex Workers, Police Officers, and Public Health Officials
Margaret L. Boittin

Immoral Traffic: An Ethnography of Law, NGOs, and the Governance of Prostitution in India
Vibhuti Ramachandran

From Manners to Rules: Advocating for Legalism in South Korea and Japan
Celeste L. Arrington

Risk and Resistance: How Feminists Transformed the Law and Science of AIDS
Aziza Ahmed

Moral Autopsy: Truths, Secrets, and the Judicial Afterlives of Communist Secret Service Archives
Saygun Gökarıksel

Courts, Constitutions and Karma: Buddhism, Monasticism and Connection in Sri Lanka's Legal Multiverse
Ben Schonthal

Terror on Trial: An Ethnography of French Courts
Sharon Weill, Dénis Salas, Antoine Mégie, and Christiane Besnier

Labor in Hard Times: Workers' Legal Mobilization at the European Court of Human Rights
Filiz Kahraman

For EU product safety concerns, contact us at Calle de José Abascal, 56–1°, 28003 Madrid, Spain or eugpsr@cambridge.org.

www.ingramcontent.com/pod-product-compliance
Ingram Content Group UK Ltd.
Pitfield, Milton Keynes, MK11 3LW, UK
UKHW021911220726
473566UK00004B/86

* 9 7 8 1 0 0 9 3 3 3 2 2 1 *